THE RISE OF HITLER'S THIRD
REICH

THE RISE OF HITLER'S THIRD

REICH

GERMANY'S VICTORY IN EUROPE 1939–42

CHRIS BISHOP

amber
BOOKS

First published in 2004

Published by
Amber Books Ltd
Bradley's Close
74–77 White Lion Street
London N1 9PF
United Kingdom
www.amberbooks.co.uk

ISBN: 1-904687-21-0

Project Editor: Michael Spilling
Copy Editor: Chris McNab
Design: Graham Curd

Printed in Italy

PICTURE CREDITS
All photographs courtesy of TRH Pictures, except:
POPPERFOTO: 20, 25, 32, 58, 84;
Ukrainian State Archive: 152–153, 160, 164, 165,
168, 177
Will Fowler: 157

Maps produced by Cartographica

Contents

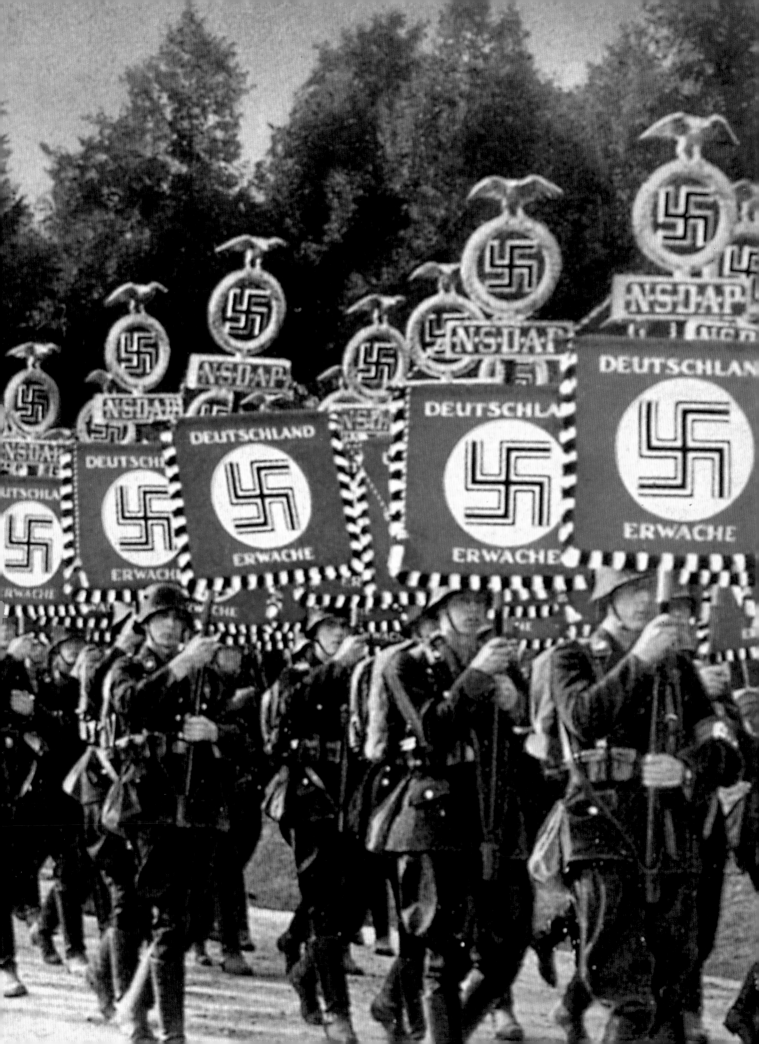

The Road to War

Adolf Hitler never made the slightest attempt to conceal his determination to achieve mastery first of Europe and then of the world, and to do so by force of arms. In the process, he would avenge Germany's defeat in the Great War.

The Treaty of Versailles that ended World War I sowed the seeds of another conflict by handing large parts of eastern Germany to Poland. Demands for vengeance amongst the German citizenry were given added stimulus by economic depression and, to many Germans, Adolf Hitler and the Nazi party offered the only real leadership.

The Origins of a Dictator

Confused and bitter, Hitler had returned to Munich after the end of the Great War, searching for reasons to explain Germany's defeat. Along with many returning soldiers, he felt that they, the front-line troops, had been 'stabbed in the back' by traitors, social democrats, communists and Jews at home in Germany. Pacifists and liberals came in for their share of the blame, but to Hitler and those who shared his opinions, the real villains were the Bolsheviks and the Jews. They were seen as one and the same, since Jewish agitators led many of the soviets set up in the German army and navy late in 1918. In his earliest political speeches, Hitler often referred to Jews as 'November criminals', alluding to the date of the Bolshevik takeover in Russia.

After the war, the army employed Hitler as a spy. His job was to report on right-wing nationalist groups in Munich. One small group was known as the *Politische Arbeiterzirkel* (Political Worker's Circle). Renamed the *Deutsche Arbeiterpartei* (German Worker's Party), it held its first meeting in January 1919. Hitler joined later that year. In an astonishing transformation, given his unpromising early career, Hitler proved to be a politician of demonic gifts and mesmerizing character. He quickly took control of what had been little more than a debating society, and turned it into the *Nationalsozialistiche deutsche Arbeiterpartei* (NSDAP) – National Socialist German Worker's Party. He spent the next decade using the party to build a power base, which was eventually to make him the absolute ruler of Germany.

Opposite: From the moment Adolf Hitler came to power in 1933, a general European conflict was inevitable. The pomp and pageantry of the Parteitage at Nuremberg would soon be followed by war, and the SS would trade in their black uniforms and banners for camouflage gear and Mauser rifles.

After a period in obscurity following the failed Munich putsch of 1923, the Nazi Party began to rise again in the mid-1920s. In 1930, the Party gained more than 100 seats in the Reichstag, winning strong support among the middle classes and in the Protestant north, which had been hit hard by the depression. The two bitterly fought elections of 1932 made the Nazis the largest party in the Reichstag, but without an overall majority. A coalition of right-wing interests invited the Nazis into government, but Hitler would accept only if he were made Chancellor. Believing they could control the Nazi leader, the politicians accepted, and on 30 January 1933, Hitler became Chancellor of Germany.

In February 1933, three days after taking office as Chancellor of the German Reich, Hitler addressed a huge gathering of Nazi Party officials and senior officers of the German armed services upon the necessity of 'unqualified Germanization' in the east as far at least as the Urals. On 27 February, an arson attack on the Reichstag (which the Nazis blamed on communist revolutionaries) gave Hitler the excuse to suspend all civil liberties in Germany. By the end of March, the so-called Enabling Act had given him dictatorial powers.

The *Wehrmacht* (armed forces) was the one institution that could have stopped Hitler coming to power. Indeed, the knowledge that the army could make or break a government had haunted the Weimar republic throughout its short life. Even after 1933, the army could have removed Hitler before he began the war and, once the war was obviously lost, a military coup could have beheaded the highly centralized Nazi regime in an afternoon. Since, according to so many of their post-war accounts, it was only Hitler's idiocy that prevented them winning the war, or at least making peace

THE *FREIKORPS*

The *Freikorps* were private armies of ex-soldiers formed in Germany in the chaotic years after the end of World War I. Usually raised by their former regular officers and given tacit support by right-wing authorities, they used their battle-proven tactics to defeat communist attempts to foment revolution in Germany. The communists in Bavaria and the Spartacists in Berlin were crushed by the *Freikorps*, and workers in the Ruhr who attempted to organize on socialist lines were also repressed. The tiny *Reichswehr* allowed to Germany by the Treaty of Versailles also made use of the *Freikorps* as auxiliary troops. Captain von Schleicher, a staff officer in the political department of the German Army HQ, secretly paid and equipped *Freikorps* units fighting on the eastern borders against the Poles and Lithuanians. Von Schleicher would later become a general and Chancellor of Germany.

In 1921, the *Freikorps* were officially disbanded. Many *Freikorps* members drifted south to Munich, where they formed much of the initial strength of the Nazi *Sturmabteilung*, or SA.

with the West, why didn't the generals kill Hitler? The truth was that Hitler and the Nazis, no matter how distasteful they were to the Prussian officer class, were providing what they wanted.

Had Hitler attempted to seize power by another putsch, as he was urged to do by the *Sturmabteilung* (SA) – 'Storm Detachment', the thuggish private army of the NSDAP – throughout 1932, there is little doubt that the army would have shot down the brownshirts and probably their leader too. But Hitler was handed power constitutionally. The army high command regarded Hitler, the former corporal, with disdain and was profoundly hostile to the SA, but most generals objected to the methods – street violence – rather than the declared aims of the movement. When Hitler addressed the generals in February 1933, it was, he later claimed, 'the hardest speech of my life'. They heard him

in silence, deaf to his impassioned oratory. Even so, they were hearing what they wanted to hear. Hitler's foreign policy boiled down to revenge for 1918. His domestic plans emphasized public order and a massive rearmament programme. There were no objections from the generals, who felt that they had chafed under the restrictions of Versailles for long enough.

Undoing the Versailles Treaty
The Versailles Treaty had been signed on 28 June 1919. It was designed by the Allies to emasculate post-war Germany. War reparations insisted on by France were crippling. The treaty so limited German power that her armed forces could not guarantee the integrity of her borders.

As Germany was not allowed to participate in the negotiations, the treaty was rejected at home as a 'dictated peace'. The onerous terms ensured a foothold for anti-democratic forces, among which was the small right-wing group that would become the NSDAP.

For a proud nation with a strong military tradition, the treaty was felt to be insulting. Germany was to be limited to a 100,000-man army. The navy was allowed to retain a few obsolete warships, which it could man with no more than 15,000 sailors. The air force and naval air force were disbanded. The production and acquisition of heavy weapons such as tanks and aeroplanes was prohibited.

From the outset, the Weimar government attempted to lessen the harshest terms. This revisionist policy had some little success, although an attempt to reduce the reparations in 1923 led to a brutal French occupation of the Ruhr, Germany's industrial heartland.

Above: In the chaotic state which Germany fell in to at the end of the Great War, political rivalries between left and right spilled out onto the streets. The right-wing Freikorps, *established to defend Germany's eastern borders, were also used in street battles with socialists and communists.*

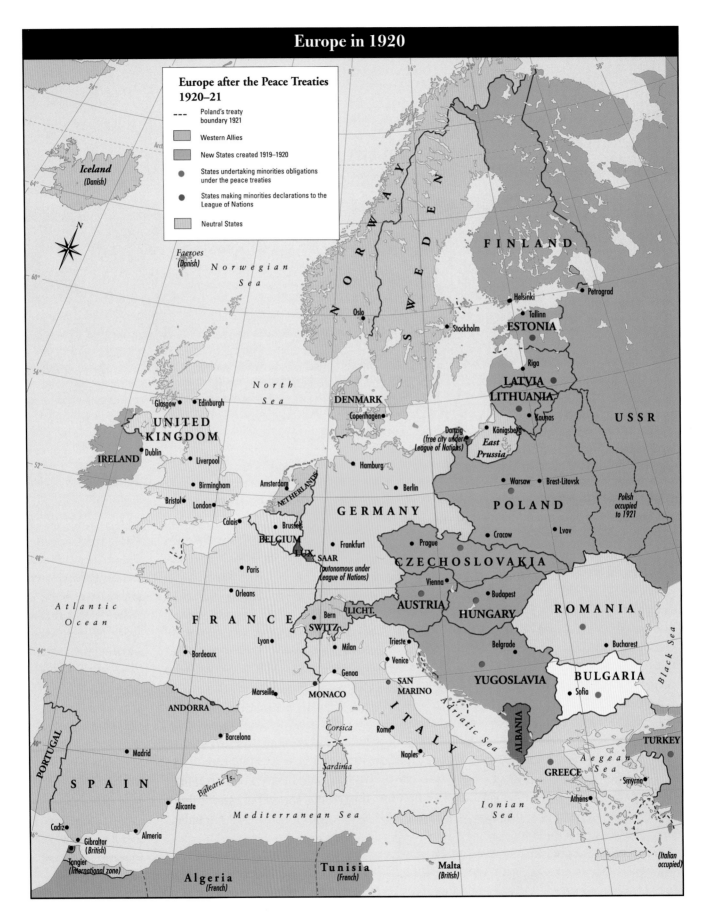

Europe in 1920

Europe after the Peace Treaties 1920–21

- - - Poland's treaty boundary 1921

Western Allies

New States created 1919–1920

● States undertaking minorities obligations under the peace treaties

● States making minorities declarations to the League of Nations

Neutral States

Although avowedly socialist, the Weimar government embarked upon a policy of secretly expanding its forces. Even limited to 100,000 men, the post-war *Reichswehr* was a significant military weapon. All of its men were superbly trained career professionals, and they would form the nucleus of a later field army. The *Reichswehr* was composed of former members of the imperial army and navy; as such, it was highly anti-republican in nature. Hitler openly courted this significant power base. Within three days of achieving the chancellorship, he announced plans to the *Reichswehr* generals for the rearming of Germany – plans he would not reveal to the rest of the world for another two years. But first, he had to do something abut the tension between the stormtroopers of the SA, who had brought the Nazis to power, and the army, which was the instrument that would enable him to dominate Europe. Hitler was a pragmatist, and he knew which was more important to his future plans.

In June 1934, Hitler decided to deal with Ernst Röhm, head of the SA and Hitler's major rival in the Nazi leadership. Röhm's desire to disband the army and absorb it into the SA offended the generals. Additionally, the SA had upset two other groups that Hitler needed: its violent radicalism offended the *Führer's* conservative supporters, and Röhm's increasing power on the streets worried Nazi rivals like Göring, Goebbels and Himmler.

Night of the Long Knives
On the night of 30 June 1934, Hitler unleashed the Gestapo and the SS, who had been provided with weapons and logistics support by the army. SS squads arrested or

Above: Stormtroopers of the SA parade through Berlin's streets in 1929. Leading the parade is the prominent young Nazi Horst Wessel. Killed in a brawl, Wessel had a song written about him that became a Nazi anthem – 'Horst-Wessel Leid'.

Opposite: Central Europe changed drastically in the years following World War I. The Austro-Hungarian empire disappeared, replaced by several new states, and large parts of Eastern Germany had been absorbed by Poland.

ORIGINS OF THE SS

In the violent politics of the Weimar Republic, most political leaders employed bodyguards for close protection. Adolf Hitler formed his first bodyguard in 1923. Calling themselves the *Stabswache*, its members were a handful of party fighters who swore to protect Hitler from all enemies within and without the party. This evolved into the *Stosstrupp-Hitler*, an assault squad headed by Julius Schreck and Joseph Berchtold, which was used in the Munich putsch. These units formed the kernel of the protection squads known as *Schutzstaffel*, or SS, from 1925. Hitler's personal bodyguard became known as the *Leibstandarte*, and under the command of Josef 'Sepp' Dietrich was to grow into a powerful military unit. Although nominally part of the stormtroopers of the SA, the SS always considered itself an elite.

murdered SA leaders all over Germany, starting with Röhm, who was arrested by Hitler himself at the head of a unit of his SS bodyguard. A number of private scores were settled at the same time. Estimates on the number killed reach as high as 1000, with 70 or 80 senior SA commanders being executed or 'shot while resisting arrest'.

Hitler proclaimed himself Chancellor and *Führer* of the German Reich in August 1934, upon the death of President von Hindenburg. He ordered the creation of a German air force (forbidden to Germany under the terms of the Versailles Treaty) and the rapid expansion of the German army and navy – the tools with which he intended to achieve his ends. In October 1933, Germany left the League of Nations and the Disarmament Conference. Early in 1934, the army was instructed to treble its strength to 300,000, but in secret.

In March 1935, Hitler came out into the open. He had Göring announce the repudiation of the Treaty of Versailles and the reintroduction of conscription. The peacetime German army would consist of 36 divisions organized into 12 Corps: a strength of around half a million men. Armaments for this vastly expanded army would be provided by concerns like Krupp, which had been carrying out clandestine research and development programmes since the 1920s, and which had been preparing modern armour and artillery designs since 1933.

Development of modern aircraft types had proceeded in parallel with the growth of the army. The result was that at the outbreak of war, the *Luftwaffe* enjoyed technical, if not numerical superiority over potential opponents. It also enjoyed tactical superiority, thanks to a cadre of pilots with real combat experience gained in the Spanish Civil War. Only the *Kriegsmarine* lagged behind: its rearmament plans needed much longer to come to fruition. Britain, France and the League of Nations protested, but did little else. Britain was appeased by an offer from the *Führer* to limit naval expansion.

Under the terms of an Anglo-German naval agreement of June 1935, the *Kriegsmarine* would be limited to 35 per cent of the total British naval tonnage. More importantly, the British would allow Germany to match the Royal Navy's submarine tonnage – a curious agreement from a country that had been on the receiving end of unrestricted U-boat warfare in 1917 and 1918. However, the Germans never intended to be bound by such an agreement: they were already building two 26,000-tonne (25,584-ton) battlecruisers

'My motto is, "Destroy by all and any means. National Socialism will reshape the world".'

Adolf Hitler
Mein Kampf

in contravention of the agreement, and plans were being made to build a fleet of the world's largest battleships by the early 1940s.

Training and Equipping

Hitler benefited from rearmament, but he did not start it. Because of the ban on offensive weapons like tanks, poison gas, aeroplanes and U-Boats, the *Reichswehr* had to keep training with such weapons hidden from the outside world. Thanks to a secret deal with the Soviets, German officers had trained with the Red Army throughout the 1920s.

The Allied Control Commission, which monitored compliance with the terms of the Treaty of Versailles, left Germany at the beginning of 1927. Almost immediately, the Weimar government stepped up design and testing of new weapons and the training of troops in Germany itself. Training troops and expanding the armed forces was all very well, but Hitler knew that his fleets and divisions and squadrons would need weapons. These would have to come from the industrial heartlands of the Saar and the Rhineland – the areas until recently occupied by troops of the Allied powers of 1918, still 'demilitarized' and still denied by treaty to German control.

The Saar region he regained in January 1935 by the simple expedient of holding a plebiscite, which naturally he won, enabling him to present the resumption of German control as a fait accompli to a generally uninterested and as yet unsuspicious world. Next, in March 1936, he sent his troops into the Rhineland – with some trepidation – and watched while Britain and France rationalized both his aggression and their own inaction with such evasions of responsibility as 'He is, after all, only walking into his own back yard.' If Hitler's ambition was the main cause of the world conflict that followed, the pusillanimity and short-sightedness of other European leaders were major contributory factors.

Two months after the reoccupation of the Rhineland, the Spanish Civil War broke out.

Below: Adolf Hitler addresses the party faithful at Nuremberg. He is wearing the brown shirt of the Sturmabteilung, *or SA. He needed the Brownshirts on his road to power, but they became an embarrassment when he was elected Chancellor.*

Right: The effects of the great depression were felt all over the world, but nowhere more than in Germany. Hyper-inflation and massive unemployment left the Weimar Republic ripe for an authoritarian takeover by a party promising to provide work – Hitler and his National Socialists.

The Great Depression

The Depression in Europe

Percentage of industrial workers unemployed
- 31.7
- 28
- 23
- 18
- 13
- No data

- ★ Strike waves
- ☆ Sit-down strikes
- ✦ Riot, demonstration or single strike

Fascist States in Europe

- Democratic countries
- Repressive or conservative countries
- Fascist countries
- Communist dictatorship
- ● Right-wing activity

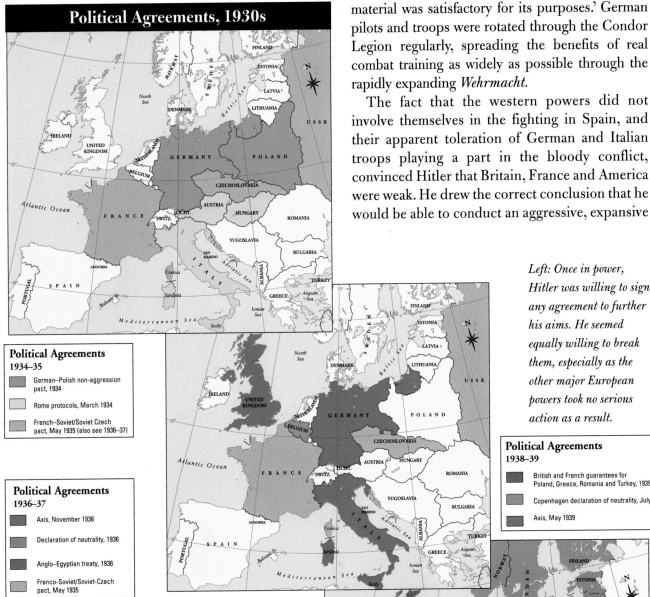

Political Agreements, 1930s

**Political Agreements
1934–35**

German–Polish non-aggression pact, 1934

Rome protocols, March 1934

French–Soviet/Soviet Czech pact, May 1935 (also see 1936–37)

**Political Agreements
1936–37**

Axis, November 1936

Declaration of neutrality, 1936

Anglo-Egyptian treaty, 1936

Franco-Soviet/Soviet-Czech pact, May 1935

**Political Agreements
1938–39**

British and French guarantees for Poland, Greece, Romania and Turkey, 1939

Copenhagen declaration of neutrality, July 1938

Axis, May 1939

material was satisfactory for its purposes.' German pilots and troops were rotated through the Condor Legion regularly, spreading the benefits of real combat training as widely as possible through the rapidly expanding *Wehrmacht*.

The fact that the western powers did not involve themselves in the fighting in Spain, and their apparent toleration of German and Italian troops playing a part in the bloody conflict, convinced Hitler that Britain, France and America were weak. He drew the correct conclusion that he would be able to conduct an aggressive, expansive

Left: Once in power, Hitler was willing to sign any agreement to further his aims. He seemed equally willing to break them, especially as the other major European powers took no serious action as a result.

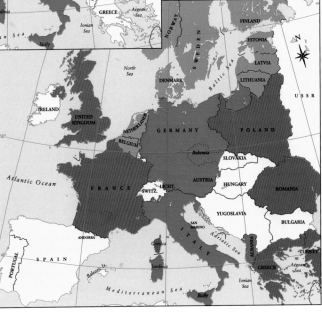

Sympathies between the rebel leader General Franco and the two dictators Mussolini and Hitler were quickly cemented by material help in the form of weapons, 'advice' and troops.

Spain would provide an ideal theatre in which to experiment with new military techniques and to train young officers in their use. Italy sent some 20,000 troops together with a 'volunteer militia' of 27,000. Germany sent the 6000 men of the Condor Legion, whose equipment included modern aircraft, tanks, transports and communications gear. In the words of Hermann Göring, the Germans found Spain to be 'a place where we had the opportunity to test with live ammunition whether our military

Right: Neville Chamberlain returns from Munich in 1938, with an agreement by Hitler that Germany would refrain from further acts of expansion. Chamberlain's hopes for 'Peace in our time' were to be sorely disappointed, as the Führer *had no intention of abiding by any such agreement.*

'In spite of the hardness and ruthlessness I saw in Herr Hitler's face, I got the impression that here was a man who could be relied upon when he had given his word.'

Neville Chamberlain, Munich 1938

foreign policy without risking more than disapproval and complaint from the other European powers. However, Germany's rearmament and Hitler's aggressive speeches eventually began to get through to the governments in London and Paris.

Annexations

During 1937, France and Britain began reluctantly to stir themselves into action. An extension of France's main defences against possible German aggression – the Maginot Line – was agreed and construction actually began. Britain passed an Air Raid Precaution Bill through Parliament, though any further or more rigorous preparation for war by the British was nullified by the succession to the office of Prime Minister of Neville Chamberlain. He was an individual whose whole character and ambition were devoted to entering the history books as the man who saved Europe from war.

On 12 March 1938, Hitler sent his troops across the Austrian border and into Vienna to a rapturous welcome. The following day, he himself travelled to Vienna to declare the *Anschluss* – the indissoluble reunion of Austria and Germany into the Greater German Reich. The German General Staff used the operation as an exercise in moving large numbers of troops by road. All did not go smoothly, but valuable logistic lessons were learnt in the bloodless takeover, lessons that would be put into practice in combat some 18 months later.

Next, Hitler's eyes turned towards the Czechs. The Sudetenland, Czechoslovakia's western and northern border areas facing Germany and Austria, had a German-speaking population of three million. The area of Bohemia had been awarded to Czechoslovakia by the Treaty of Saint-Germain en Laye between Austria and the Allies. The area had rich mineral resources, and it also housed major munitions factories at Pilsen. The indigenous Nazi movement, the *Sudeten deutsche Partei* (SdP) created by Konrad Henlein, kept up pressure for the

Sudetenland to be united with Germany. In 1933, the 9500-strong SdP was banned by the Czech Government, but this seemed only to encourage it. In 1934, Henlein held his first mass meeting and gathered 20,000 people, and by 1938 membership had grown to 1.3 million.

Disregarding any vague promises he may have made to the British the previous November, the *Führer* announced in a secret directive on 30 May 1938 his irrevocable decision to destroy Czechoslovakia, and mobilized what had now become 'his' *Wehrmacht*. Hitler had assumed supreme military command of all Germany's forces in February.

'Peace in Our Time'

Throughout the summer, Hitler could watch with detachment the diplomatic traffic racing to and fro between London, Paris and Prague. His patience was rewarded. On 15 September, Chamberlain flew to Germany to try personally to persuade Hitler not to

Right: Between 1936 and 1939, Hitler nearly doubled the size of the Third Reich. With little opposition, his troops were allowed to march into the Saar, the Rhineland, Austria, the Sudetenland and Czechoslovakia. It was not until the invasion of Poland in September 1939 that Britain and France declared war.

Hitler's Annexations

**Hitler's Annexations
1936–39**

- Germany after 1919
- Troops into demilitarized Rhineland March 1936
- Anschluss (union with Austria), March 1938
- Occupation of Sudetenland October 1938
- Original Czechoslovakian border
- Formerly Czechoslovakia occupied March 1939
- Moravian territory to Poland October 1938
- Memel territory to Germany March 1939
- Protectorate of Slovakia territory to Hungary Nov. 1938
- Czechosovakian territory to Hungary March 1939

carry out his threats against the only true democracy in mid-Europe. On 22 September, Chamberlain was back with Hitler at Bad Godesberg for a further talk upon the European predicament, and on 30 September in Munich Chamberlain, Daladier, Mussolini and Hitler agreed that the German-speaking Sudetenland should after all be transferred to the Reich as the final stage of Hitler's territorial aggrandizement. Chamberlain then returned to England, waving the signed agreement and declaring, 'I believe it is peace for our time!'

Yet by mid-March of 1939, the British Prime Minister was facing a bitter reality. German troops had moved forward from the Sudetenland, first to Prague and then on into the whole of Bohemia and Moravia. Before leaving Berlin to make another triumphant entry, this time into Prague, Hitler announced that 'Czechoslovakia has ceased to exist' – and Chamberlain was sadly complaining that the *Führer* had broken his word. It was obvious that Hitler now intended for Poland to be his next victim.

'This is a sad day for all of us, and to none is it sadder than to me.... I trust I may live to see the day when Hitlerism has been destroyed and a liberated Europe has been re-established.'

Neville Chamberlain, BBC broadcast, 3 September 1939

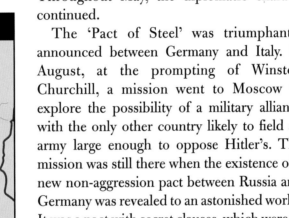

Throughout May, the diplomatic charade continued.

The 'Pact of Steel' was triumphantly announced between Germany and Italy. In August, at the prompting of Winston Churchill, a mission went to Moscow to explore the possibility of a military alliance with the only other country likely to field an army large enough to oppose Hitler's. The mission was still there when the existence of a new non-aggression pact between Russia and Germany was revealed to an astonished world. It was a pact with secret clauses, which were to become all too obvious only too soon. In response, Chamberlain announced Britain's guarantee of Poland's independence.

On 31 August, Hitler ordered the invasion of Poland. At 4.45 on the morning of 1 September 1939, bombers and fighters of the German *Luftwaffe* crossed the Polish frontier. They began the systematic destruction of Polish airfields and aircraft, of road and rail centres, of concentrations of troop reserves, and of anything which intelligence or observation had indicated as likely to house command headquarters of any status. The first *Blitzkrieg* had begun.

The following day, Britain and France demanded the instant withdrawal of all German forces from Polish soil. An ultimatum was sent – and duly ignored. At 11 a.m. on Sunday, 3 September 1939, Chamberlain broadcast the news that Britain was now at war with Germany.

Blitzkrieg and the Phoney War

At 4.45 on the morning of 1 September 1939, without Germany formally declaring war, aircraft of the *Luftwaffe* – Germany's air force – crossed the Polish frontier. The mission of almost 1400 fighters, bombers and dive-bombers was simple: the systematic destruction of Poland.

German Messerschmitts rapidly established air superiority, ruthlessly knocking Polish fighters from the skies while German bombers pounded Polish military and civil targets. Working under the protective fighter cover, German land forces were unleashed against the Polish army. From the start, the outcome was never in doubt. In little more than a month, all resistance had been crushed and the Polish state ceased to exist. Poland had succumbed to a new form of warfare, which would conquer most of western Europe in the next eight months. The Nazis called it *Blitzkrieg* – Lightning War.

The Invasion of Poland

The attack on Poland was a natural development of Hitler's hunger for conquest. He had already absorbed Austria and Czechoslovakia: Poland was his next target. Rivalry between the two countries had already soured relations, and armies on both sides of the German-Polish border were preparing for war.

Planning for the invasion of Poland had begun in April 1939, and Hitler ordered the German General Staff to launch the operation, known as *Fall Weiss* ('Case White') five months later. In many ways, Poland was an ideal theatre for the new kind of combined arms operations being developed by the *Wehrmacht*. It was fairly flat, and therefore suitable for mechanized operations, while its long borders meant that the Polish army was over-stretched.

One hour after the initial *Luftwaffe* strikes, it was the turn of German ground forces to swing into action. Over 40 German combat divisions were committed to the Polish campaign. Providing the spearhead of the German invasion force were six Panzer divisions and eight motorized infantry divisions. These were supported by 27 foot-slogging infantry divisions.

Opposite: The tank force with which Germany launched its Blitzkrieg *in 1939 was not the mighty juggernaut it was to become. Speed and mobility was the key to the* Wehrmacht's *success, and the bulk of its armoured strength in Poland was provided by light tanks armed with machine-guns, like this Panzer I.*

Invasion of Poland

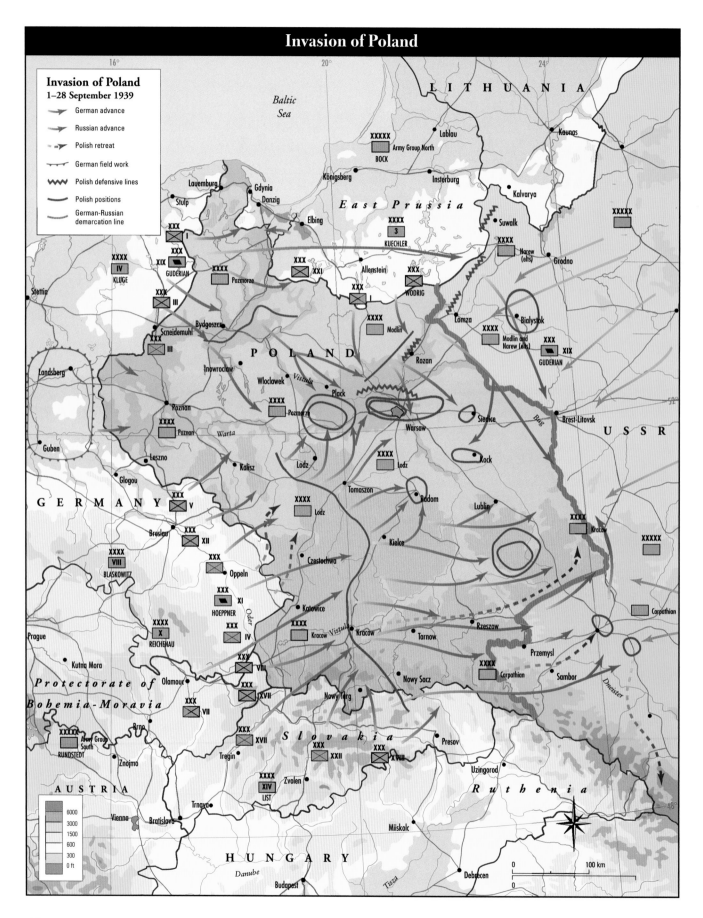

Invasion of Poland
1–28 September 1939

→ German advance
→ Russian advance
→ Polish retreat
↗ German field work
〰 Polish defensive lines
～ Polish positions
～ German-Russian demarcation line

LITHUANIA

Baltic Sea

East Prussia

Lablau
Kaunas
Königsberg
Insterburg
Kalvarya

XXXX Army Group North
BOCK

Lauemburg
Stulp
Gdynia
Danzig
Elbing

Suwalk

XXXX 3 KUECHLER

Narew (elts)
Grodno

XXX XIX GUDERIAN

XXXX IV KLUGE

XXX I

XXX XIX GUDERIAN

XXX XXI

Allenstein

XXX I

XXX WODRIG

Pozmorze

Lomza
Bialystok

XXXX Modlin

XXXX Modlin and Narew (elts)

XXX XIX GUDERIAN

Stettin

XXX III

Scneidemuhl

XXX III

Bydgoszcz

POLAND

Inowroclaw

Wloclawek
Vistula
Plack

Rozan

Landsberg

XXXX Pozmorze

Siedlce

Warsaw

Brest-Litovsk

USSR

Poznan

XXXX Poznan

Warta

Lodz

Kock

Guben

Leszno

Kalisz

XXXX Lodz

Tomaszon

Radom

Lublin

Glogou

GERMANY

XXX V

Breslau

XXX XII

Kielce

XXXX Kracow

XXXX VIII BLASKOWITZ

XXX Oppeln

Katowice

Kracow *Vistula* Kracow

Tarnow

Rzeszow

XXXXX

Carpathian

XXX XI HOEPPNER

Oder

XXXX X REICHENAU

XXX IV

Prague

XXX VIII

Nowy Sacz

Przemysl

Sambor

Kutna Mora

Olamouc

XXX IXVII

XXXX Carpathian

Dneister

Protectorate of Bohemia-Moravia

XXX VII

Brno

Nowy Torg

Presov

Uzingorod

XXXXX Army Group South RUNDSTEDT

Znojmo

XXX XVII

Slovakia

XXX XXII

XXX XVIII

Ruthenia

Tregin

Zvolen

Miiskolc

XXXX XIV LIST

AUSTRIA

Trnaya

Bratislava

Vienna

HUNGARY

Danube

Budapest

Tisza

Debrecen

6000
3000
1500
600
300
0 ft

0   100 km

'CANNED GOODS'

Canned Goods was the codename for a series of fake attacks on German border posts, fabricated in August 1939 to justify the German attack on Poland. Conceived by Himmler, Heydrich and Heinrich Müller, and initiated with Hitler's approval, the operation used about a dozen condemned German criminals and camp inmates, who were dressed in Polish uniforms, given lethal injections and then torn apart by small-arms fire. The international press were then invited to view the bodies, which had been positioned to look as if they had been killed in a cross-border raid. The most important 'target' for these attacks was the radio station at Gleiwitz, where disguised SS troops under command of Alfred Helmut Naujocks added to the effect by storming the radio station, beating up the staff and making crude anti-German broadcasts.

'Poland's existence is intolerable, incompatible with the essential conditions of Germany's life. Poland must go and will go...'

General von Seeckt, speaking in 1922

The main role of the infantry was to engage the bulk of the Polish army while the German mobile forces raced around the flanks, cutting through supply lines and striking at command-and-control centres to the rear.

The role of the *Luftwaffe* was to provide close air support for the German ground forces. However, German aircraft also played a more strategic role, striking at Polish airfields and aircraft, road and rail centres, concentrations of troop reserves, and military headquarters. A number of Polish aircraft survived the initial attacks and put up stiff – if limited – resistance over the following week. But it was too little, too late.

The world was stunned by the pace of the attack. While German Panzers crossed the River Warta, Britain and France demanded the instant withdrawal of all German forces. In the face of the contemptuous silence with which this was greeted in Berlin, the Allies consulted on how best to implement their promises to Poland.

A final ultimatum was sent to Berlin – and ignored. At 11 a.m. on Sunday, 3 September, British Prime Minister Neville Chamberlain broadcast the news that Britain was now at war with Germany. The world would realize, he felt sure, what a bitter personal disappointment this was. After all, Hitler had given his word he would not attack.

The Land Campaign

The campaign was planned as a massive double pincer movement. The inner pincer was designed to close on the Vistula river, surrounding the bulk of the Polish field army, while the outer, faster-moving forces were targeted on the Bug, cutting off any possibility of escape.

The operation was conducted by two German Army Groups – North and South. Von Rundstedt's Army Group South comprised three armies. The Eighth Army on the left flank drove for Lodz, while Fourteenth Army on the right aimed for Krakow. In the centre, von Reichenau's Tenth Army had the bulk of the group's armour. Its mission was to pierce the gap between the Polish Lodz and Krakow armies, link with Eighth Army mobile units and push on to Warsaw. Attacking simultaneously was von Bock's Army Group North. Kuechler's Third Army drove south from East Prussia while von Kluge's

Opposite: The German campaign in Poland was not a true Blitzkrieg *– it was a classical double envelopment. Two great pincers cut off and isolated the main Polish field armies, with the outer pincer being spearheaded by the new panzer corps under Guderian and Hoeppner.*

Fourth Army struck from the west, across the Polish Corridor. This attack was spearheaded by the Panzers of Guderian's XIX Corps.

The plan worked brilliantly. Never before had so much territory been gained in such a short space of time. After just three days of fighting, leading elements of the German army had pushed 80km (50 miles) into Poland. Whole Polish armies were in danger of being isolated. By the end of the first week, the Polish Government had fled from Warsaw. In spite of some successful counterattacks early in the campaign, the Polish air force had been all but wiped out. With the elimination of any aerial threat, German Stuka dive-bombers were free to probe ahead of advancing Panzer columns.

The momentum of the German advance continued virtually unchecked. By 8 September, the German 4th Panzer Division had advanced nearly 241km (150 miles), an average of more than 29km (18 miles) per day. In the same period, the Poles began to prepare Warsaw's defences. The next day, initial German attempts to storm Warsaw were rebuffed. This was followed by a spirited Polish counterattack in the Bzura region, marking the start of the biggest battle of the campaign.

Encirclement

By now, the entire Polish army was becoming trapped inside an ever-decreasing circle of German forces. On 10 September, the *Luftwaffe* began to launch heavy raids on Warsaw, and the Polish Government ordered a general military withdrawal to the southeast. On 15 September, the Germans issued an ultimatum to Warsaw – surrender or be destroyed. The garrison, supported by as many as 100,000 civilians, chose to fight on.

Army Groups North and South met at Wlodawa on 17 September, completing the outer ring of the German double pincer. From this double encirclement, only a small fraction of the Polish army could hope to escape, and on the same day even this hope was dashed. Surrounded and besieged, the Poles received yet another crushing blow with the news that Soviet forces had entered the war on the German side.

Signed the previous month, the secret Russo-German Pact called for the division of Poland. While the Germans crushed any remaining Polish resistance in the east, the Red Army advanced on two fronts north and south of the impassable Pripet marshes, meeting negligible opposition. The Polish Government, which had already changed its location five times, fled into Romania. On 19 September, the Polish

ATROCITIES IN POLAND

It was in Poland that the Nazi state showed its true colours. Following on the heels of the German Army as it smashed the Polish military came 15 *Einsatzkommandos*, or Special Units, staffed mainly by members of the SS and the SD (the *Sicherheitsdienst*, or SS security service). The *Einsatzgruppen* were originally established to eliminate political opposition in Austria following the *Anschluss* in 1938.

The task of the SD officers in Poland was to 'combat hostile elements', which in practice meant that the *Einsatzkommandos* conducted terror operations against Jews, the Polish army and the Polish intelligentsia.

In the two months when they were active, the *Einsatzkommandos* in Poland murdered some 15,000 people – a foretaste of even more horrific massacres that were to come after the invasion of the Soviet Union in 1941.

The Soviet NKVD was carrying out similar activities on their side of the line. In March 1940, Stalin signed an order to execute over 25,000 Poles, the most notorious massacre being of 4000 captured Polish officers in the Katyn Forest.

army in the Bzura pocket was finally defeated: more than 100,000 men were taken prisoner. Two days later, the Germans launched a massive bombardment of Warsaw. The next day, the Soviets occupied Lvov, and mounted a joint victory parade with the Germans in Brest-Litovsk. A further ultimatum was issued on 25 September to the citizens and defenders of Warsaw, emphasized by attacks by more than 400 bombers. Polish resistance began to weaken, and on 26 September the *Wehrmacht* launched an infantry assault on the city. Within a day, the Germans had taken control of the outer

Left: Poland's armies could do little to stop the Germans, and it soon became clear to the inhabitants of Warsaw that they would come under attack in a very short time. The population turned out en masse *to help dig defences – these school girls are preparing trenches to provide protection from air attack.*

Above: Legend has it that the gallant but doomed Polish cavalry charged German panzers with lances. The truth is more prosaic. A Polish cavalry unit was cut off by panzers and to escape had no choice but to try to ride through the enemy armour. Not surprisingly, casualties among men and horses were heavy.

suburbs, and the Polish commander, recognizing a lost cause, offered to surrender. A ceasefire came into effect the next day, 28 September.

The First Triumph

To the victors went the spoils of war. The Soviet-German partition of Poland came into force immediately with the signing of a 'treaty of frontier regulation and friendship' on the 29th. Poland as a nation ceased to exist.

To seal his triumph, Hitler flew into Warsaw on 5 October and took the salute at a victory parade. Organized Polish resistance ceased the next day with the surrender of 8000 troops southeast of Warsaw. For the Poles, defeat was now complete. Despite the desperate gallantry of its soldiers, the Polish army had been outclassed by a vastly more efficient military machine. The fatal weakness in Poland's defences lay in her lack of armour and mobile forces. At the start of the war, 30 Polish infantry divisions had been supported by 13 cavalry brigades, just two of which were motorized: the remaining 11 still used horses.

The whirlwind German campaign introduced a new type of warfare, making use of classic principles of fire and manoeuvre allied to the utilization of the latest weapons in both the air and on the ground. Speed was a major contribution to the *Wehrmacht's* success, as was good intelligence. German troops unerringly found the weak spots in the Polish defences, which were exploited by fast-moving armour and mechanized infantry, driving towards their objectives while all but ignoring flank security. They relied on their speed of penetration to disrupt any potential Polish counterattacks, leaving consolidation to the slower moving infantry following on foot.

The *Wehrmacht's* triumph was recorded by scores of Joseph Goebbels' Propaganda Company cameramen, whose work was soon being shown in cinemas all over the world. This contributed greatly to the myth of *Blitzkrieg*, which would soon be terrifying Germany's enemies. Curiously, many western military professionals did not give the new tactics much attention, wrongly assuming the magnitude of the *Wehrmacht's* victory to be due to the incompetence of the Poles.

For Hitler, the Polish campaign had been a gamble that he'd taken. . . and won. The *Wehrmacht* had committed most of its forces to operations in Poland. No more than a token covering force in the west was left to face an overwhelming French army of 70 divisions and a small British Expeditionary Force. Although dangerously overexposed, Hitler had calculated correctly that the Allies would do nothing if he invaded Poland. Once the subjugation of Poland was completed in early October, Hitler was free to turn his attention to further campaigns in the west. However, fighting in Eastern Europe was

Below: The Luftwaffe's *Ju 87 Stuka dive-bombers gained an awesome reputation in Poland. The crank-winged machines with their screaming sirens and ability to make precision attacks ranged ahead of the advancing* Wehrmacht. *Acting as flying artillery, they destroyed a variety of Polish targets, including bridges, railways, road junctions, field fortifications and strongpoints.*

far from over, and while there was no direct German involvement, the Winter War of 1939–1940 was a direct result of the success of the *Wehrmacht* in Poland.

The Winter War

The Russo–Finnish war began when Finland, formerly a Russian province, refused Soviet demands for border adjustments. The Soviets, fearful of Hitler's future plans, wanted to consolidate their grip on the Baltic states to provide a position of strength on the northern flank of the expanding Third Reich.

First to fall were the Baltic states of Latvia, Lithuania and Estonia, which had been independent since the fall of the Tsarist empire. After the partition of Poland, Stalin bullied the small republics into accepting mutual 'defence' pacts with the USSR. Once the treaties were signed, the Red Army moved large forces into the three countries. Ostensibly these were to provide for their protection, but they were occupying forces in all but name. The citizens of the three Baltic republics could do little in the face of overwhelming force, but their resentment remained, which explained why many greeted the Germans as liberators when they invaded two years later.

Finland had also been part of the Tsarist empire, and the Soviets demanded a similar accommodation with the Finns. Stalin demanded that the Helsinki government must cede southern Karelia to the USSR, as well as allowing the Red Army to base troops on numerous islands in the Baltic as well as on the Finnish mainland. The Finns rejected the Soviet demands outright, and began mobilizing forces along the frontier. Commanding the Finnish defences was Marshal Carl von Mannerheim, a veteran of the Russo-Japanese War of 1905 and a cavalry general in the Imperial Russian army during World War I.

Mannerheim had first planned a line of defences across the Karelian Isthmus after World War I, and over the next 20 years a series of some 200 concrete defensive positions were constructed. Stretching from the Gulf of Finland through Summa to the Vuoksi river at Taipale, these became known as the Mannerheim line. On 30 November 1939,

Right: The bodies of Red Army soldiers lie frozen in the Karelian forest, victims of a poorly planned and executed Soviet invasion of Finland. The Winter War was to cost the Soviets more than a quarter of a million men.

the Red Air Force launched a surprise attack on Helsinki, followed by a full-scale invasion. Almost a million Soviet troops smashed into Finland from the east, the southeast, and from across the Gulf of Finland. Facing them were around 300,000 Finnish troops, 80 percent of whom were reservists.

Stalin reckoned that with such overwhelming force the Red Army would have occupied Finland in less than a month, but he was rudely disillusioned. The Finns proved to be ferocious fighters, and familiarity with the terrain and weather meant that they put up incredible resistance to the Soviet attack. A Russian column attacking at Petsamo in the north made brief progress before being stopped in their tracks, while the amphibious assaults in the south were all beaten back. The main Russian thrust through the Karelian isthmus was beaten back with heavy losses at the Mannerheim line. Other Soviet columns attempting to move through the seemingly endless forests and lakes of central Finland were run ragged by small Finnish ski units fighting a guerrilla-style war to which the Red Army had no answer.

The initial Soviet attack ended with a fierce battle around the village of Suomussalmi, lasting through December and into the first week of January. Harassing Finnish attacks cut the Soviet supply routes, trapping two Russian divisions in and around the village. In a series of slashing assaults, the Finns cut the Soviet troops to pieces. Total Soviet losses exceeded 27,000 killed or frozen to death, while the Finns lost less than 1000.

Above: Finnish irregular ski troops on patrol. Vastly outnumbered by the Red Army, the Finns used their winter warfare ability and familiarity with the terrain to hold the Soviets back for more than three months.

Right: Operations in the Winter war stretched from the Gulf of Finland to the Arctic Ocean. The main thrust was in the south, where the Soviets eventually broke through the Mannerheim Line by using brute force and by ignoring horrendous casualties.

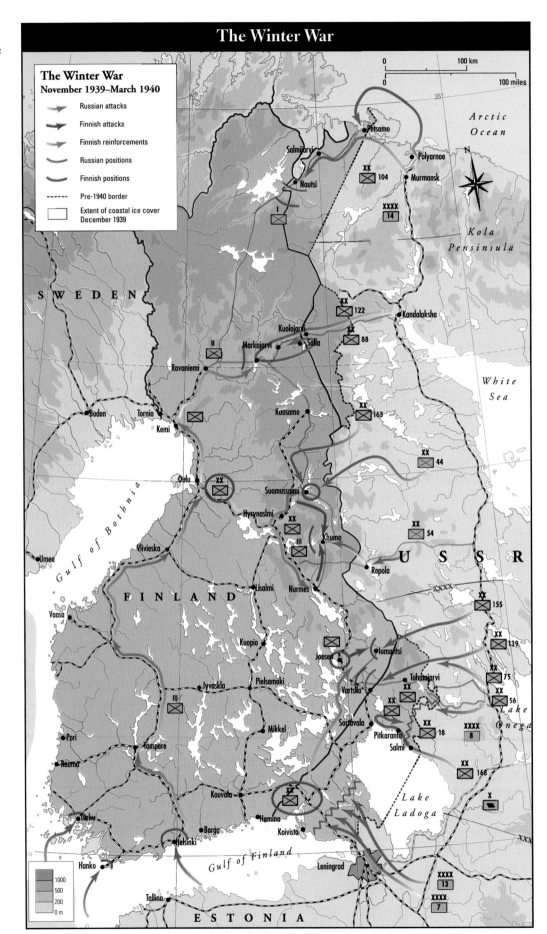

The Winter War

The Winter War
November 1939–March 1940

- Russian attacks
- Finnish attacks
- Finnish reinforcements
- Russian positions
- Finnish positions
- Pre-1940 border
- Extent of coastal ice cover December 1939

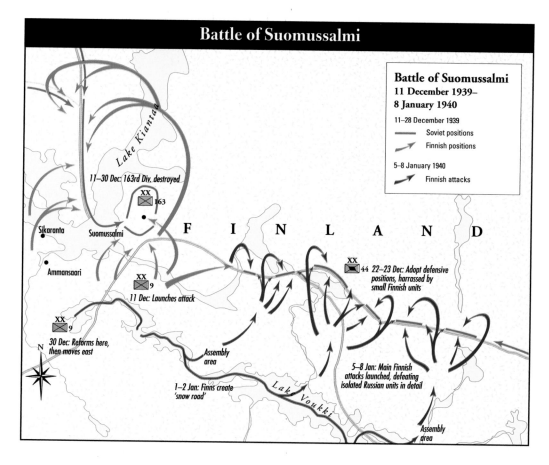

Battle of Suomussalmi

Battle of Suomussalmi
11 December 1939–
8 January 1940

11–28 December 1939

Soviet positions

Finnish positions

5–8 January 1940

Finnish attacks

Lake Kianta

11–30 Dec: 163rd Div. destroyed

XX 163

Sikaranta

Suomussalmi

F I N L A N D

Ammansaari

XX 9
11 Dec: Launches attack

XX 44 22–23 Dec: Adopt defensive positions, harrassed by small Finnish units

XX 9
30 Dec: Reforms here, then moves east

N

Assembly area

1–2 Jan: Finns create 'snow road'

Lake Voukki

5–8 Jan: Main Finnish attacks launched, defeating isolated Russian units in detail

Assembly area

Left: The Battle of Suomussalmi saw the Finns using guerrilla tactics to harass and blunt the main Soviet probe into central Finland.

The humiliating defeat forced the Red Army to regroup, and a further half million men were committed to the battlefront under the command of Marshal Timoshenko. The Soviets planned a massive battle of attrition in the Karelian isthmus, aiming to smash through the Mannerheim line by brute force. On 1 February, two Soviet armies, totalling 54 divisions, began battering at the Finnish defences, mounting four or five attacks each day. The Finns inflicted horrific slaughter on the wave after wave of Soviet infantrymen pushing through the snow, but the Soviet high command was willing to accept any losses to achieve its aim. Eventually, on 13 February, the Russians broke through at Summa, and began to roll up the Finnish defences. Over the next month the Finns were forced back, and on 12 March they sued for peace.

The Finns signed an armistice after losing some 25,000 men. Soviet losses were at least 10 times higher, many soldiers freezing to death in the Arctic cold, which on occasion fell to –50°C (–58°F). Stalin did not impose any demands beyond those asked for before the fighting started, knowing that too much repression would probably force the stubborn Finns into a guerrilla war – and nobody on the Soviet side wanted to face that.

The original Soviet invasion had been incompetently planned, led and executed, with little regard to the terrain or the weather. Success came only because the Red Army was willing to accept huge casualties to achieve its aims. The Soviet failure to dominate Finland convinced many Germans – Adolf Hitler and the German high command included – that the Soviet Union was a paper giant, and that an invasion of the USSR was possible.

Above: Over the winter of 1939/1940, the Western Allies believed that the war would never come to anything serious. To many British people, the comfort of the troops was a more important concern. Here, a consignment of new dartboards is about to be shipped to the British Expeditionary Force in France.

The 'Phoney War'

Although the Russo-Finnish War excited great interest among the British and French, in practice it did not affect them a great deal, for their main enemy – Germany – was not involved. Thus once the subjugation of Poland was completed in early October, it almost seemed to the peoples of Western Europe that military operations had ceased. There had been some idea of helping the Finns, but neutral Norway and Sweden had refused permission for Anglo-French supplies or troops to cross their territories, and nothing came of it. Naval operations aside, the 'fighting war' was apparently over and what United States Senator Boragh dubbed the 'Phoney War' began. British Prime Minister Neville Chamberlain called it the 'Twilight War', the Germans called it the *'Sitzkrieg'* ('seated war'), and one perspicacious observer called it the 'Winter of Illusion'.

This it certainly was for the British people and their leaders, for there grew in Britain (and in the United States, though to a lesser degree in France) a dangerous feeling that perhaps it would be possible to get through this war without too much unpleasantness, such as actual battle. True, there had been losses at sea – the aircraft-carrier *Courageous* had been torpedoed and sunk in September and the *Royal Oak* inside Scapa Flow in October – but the defeat of the *Graf Spee* levelled these losses out to some extent. In Britain, there was a growing impression that, ever since the torpedoing of the passenger liner *Athenia* a few hours after the declaration of war, the whole conflict was a sad mistake.

Chamberlain would, of course, allow no suggestion that any sort of deal could be done with Hitler, but once the German people 'had realized that they can't possibly win this war' – a condition he visualized developing by spring 1940 – they would undoubtedly rid themselves of their *Führer,* and probably an agreement could then be arrived at with some other German statesman – Marshal Göring, for instance.

In the meantime, 18,000,000 printed leaflets informing the Germans of the wickedness of their *Führer* would be dropped over Germany by the RAF, who would doubtless continue to suffer their resultant losses with knightly forbearance, at the same time ensuring that no damage whatsoever occurred to German citizens' private property, in case it upset them.

As winter approached, the British Expeditionary Force, some 400,000 strong, had crossed the Channel, and proceeded smoothly to their positions along the Franco-Belgian border around Arras and Lille, where they built pill-boxes and dug trenches. When Major-General Montgomery visited his division in December, Chamberlain queried, 'I don't think the Germans have any intention of attacking us, do you?' The general's reply is not recorded, but the Prime Minister's feelings reflected those of the British population as a whole, and was echoed in France, especially at the top of the French command.

There, the French generals believed they were arguing from a position of strength. Following the end of World War I, France had spent billions of francs on the construction of border fortifications known as the Maginot Line. Stretching from the Swiss border to the Belgian border, the Maginot Line consisted of a series of immense concrete fortresses. They were designed to be impregnable to conventional attack. Manned by more than 400,000 troops, they also sucked up a large proportion of France's available manpower. However, for political reasons, the Line did not extend along the Belgian border. There, the defences consisted mainly of a series of unconnected fortifications, many dating back to before World War I.

Manning the Defences

Both Britain and France still believed that all-out war with Hitler could be avoided. Certainly, there had been no attempt to take pressure off the Poles during their ordeal by military action across the Rhine – much to the relief and astonishment of some of the senior *Wehrmacht* officers, who revealed after the war that a powerful thrust into the Saar during the first month of the war would have been almost uncontested and could quite possibly have precipitated that popular revolt against the Nazi Party and the *Führer* of which Chamberlain so ardently dreamed.

But nothing happened, and once the Poles had been beaten, the combat-tested and battle-proven German divisions moved swiftly back across their country to Germany's western defence, the West Wall (known as the Siegfried Line to the British). Here they settled down to do little for the moment but glower at their opposite numbers and exchange insults with them daily through loudspeakers – but neither side did much to disturb the other's physical comfort. However, remaining on the defensive formed no part of the *Führer's* plans, and behind the fortifications German troop numbers rose dramatically as the *Wehrmacht* began to prepare for the next, even more deadly phase in the fighting.

The Allies expected the Germans to follow their standard plan for the invasion of France. First drawn up by General Count Alfred von Schlieffen in the first years of the 20th century, the Schlieffen Plan envisaged drawing the main French field forces into a battle in Alsace, after which the bulk of the German armies would smash through the

'The French army, the strongest in the world, faced no more than twenty-six German divisions. It sat still, sheltering behind steel and concrete while a valiant ally was being exterminated.'

J. F. C. Fuller,
On the 'Phoney War'

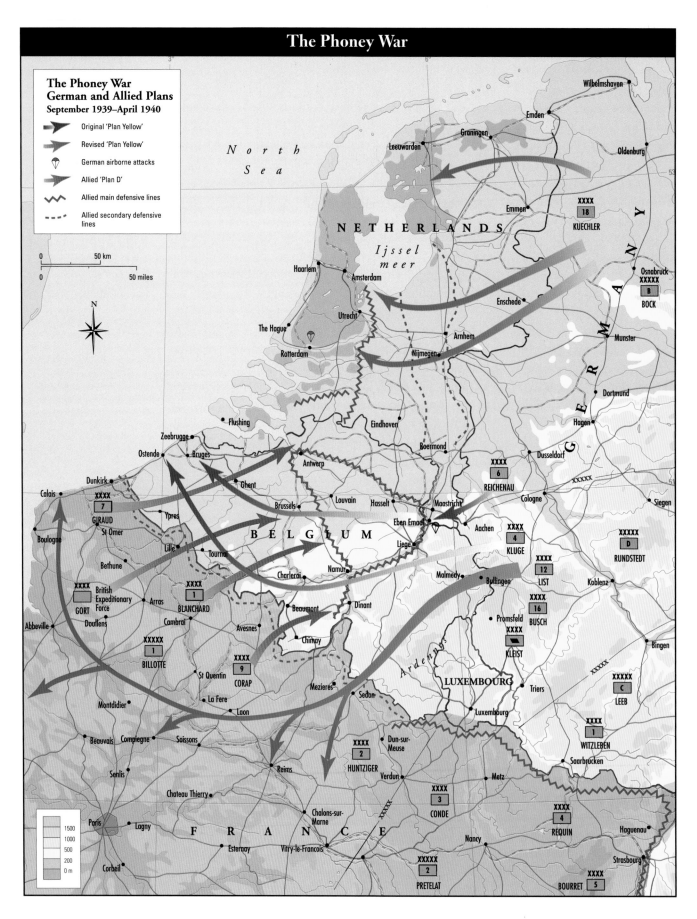

The Phoney War

The Phoney War
German and Allied Plans
September 1939–April 1940

- Original 'Plan Yellow'
- Revised 'Plan Yellow'
- German airborne attacks
- Allied 'Plan D'
- Allied main defensive lines
- Allied secondary defensive lines

0   50 km

0   50 miles

N

N o r t h
S e a

NETHERLANDS

Ijssel
meer

Wilhelmshaven
Emden
Graningen
Leeuwarden
Oldenburg
Emmen
Osnabruck
Enschede
XXXX
18
KUECHLER
XXXXX
B
BOCK
Munster

Haarlem
Amsterdam
Utrecht
The Hague
Rotterdam
Nijmegen
Arnhem
Dortmund
Hagen

Flushing
Eindhoven
Roermond
Dusseldorf
XXXX
6
REICHENAU
Cologne
Siegen

Zeebrugge
Ostende
Bruges
Ghent
Antwerp
Louvain
Hasselt
Maastricht
Eben Emael
Aachen
XXXX
4
KLUGE
XXXXX
D
RUNDSTEDT

Dunkirk
Calais
XXXX
7
GIRAUD
Ypres
St Omer
Lille
Tournai
BELGIUM
Brussels
Liege
XXXX
12
LIST
Malmedy
Bullingen
Koblenz

Boulogne
Bethune
Charleroi
Namur
Dinant
XXXX
16
BUSCH
Promsfeld
Bingen

XXXX
British
Expeditionary
Force
GORT
Arras
XXXX
1
BLANCHARD
Beaumont
Chimay
Ardenns
XXXX
KLEIST

Abbeville
Doullens
Cambrai
Avesnes
LUXEMBOURG
Triers
XXXXX
C
LEEB

XXXXX
1
BILLOTTE
St Quentin
XXXX
9
CORAP
Mezieres
Sedon
Luxembourg
XXXX
1
WITZLEBEN
Saarbrücken

Montdidier
La Fere
Laon

Beauvais
Compiegne
Soissons
Reims
XXXX
2
HUNTZIGER
Dun-sur-Meuse
Verdun
Metz
XXXX
3
CONDE
XXXX
4
REQUIN
Haguenau

Senlis
Chateau Thierry
Chalons-sur-Marne
XXXXX
2
PRETELAT
Nancy
XXXX
5
BOURRET
Strasbourg

1500
1000
500
200
0 m
Paris
Lagny
F R A N C E
Esternay
Vitry-le-Francois
Corbeil

Malmedy

GERMANY

Low Countries in a massive sickle manoeuvre, taking the French armies in the flank and rear and leaving the road to Paris wide open.

It was partly to counter this that the Allies planned to advance into Belgium and Holland, setting up defences along the Dyle Line, using the many waterways of the area as natural obstacles to a German advance. But both Belgium and Holland were maintaining a strictly neutral posture, which meant that their military commanders did not dare make contact with French and British military planners to coordinate defensive plans. Similarly, the Anglo-French forces could not set up fortifications on the locations where they planned to fight. As the Allies sat and built their defences, the Germans were preparing an invasion force behind the Siegfried Line border. From northern Holland to Switzerland, the *Wehrmacht* amassed more than two million men, deployed in 104 infantry divisions, nine motorized divisions and 10 Panzer or armoured divisions.

A Pause in War

While the two armies faced each other across the Franco-German frontier, the war was having little effect on the life of ordinary Germans. German rearmament had been carried out as a short, sharp process, and no plans had been made to place the German economy on a true war footing. Military production had not risen above pre-war levels, the production of civilian goods was hardly reduced, working hours were not extended, and in spite of severe labour shortages caused by so many men in uniform, no attempt was made to make use of Germany's women, the majority of whom did not work. To farmers and city dwellers alike, the war was something they read about or saw in newsreels, not something they were experiencing.

The British were much more realistic. The lives of British civilians were disturbed by the torrent of bureaucratic regulations that descended upon them from every old and several new departments of government, and their homes were either emptied of their own children if they lived in important cities or filled with other people's children if they lived in the country. A lot of them suffered disability or even death as a result of accidents in the black-out, and life, commented one observer afterwards, 'seemed to have become a continual exhortation, as posters sprouted everywhere enjoining every civic virtue from thrift to celibacy'.

As winter passed and the first signs of spring began to appear in 1940, boredom with the war and all its petty nuisances was a general feeling. But things were about to change.

Opposite: The Allied High Command expected that any German attack would be a repeat of the Schlieffen Plan of World War I – an attack through the Low Countries. Allied forward deployments were based on that assessment – so British, French and Belgian troops were totally unprepared when the Panzers burst through the Ardennes and raced for the coast.

THE WEST WALL

Germany's western defence, the West Wall, had been built in the 18 months before the outbreak of war. Heavily featured in propaganda films of the time, it consisted of more than 14,000 bunkers, gun positions and dugouts, stretching more than 600km (373 miles) from the Swiss border through the Upper Rhine, the Palatinate and the Saar as far as Aachen. Its building consumed more than 7.3 million tonnes (8 million tons) of concrete, 1.8 million tonnes (2 million tons) of steel, and over 18 million tonnes (20 million tons) of rubble and other filler material.

War in the West

The last time German soldiers had poured into France, in 1914, their initial drive had taken them close to Paris. But they were driven back, and had to endure four bloody years of trench warfare. This time, *Blitzkrieg* tactics would ensure a different outcome.

This time, they would break the back of enemy resistance in a single week. After a little more than a fortnight, the British would be evacuating their soldiers, and France would be at Hitler's mercy. The humiliation of 1918 would be avenged – and it would be the *Führer's* master strategy that did it, not the General Staff's. But before Hitler's *Wehrmacht* could achieve its triumph against the enemies of the Great War, Germany's soldiers would have to secure their flanks, in Scandinavia and the Low Countries.

In September 1939, when Hitler unleashed his forces against Poland, the *Wehrmacht* left no more than a covering force in the west to face a French army of 70 divisions, which was supported by 3000 tanks and had complete air supremacy – but only if the *Armée de l'air* had been ordered to fight. Hitler had a feeling that the French would do nothing, and his intuition paid off. The huge French army sat still, while a small British Expeditionary Force (BEF) was shipped to northern France.

The 'Phoney War' lasted through the winter and into the spring, until German forces invaded Denmark and Norway, forestalling an Allied landing by a matter of days. It was not until 10 May, eight months after the outbreak of war, that Hitler sent his armies west.

Exercise Weser

The Scandinavian attack had not been intended to happen, though planning had started at the beginning of the year, just in case it was necessary. It became necessary in April 1940. On 8 April, the First Lord of the Admiralty, Winston Churchill, announced that the Royal Navy was laying mines in Norwegian waters in order to stop the iron ore traffic between Narvik and Germany. This flagrant violation of Norway's neutrality was justified on the curious ground that Germany's reaction was likely to be even more flagrant. As Norway was a distinctly friendly neutral, this struck many British people as odd. But not so odd as the news next morning.

Opposite: When combat erupted on the Western Front, it was not in the Low Countries, as had been expected by the Allies. German troops went into action in Scandinavia, primarily to secure Germany's supplies of Swedish iron ore.

Right: A Luftwaffe *Heinkel He 111 bomber sweeps low over the approaches to Oslo, ready to mount an anti-shipping strike in support of the German army landings.*

It had been the Winter War between Russia and Finland, and the possibility that British and French reinforcements and supplies might cross from Narvik to Lulea in Sweden and thus interrupt Germany's supplies of iron ore, which first brought Hitler's attention to Norway. Before that, his focus on the west had been concentrated on the Low Countries, but once he had seen the dangers that Allied exploitation of Norway might hold for Germany, and the advantages which would accrue to his *Kriegsmarine* by possession of Norwegian ports and control of her coastline, he ordered planning for what became known as *Weserubung,* or Exercise Weser.

Following the *Altmark* incident on 16 February (see feature box, page 44), Hitler ordered a speeding-up and consolidation of the planning for *Weserubung.* Two days later, General von Falkenhorst and his staff were given control of the operation, and it was one of the ironies of fate that, at the end of March, Hitler decreed that it would be launched at dawn on 9 April – one day after Churchill's announcement.

The result was that, to the watching world, Germany's reaction to the Royal Navy's mining of the Norwegian waters, flagrant violation or not, appeared unbelievably rapid. OKW, the high command of the German armed forces, released a message to the world's press as operations against Denmark and Norway were launched: 'In order to counter British preparations to take away the neutrality of Denmark and Norway, the *Wehrmacht* is taking over the armed defence of both nations.'

Denmark and Norway

The first step was to occupy Denmark, which would provide a springboard into Norway. As of April 1940, the Danish army had fewer than 14,000 men under arms, including 8000 men conscripted in February and March. The men were poorly trained and equipped with little or no armour.

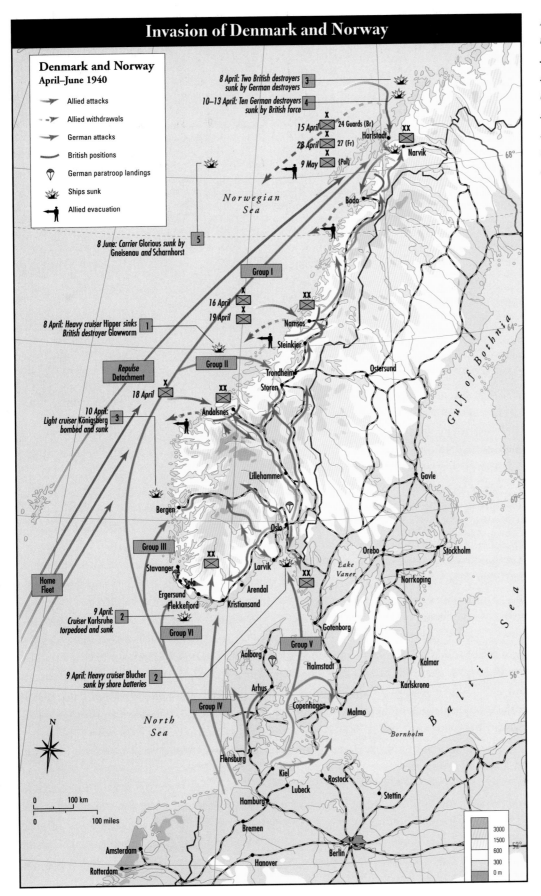

Invasion of Denmark and Norway

Denmark and Norway
April–June 1940

→ Allied attacks
⇠ Allied withdrawals
→ German attacks
⌒ British positions
⛳ German paratroop landings
✹ Ships sunk
🔫 Allied evacuation

8 April: Two British destroyers sunk by German destroyers **3**

10–13 April: Ten German destroyers sunk by British force **4**

15 April ☒ 24 Guards (Br)
28 April ☒ 27 (Fr)
9 May ☒ (Pol)

Harlstadt
Narvik

Norwegian Sea

8 June: Carrier Glorious sunk by Gneisenau and Scharnhorst **5**

Bodo

Group I

16 April ☒
19 April ☒

Namsos
Steinkjer

8 April: Heavy cruiser Hipper sinks British destroyer Glowworm **1**

Repulse Detachment

Group II

Trondheim
Storen
Ostersund

18 April ☒

10 April: Light cruiser Königsberg bombed and sunk **3**

Andalsnes

Lillehammer
Gavle

Bergen

Oslo

Group III

Stavanger
Sola
Ergersund
Flekkefjord

Larvik
Arendal
Kristiansand

Orebo
Stockholm

Norrkoping

Lake Vaner

9 April: Cruiser Karlsruhe torpedoed and sunk **2**

Group VI

Home Fleet

Group V

Aalborg
Halmstadt
Kalmar

9 April: Heavy cruiser Blucher sunk by shore batteries **2**

Arhus

Gotenborg

Karlskrona

Group IV

Copenhagen
Malmo

Bornholm

North Sea

N

Flensburg
Kiel
Rostock
Lubeck
Stettin

Hamburg

Bremen

Berlin

Amsterdam
Rotterdam

Hanover

0 — 100 km
0 — 100 miles

3000
1500
600
300
0 m

Gulf of Bothnia

Baltic Sea

Left: After the rapid takeover of Denmark, Norway was invaded in a series of widely separated but coordinated attacks stretching from Kristiansand in the south to Narvik, far to the north of the Arctic Circle.

'We have concluded a non-aggression pact with Denmark. Germany never had any conflict with the Northern States and has none today.'

Adolf Hitler, before the attack on Scandinavia

At 5 a.m. on 9 April, German *Fallschirmjäger* paratroopers were dropped at the unused fortress of Madneso and then at Aalborg airport. At 6 a.m., a battalion of infantry that had been hidden in a merchant ship in Copenhagen harbour, emerged to seize the Danish King and his government. Two divisions of the German XXI Infantry Corps crossed the border and moved into Jutland. Totally outmatched, the Danish army put up little resistance except in North Schleswig, and there was a brief firefight for possession of the Royal Palace in Copenhagen.

At 9.20 a.m., after Germany threatened to use the *Luftwaffe* to bombard Copenhagen, the Danish Government ordered a cease-fire. By the end of the day, Germany controlled all of Denmark. In addition to providing a platform for operations in Norway, occupation of Denmark provided the *Kriegsmarine* with bases for operations in the North Sea and Atlantic. It also provided flank security for the vital supplies of Swedish steel coming to Germany across the Baltic.

At dawn on the same day, German troops were swarming ashore at Oslo,

'Operation Weserübung warrants examination because it was one of the first "joint" operations, with the German army, navy, and air force fighting as a team in spite of inter-service rivalries.'

R. Hooker/ C. Coglianese, modern US Department of Defense analysis

Bergen, Trondheim and even – to the astonishment of a world steeped in the tradition of British supremacy at sea – at Narvik, over a thousand miles from the German homeland. German paratroops seized Sola airport near Stavanger and dropped later on to Fornebu airport near Oslo, while the *Kriegsmarine* ferried the army formations across the Skagerrak and Kattegat, though not without loss. Both the heavy cruiser *Blücher* and the light cruiser *Karlsruhe* were sunk, the first by Norwegian coastal guns and the second by the British submarine *Truant*. The heavy cruiser Admiral Hipper had 37m (120ft) torn out of her starboard bow when she was rammed by the British destroyer *Glowworm* in a self-sacrificial attack, an action that won her commander, Lieutenant-Commander G.B. Roope, the first posthumous Victoria Cross of the war.

On land only the Norwegian forces, reacting with admirable determination after the first shock, could offer any resistance, but the Royal Navy could at least help up at Narvik. Five destroyers led by Captain Warburton-Lee created chaos among the German warships in the harbour, sinking two German destroyers but losing two in the process. On 12 April, the old battleship *Warspite*, accompanied by nine destroyers, raced up the Ototfjord and completed the destruction; but to the south the preponderance of German artillery and trained battalions – and the complete domination of the air by the *Luftwaffe* – ensured the *Wehrmacht's* ultimate success.

*Above: German
Gebirgsjäger, or mountain
troops, paddle up a
Norwegian fjord. Under
the command of General
Dietl, the 3rd Mountain
Division captured Narvik.
However, it was
recaptured by the British
in May.*

In eight days, brigades of the German 163rd and 196th Divisions had advanced 290km (180 miles) and now controlled the vital southern region. When hastily landed British reinforcements eventually arrived, they were incorporated piecemeal into the ragged defences, and beaten, as were the Norwegians, by better trained, better armed, and much better coordinated and commanded German troops. The survivors of two British brigades, landed at Andalsnes in the middle of April, were re-embarked and evacuated by 1 May, and central and southern Norway was virtually abandoned to the Germans.

However, in the far north at Narvik, the situation for the German General Dietl and his 2000 mountain troops was not at first so favourable. Their naval transport and supply had been destroyed and they were chased out of Narvik itself by a combined force of British Guardsmen, French *Chasseurs Alpins* and Polish *Chasseurs du Nord*. By 28 May, Narvik was at last firmly in Allied hands. Thus it was somewhat ironic that orders had already been issued for the rapid return home of all Allied forces, as they and their weapons were urgently needed elsewhere.

Perhaps the most illuminating comment upon the Allied conduct of the Norwegian campaign was written years after the war by the man appointed to command the British reinforcements in central Norway. As Major-General Carton de Wiart, VC walked along

Whitehall to answer an urgent summons to the War Office in early April, 'It dawned on me that it might be Norway, as I had never been there and knew nothing about it!'

But if the Norwegian campaign was a setback for the British Army, it was a disaster for the Prime Minister.

Political Retribution

The House of Commons was packed, the mood of the members frustrated and angry. The anger concentrated on the figure of Neville Chamberlain sitting in his usual place on the front bench, so pale with fury and humiliation that Churchill, despite the bitter arguments of the past few years, was filled with sympathy for his harassed leader.

The First Lord of the Admiralty could hardly remember such bitter attacks being mounted in the House before. These were attacks against the policies of appeasement to which the Government had clung for so many months, against the pathetic optimism exhibited by the Prime Minister both in his dealings with Hitler before the war and in his attitude to Britain's defences since its outbreak, and especially against the contents of a speech Chamberlain had made but a month before, which had included the unfortunate statement that he believed 'Hitler has missed the bus!'

Nor was the attack delivered entirely by members of the Opposition, for it reached its zenith with a speech from one of Chamberlain's oldest friends and political colleagues, Leo Amery. Quoting Cromwell's scathing indictment of the leaders of Hampden's army as 'old decaying service men,' he turned directly on the Prime Minister and quoted Cromwell for the second time: 'You have sat here too long for any good you have been doing,' he proclaimed. 'Depart, I say, and let us have done with you! In the name of God, go!'

It was a devastating shock to the Prime Minister's ego, underlined by howls from the backbenchers chanting 'Go! Go! Go!' as he left the House. Later that day, he admitted to Churchill that he felt that he could not continue to lead a one-party government in the prosecution of the war, and that a national government embracing members of all parties should be formed. However, he doubted if the Labour leaders would serve under his own direction.

So, in fact, it proved during the somewhat involved talks and negotiations of the next 48 hours. By 11 a.m. on 10 May, Chamberlain had accepted that he must give way to another leader, and sent for the two men between whom he felt the choice must be made: Lord Halifax and Winston Churchill.

'I have had many important interviews in my public life,' Churchill later wrote, 'and this was certainly the most important. Usually I talk a great deal, but on this occasion I was silent.' It must have been a remarkable scene: Chamberlain, still icily certain of the rightness of his every action since taking office but prepared to yield in the face of such uncomprehending and

Below: Scandinavia saw the first major parachute operations of the war, when German Fallschirmjäger *were used to capture key Norwegian and Danish airfields, thus allowing safe landing of additional more conventional forces and supplies.*

Left: Wehrmacht *troops stand at the ready, poised with an MG-34 machine gun and Kar-98 rifles. By the end of April, the Germans controlled the major cities of Norway.*

incomprehensible hostility, now sure that his preference for Lord Halifax was justifiable; Churchill silent, feeling no doubt the weight of history already pressing about him; Halifax uncertain, his sense of duty unsustained by any driving ambition. It was, as Churchill wrote, 'a very long pause.... It certainly seemed longer than the two minutes which one observes in the commemoration of Armistice Day.'

It was broken, at last, by Halifax. It would be, he said, very difficult for him to direct the War Cabinet from outside the House of Commons, where all the major decisions must be debated, and where, as a member of the House of Lords, he was barred from speaking. It should be remembered that these were the days before a peer could disclaim his title. When he had finished, it was evident that Churchill's would be the name recommended to His Majesty, and after a little more desultory talk the three men parted. The call to Churchill came late in the afternoon, and at 6 p.m. he was shown into the

'I would say to the House, as I said to those who have joined this government: I have nothing to offer but blood, toil, tears and sweat.'

Winston Churchill, 13 May 1940

presence of the King, whom he was to serve so devotedly through such crucial years.

'I suppose you don't know why I have sent for you?' asked the King with a smile.

'Sir, I simply couldn't imagine why,' replied Churchill, matching his mood.

'I want to ask you to form a government'.

So began the premiership of one of the most remarkable men in British history and it is hard to believe that, for most of the rest of the world, the appointment itself and the events surrounding it passed for the moment almost unnoticed.

One of the few who might have taken heed of the new appointment was Adolf Hitler, who had been well aware of Churchill's opposition to the Nazis in the 1930s. Via the Nazi Foreign Office official Ernst Bohle (who had been born of German parents in Yorkshire and brought up in South Africa), Hitler had invited Churchill to Germany for talks, but the Englishman refused. At the time, the Germans considered Churchill to be too much of an outsider to be much of a threat, but now the biggest foe of appeasement was in charge in London. However, they thought that Churchill would be only a minor irritant, who would be swept aside as the full might of the *Wehrmacht* was unleashed.

On the morning of Churchill's appointment, the *Wehrmacht* launched a massive offensive into Belgium and Holland, both of which had been neutral up to that time. As army and SS spearheads crossed the border into the Low Countries, the *Luftwaffe* bombarded Rotterdam and German *Fallschirmjäger* were dropped onto key points along a carefully planned attack route. The days of the 'Phoney War' were gone for ever.

Into the Low Countries

The original army plan for the invasion of western Europe was based on Germany's opening attack in World War I, but was actually less ambitious than the Schlieffen Plan of 1914. The generals intended to occupy Belgium and France's northern industrial regions but no further. They had no intention of repeating the ill-fated march on Paris tried in 1914. Indeed, the army high command believed that the ratio of forces and the power of modern defence admitted no other strategy; new objectives would require a further campaign in 1941. The German generals were not alone in thinking that this was how it would be: the French and British generals agreed too, drawing up plans to push their main mobile forces into Belgium the moment that hostilities began.

Had the attack been delivered when first ordered in autumn 1939, the generals would have had the war they planned. But Hitler had other ideas. He had fought in Belgium, among the shattered villages around Ypres, where a million British and German soldiers were killed in 1917. He knew the ground, how artillery bombardments reduced the ground to a quagmire. Countless small rivers and streams offered endless obstruction to an invader. Surely it would be better to attack further south, perhaps through

RESCUE FROM THE *ALTMARK*

On 16 February 1940, British intelligence discovered that the *Altmark*, one of the *Graf Spee*'s supply ships, was steaming down the Norwegian coast. The converted tanker had a large number of British seamen aboard, taken prisoner during the *Graf Spee*'s raiding cruise. When threatened by the British 4th Destroyer Flotilla under Captain Vian, the *Altmark* took refuge in Norwegian territorial waters, putting in to Josenfjord. With typically Churchillian panache, the orders went out from Whitehall to take the *Altmark*. Vian disregarded Norwegian neutrality, entered the fjord, forced the *Altmark* aground and rescued the prisoners, his boarding party making minor popular history with the call 'The Navy's here!'

the forested hills of the Ardennes? The generals looked down their noses at the idea.

By the time the postponed offensive was ready to roll in the spring of 1940, Hitler discovered that at least some officers shared his vision. General Erich von Manstein was chief of staff to General von Rundstedt, commander-in-chief of Army Group A in the west. Manstein had studied the Ardennes region and come to the same conclusion as the *Führer*. He discussed the idea with the Germany's most influential tank expert, General Heinz Guderian. They argued for a radical strategy: to rush German Panzer divisions along the narrow forest tracks and out onto the gently rolling hills of northern France. Bursting into open country, they would punch through the enemy before the defences were ready for them. It would be difficult to bring enough artillery with these fast-moving formations, and other German commanders envisaged a pause while the guns were brought forward; a World War I-style battle would then take place along the river Meuse. Guderian and his tank men were far more sanguine, confident that they could storm the French defences. The *Luftwaffe's* bombers, especially its fearsome Ju-87 'Stuka' dive-bombers, would provide close support in place of artillery.

Hitler adopted the Manstein plan and changed the orders to his commanders in the west. Manstein would receive due credit in time, but the orthodox generals resented having a relatively junior officer's plan thrust upon them, and posted von Manstein to command an infantry corps in the rear. One thing Hitler could not change was the odds. Although Germany enjoyed superiority in the air, with 4000 aircraft against 3000 Allied, the *Wehrmacht* had only 141 divisions with which to attack 144 Allied divisions. The Allies had some 3383 tanks compared to the German total of 2335 – many of these being light tanks of limited fighting capacity.

Above: British troops captured in northern Norway are marched towards the ships in Trondheim harbour which will take them to prisoner of war camps in Germany.

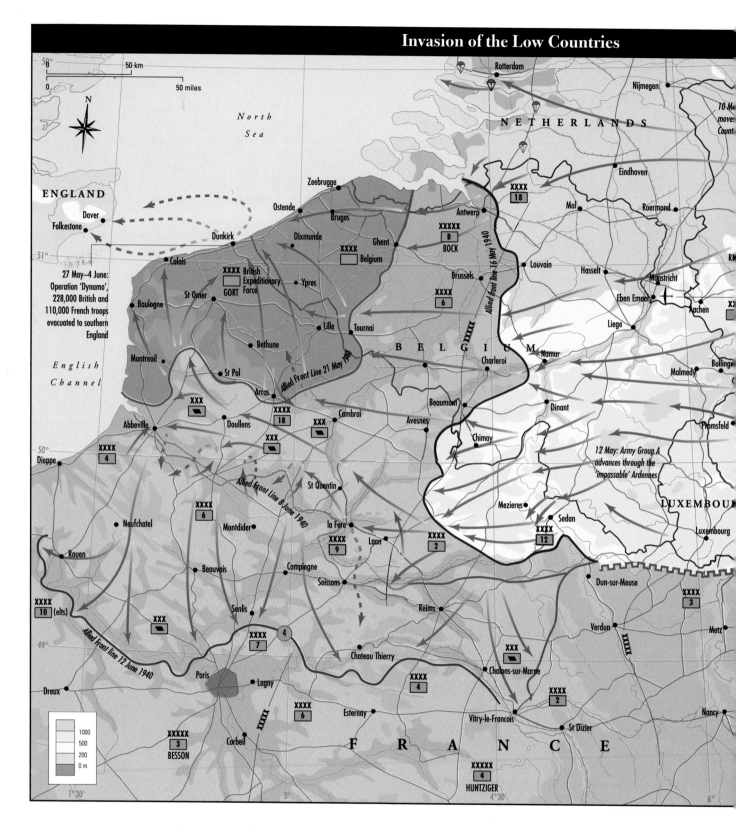

Invasion of the Low Countries

27 May–4 June: Operation 'Dynamo', 228,000 British and 110,000 French troops evacuated to southern England

12 May: Army Group A advances through the 'impassable' Ardennes

Operations Begin

Shortly after 2.30 on the morning of 10 May 1940, 64 men of the German army crossed the Dutch frontier; this was the very spearhead of the *Wehrmacht's* advance. Paratroopers were dropped on key bridges near Rotterdam, the Hague, Dordrecht and

Invasion of the West
May–June 1940

→ German attacks
→ Allied counter-attacks
- -► Allied retreats
— Allied front lines
ᔐᔐ Allied defensive lines
ᕀ German paratroop drops
✝ German glider assault

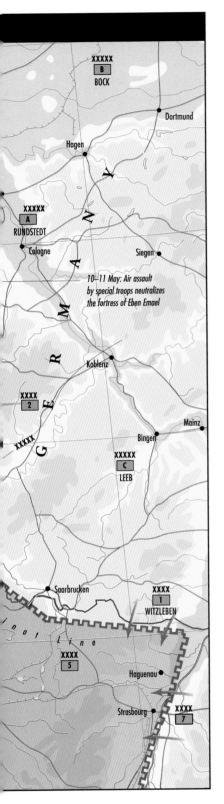

10–11 May: Air assault by special troops neutralizes the fortress of Eben Emael

Moerdijk, paralyzing any effective Dutch response to the flood coming across the border. More troops crossed the Albert Canal into Flanders. They should have been held back by the huge Belgian fort at Eben Emael, but at 5.30 a.m., glider-borne troops had dropped over the Belgian border to capture and demolish the massive strongpoint.

Five minutes later, the 30 divisions of Army Group B under General Fedor von Bock flooded forward across the frontiers from Maastricht up to the coast at the Ems estuary, while to the south General von Rundstedt's Army Group A of 44 divisions, including the main striking force of seven Panzer divisions under General Kleist, moved forward into the Belgian Ardennes – the wooded country which French military commanders had been describing as impassable for tanks since 1919.

With an almost suicidal alacrity that brought tears of joy to Hitler's eyes, the Allied armies in the north – five divisions of the BEF, eight divisions of the French First Army on their right and seven divisions of the French Seventh Army up on the coast around Dunkirk – left the defensive positions they had spent the bitterly cold winter so arduously preparing, and moved forward to join the Belgian army in accordance with the Dyle Plan, which envisaged a defensive line running along the Dyle and Meuse rivers.

There were obviously some difficulties to be overcome on the way, for the *Luftwaffe* was busy overhead all the time, and it provided the baptism of Allied troops by dive-bombing. It took time for them to become accustomed to the nerve-shaking howl which accompanied it. Moreover, the violence and speed of the German advance and the seemingly continuous *Luftwaffe* attacks had spread panic among the civilian population, and the roads over which the Allied troops were travelling were soon choked by refugees fleeing ahead of Bock's advancing infantry.

Nevertheless, by the evening of 14 May, the Allied line was formed. From the mouth of the Scheldt to just north of Antwerp stood three divisions of the French Seventh Army; the 80km (50 miles) southeast to Louvain were held by 13 divisions of the Belgian army; between Louvain and Wavre, the front was held by the BEF and from Wavre to Namur by six divisions of the French First Army. Many of the battalion and brigade commanders were dismayed by the fragmentary

Left: German operations in the West began as the Allies expected, with an advance into Holland and Belgium. What came as a surprise was the massive armoured assault through the Ardennes.

47

Above: A German MG34 machine gun team in action. The MG34 was the first true general-purpose machine gun, able to lay down sustained fire from a tripod but light enough to be used as a squad support weapon when fitted with a bipod.

nature of the defences they now occupied, and their troops were equally unhappy. They had spent the winter preparing extensive field fortifications along the French border, and now they were expected to hold back the advancing *Wehrmacht* from defensive positions which at best were rudimentary, and many cases were non-existent. At the same time, the divisional and higher commanders were alarmed by news of events further to the south. But, as yet, none of them were aware of the fact that Bock's slowly advancing Army Group was in fact 'the matador's cloak' tempting the mass of the Allied armies forward into the trap that would release Kleist's Panzer Group for the killing thrust.

Allied Collapse

After sucking the Allied mobile forces northwards, Bock was tasked with securing Holland before moving southwards into Belgium and France, providing the anvil to the hammer of the Panzers heading for the French coast. The first task for the Germans was to take key fortifications around which the Dutch and Belgian defences were based. The imposing concrete and steel fortress at Eben Emael had already fallen to a glider assault. Other paratroopers were needed to secure the bridges that made it possible to operate across Holland's vast canal network and drive for the major Dutch cities near the coast.

By 13 May, the German Eighteenth Army under General Georg von Kuechler was pushing into 'Fortress Holland', crossing bridges that had been seized by paratroopers in the previous days. Near Breda they encountered the French Seventh Army under Henri Giraud, which had moved along the coast through Belgium and into Holland. The French were driven back towards Antwerp.

The Dutch destruction of the key bridges across the Ijssel and the flooding of much of the countryside meant that the German push towards Amsterdam, which was spearheaded by the *Leibstandarte* SS, was slowed considerably. Since Hitler did not want his 'show troops' to get bogged down in an infantry slogging match, they were moved south on 13 May to join with the SS-VT regiments and the 9th Panzer Division in the drive on Rotterdam. German *Fallschirmjäger* had already captured the key Moerdijk bridges intact, and the way into the city was open. On the morning of the 14th, the SS men accompanying the Panzers relieved the lightly armed paratroopers holding the Moerdijk bridge, having taken over 4000 prisoners during the advance.

Dutch resistance, though patchy, was holding up the German timetable. The German high command issued an ultimatum, threatening to destroy Rotterdam by artillery and air bombardment unless Dutch resistance ceased. The Dutch, cut off from their British and French allies, had no choice but to comply. However, although the artillery bombardment was cancelled, the orders did not reach the *Luftwaffe,* and Rotterdam was bombed into ruin. Immediately after the bombing, the *Leibstandarte* SS moved into the city. At one point, they saw a number of armed Dutch soldiers and opened fire. Unfortunately for the SS men, the Dutch soldiers had been part of a local surrender, which was being accepted by *Luftwaffe* General Kurt Student. The *Leibstandarte* fire seriously wounded Student, the founder of the German parachute force. He survived to lead the invasion of Crete a year later.

On 13 May, the Queen of the Netherlands and much of the Dutch Government took ship at the Hague, heading for England and exile. General Henri Winkelmen, the commander of the Dutch army, then surrendered. Further south, von Reichenau's Sixth Army poured across the Albert Canal into Belgium. The Belgian army fell back to the line of the River Dyle, where it was joined by elements of the BEF and by General Georges Blanchard's First French Army. By 15 May, some 35 Allied divisions were concentrated between Namur and Antwerp. The German Sixth Army was probing their hastily built defences, while the Eighteenth Army was pushing southwards out of Holland and threatening to take the Anglo/French/Belgian force in the flank.

However, even as they prepared to take on Bock's armies, the Allies were hit by shocking news from the southeast. The French centre had been shattered by new German forces, and all of the Allied troops in Belgium were in danger of being cut off. The campaign in the Low Countries was all but over, and the German plan was, with a few minor exceptions, working as predicted. Bock's advance into Holland had drawn the Allies northwards. Now Rundstedt's armour had been unleashed through the Ardennes, and the Panzers were rampaging through northern France.

'Germany has bombed Rotterdam today, and Utrecht is threatened with destruction. To save the civilian population, I believe to be justified to order the troops under your command to stop fighting.'

General Winkelman, Dutch army commander, 14 May 1940

SS COMBAT UNITS

The armed SS was established after Hitler came to power in 1933. It was designed to provide a politically reliable force to act as a counterbalance to the *Wehrmacht.* Initially it comprised the members of Hitler's bodyguard, the *Leibstandarte,* together with a number of *Politsiche Bereitschaften,* or Political Emergency Squads whose primary function had been to use violent measures against party opponents. These became the SS-*Verfügungstruppe,* or SS-VT.

By the time of the *Anschluss* with Austria, the armed SS had grown dramatically. In addition to the 2600 men of the *Leibstandarte,* there were three SS-VT *Standarten,* or regiments, derived from the *Politische Bereitschaften.* The three regiments were given the names *Deutschland, Germania* and *Der Führer* and were trained and equipped as motorized infantry. The three *Standarten* would become the nucleus of the SS-VT division, which saw action in Poland and France. In 1940, the division was renamed *Das Reich,* and it was joined by the *Totenkopf* division, formed around a nucleus of the SS *Totenkopfverbände,* Theodore Eicke's concentration camp guards.

The Battle of France

One of the principal aims of Adolph Hitler's military policy was to see the destruction of France, the enemy that had humiliated Germany after World War I. The invasion of the Low Countries was nothing more than a trap to draw the Allied armies out of position while the *Wehrmacht* prepared its killer blow – a Panzer thrust through the Ardennes.

Once the attack in the West was launched, German forces stormed across Holland and Belgium just as the Allies expected, the imposing concrete and steel fortress at Eben Emael falling to a crack unit of paratroops who landed by glider right on the roof. However, the forces under General von Bock – 30 infantry divisions of Army Group B – were actually a feint. Their intent was designed to convince the Allies that the Germans were following the same old plan which had failed in earlier wars.

The Drive through the Ardennes

The real punch came through the Ardennes, where the 44 divisions of von Runstedt's Army Group A, including seven Panzer divisions under von Kleist, planned to catch the Allies by surprise. The bulk of the French troops were contained in the massive defences of the Maginot line, guarding against an attack across the German border. But the huge works did not cover the Belgian border, French planners having considered that a major attack through the Ardennes was impossible.

The German plan quickly became a reality. Encountering little resistance from Belgian troops in the Ardennes, the Panzer divisions headed down the dirt roads in alarmingly dense columns. Crashing through the 'impassable' forests and hills as though on a peacetime exercise, brushing aside the French light cavalry unit that had been sent out to 'delay' them, the three divisions of General Guderian's Panzer Corps were across the French frontier and had reached the Meuse on each side of Sedan by the afternoon of 12 May.

Military traffic police have seldom had a more decisive impact on a campaign: thousands of vehicles kept to schedule and by the evening of 12 May, German armour controlled the right bank of the Meuse up as far as Dinant. Here, in 1870, the French Emperor Napoleon III had been decisively beaten by the Prussians, going into captivity with his surviving soldiers while revolution broke out in Paris. Seventy years later, the

Opposite: The German invasion of France came after operations in the Low Countries had drawn the main Allied field armies northwards. Bypassing the Maginot Line, the Wehrmacht *was soon rampaging through northern France, spreading havoc and confusion.*

French commander-in-chief, 68-year old General Maurice Gamelin, expected German units to emerge from the Ardennes at some stage in the battle. But since he did not anticipate anything more than a light, probing force, the 9th Army, assigned to protect the area, was stretched more thinly than other French armies.

Once they had got over the shock of the German arrival on the Meuse, the French High Command estimated that the crossing would take at least four days to organize and two to carry out. In fact, the *Wehrmacht* was across the river in strength within 24 hours. On 13 May, Guderian's infantry paddled across the Meuse in rubber dinghies. At the same time, a *Luftwaffe* force of 300 twin-engine bombers and 200 Stukas pulverized the French defences.

The dive-bombers attacked with particular accuracy, knocking out key French gun positions. The foot soldiers were across by 3 p.m. Combat engineers had a ferry

Right: Bursting through the Ardennes, the troops of von Runstedt's Army Group A reached the Meuse at Sedan on 12 May. They were across the river one day later, ahead of combat engineers who would build the bridges needed by the panzers.

operational in an hour, and by 4.30 p.m. a bridge was in place and the tanks could cross to the far bank. French counterattacks came too little and too late. All the first-line troops had been committed to the northern flank. The Allies' strategy unravelled as the Panzer divisions fanned out, racing ahead of their infantry and threatening to cut off the British and French armies in Belgium.

Pushing into France

By the morning of 14 May, Guderian had two bridgeheads consolidating, while up at Dinant the 7th Panzer Division of Colonel-General Hermann Hoth's XV Panzer Corps (commanded by Major-General Erwin Rommel) had formed yet another bridgehead in the face of desperate but sporadic French resistance.

Early on 15 May, the flood burst into France. From each of the bridgeheads, the Panzers roared out, preceded on every front of advance by a cloud of screaming Stukas, covered against attack from British or French fighters by marauding Messerschmitts. Refugees choked the roads. It was bad enough that they were being harried by the *Luftwaffe*, but the helpless civilians were also bullied by frightened and demoralized soldiers and gendarmes of their own side. All too soon, they were being forced into the ditches by strange, ominous, foreign vehicles manned by confident young Germans who waved triumphantly at them as they passed. The *Wehrmacht* troops rarely deliberately harmed fleeing civilians, but in their wake they left an impression of total invincibility.

That evening, German Panzers were reported only 19km (12 miles) from Laon. Daladier, now France's Minister of National Defence, ordered a counterattack, but the French commander-in-chief, General Gamelin, replied that he had no reserves because the bulk of French strength was locked up in the outflanked Maginot Line. At the same time, Gamelin announced that he could no longer take responsibility for the defence of Paris, and he issued orders for a general retreat of all French forces in Belgium. A copy of these orders came, solely by good fortune, to the notice of the British commander-in-chief, Lord Gort, enabling him to ensure that the British Expeditionary Force (BEF) divisions on the Dyle were not left there on their own.

The scale of the catastrophe was now apparent and the French Government prepared to evacuate Paris. With political will equally paralyzed in London – Winston Churchill had only just replaced Neville Chamberlain as prime minister – it was left to Gort to choose between abandoning the French or hazarding most of Britain's tiny regular army in a last attempt to salvage the situation.

In the face of apparently imminent disaster, Churchill flew to Paris on the evening of 16 May. He had been woken by a telephone call from the French premier, Paul Reynaud. In a devastating indication of French morale, Reynaud announced that 'We have been defeated! We are beaten; we have lost the battle!' Churchill's aim was both to put some iron into the French political backbone and to discover for himself the true state of affairs. These became distressingly obvious when in answer to his question 'Ou est la masse de manoeuvre?' ('Where is the strategic reserve?'), Gamelin answered 'Aucune!' ('None!'). But even at this unsettling news, Churchill refused to abandon hope.

There were still considerable French forces to the south of the German breakthrough, he noted, and even larger forces, including the BEF, to the north. Between them, could they not first manoeuvre to channel and then contain the German breakthrough, then counterattack from both north and south and so cut the enemy spearheads off from their main sources of supply and support?

'Well, I don't think you'll get across the river in the first place!'

General Busch's (erroneous) reaction to General Guderian's estimate of being able to operate south of the Meuse within five days of the offensive through the Ardennes.

Attempting a Defence

In the depths of their despondency, the French leaders were reluctant to admit the practicability of such a scheme, pleading lack of air strength unless Churchill were to abandon all thought of retaining RAF fighter squadrons for the defence of Britain and send them all to France instead. Even then, it seemed most likely that the German forces would be either on the Channel coast or in Paris – or both – in a matter of days, in which case the British and French armies to the north most probably faced at least disintegration and, unless a general armistice saved them, possibly total destruction.

Churchill was home by the following morning, but before he left he managed to instil something of his own dogged courage into the French leadership, so that they at least agreed to order some form of counterattack on the German spearheads as he had suggested. Yet the sluggish pace of Allied military planning meant that it would be four days before the counterattack could be attempted, and even then it was bungled. By the evening of 20 May, Guderian's Panzer spearheads had reached Abbeville at the mouth of the Somme, and at this point their line was as attenuated as it ever would be. If the *Wehrmacht* was vulnerable to a determined counterattack, it was here.

On 21 May, four British infantry brigades and a tank brigade were launched southwards from Arras, in theory supported by two French infantry divisions on one flank and one light mechanized division on the other, while equally strong French forces

Below: The French High Command estimated that it would take the Germans four days to cross the Meuse at Sedan. Guderian's troops, who had seized control of the East bank on both sides of the city, were across in force in less than 24 hours.

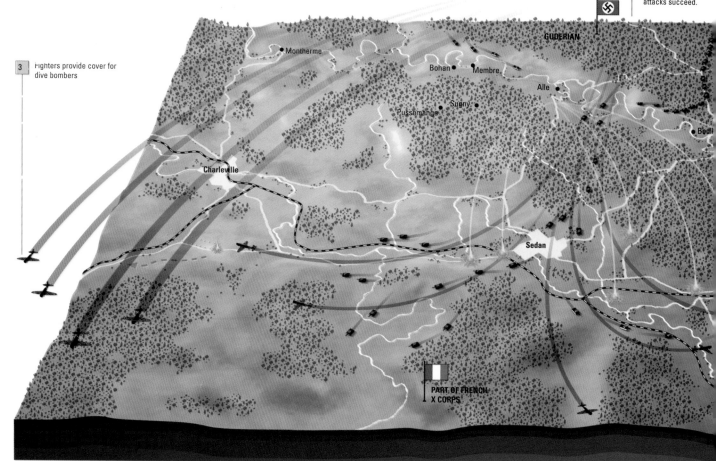

2   13 May: Guderian laun[ched] four attacks across th[e] Meuse river, covered [by] Stuka dive bombers. T[he] attacks succeed.

GUDERIAN

3   Fighters provide cover for dive bombers

Montherme

Bohan   Membre

Alle

Sugny

Pussemange

Bouil

Charleville

Sedan

PART OF FRENCH
X CORPS

were assumed to be attacking up from the south to meet them. In the event, only the British forces and the French light mechanized division moved at all. They did manage to inflict a stinging reverse on the SS *Totenkopf* Division, who later took out their frustrations by massacring 100 British prisoners of war at Le Paradis, the first of numerous such atrocities committed by the SS. The British tanks, however, quickly found themselves blocked by Rommel's 7th Panzer Division. Rommel used his 88mm (3.46in) Flak guns to engage the heavily armoured British infantry tanks, which were virtually invulnerable to smaller German anti-tank weapons. After a brisk battle, which at least managed to worry Rommel seriously, the 7th Panzer Division drove the British back to their original positions and threatened them with encirclement.

By the evening of 23 May, Gort was withdrawing the British brigades further north, and two days later it became evident to him that only a rapid retreat to the coast and

Panzer strike through the Ardennes
12–14 May, 1940

Armoured advance

Air support

Artillery support

French retreat

1 12 May: XIX Panzer Corps Commanded by Gen. Guderian advances using country lanes and tracks through the lightly defended Ardennes forest. It quickly brushes aside the French forces.

4 14 May: French forces harassed by armoured and air attacks fall back, unable to reorganize. Efforts by Ravigny's XXI Corps to mount an armoured counterstroke are defeated by the power of Guderian's Corps.

evacuation to England would save even a quarter of his command. On his own responsibility, he issued the necessary orders: the British III Corps withdrew to the beaches on each side of Dunkirk, I Corps fell back to hold the western flank with one French division on their right and the British II Corps on their left, while the Belgian army held the eastern end of the perimeter. However, on 28 May King Leopold of Belgium signed an armistice with the Germans, the Belgian army ceased to exist, and a large gap yawned on the left of the British positions.

The gap was filled during the night by a manoeuvre of extraordinary difficulty carried out with admirable efficiency by the 3rd Infantry Division under command of Major-

Above: Soldiers from the 'Das Reich' division take a break to eat during the rapid German advance through northern France.

55

General Montgomery. It is not too much to say that this operation saved the British Expeditionary Force. And then fate stepped in. The *Führer* ordered his Panzers to stop, allowing the British a breathing space in which to organize one of the greatest evacuation operations in history.

Operation Dynamo

Operation Dynamo was the attempt to evacuate the British Army, and as many French soldiers as possible, from the trap into which they had been lured. Over a thousand boats took part in this evacuation. They varied in size from a Royal Navy anti-aircraft cruiser down to dinghies, which were sailed across the Channel by their owners from a hundred tiny slips along the south coast or along the reaches of the Thames. At least 250 of these craft were sunk and many of the yacht owners were killed or wounded, but an astonishingly large number of soldiers were saved to fight again, and to form the basis of new armies. The highest hopes before the evacuation began were that perhaps 50,000 men might escape capture or worse; in the event, 338,226 reached the shores of Britain during those miraculous nine days, of which, on Churchill's insistence, over 100,000 were French. He had returned to Paris on 31 May, and there agreed that British troops would share in holding the rear guard, and that French troops in the bridgehead would be evacuated in the same proportion as the British.

HITLER'S 'STOP ORDER'

Why did Hitler order his Panzers to stop their advance against the British around Dunkirk? There have been several suggestions. It may have been a political gesture to allow the British time to come to terms with defeat and sue for peace. Hitler might also have been worried about the terrain, stopping his forces to prevent the Panzers from getting bogged down amid the canals and marshes around Dunkirk. However, the most commonly held belief is that the order was intended to allow Hermann Göring to make good on his boast that the *Luftwaffe* could finish the job. In the event, the Germans met with stiff resistance from the Spitfires and Hurricanes of the RAF, and in spite of some successes were never able seriously to impede the British evacuation from Dunkirk.

As it happened, French formations were fighting furiously to the south of the bridgehead (thus holding back powerful German forces that would otherwise have been free to attack Dunkirk), and these never reached the sea. Many of those which did arrive towards the end of the operation refused the chance to escape, and the last ships to sail were almost empty. As quite a large number of French troops who did get away, quickly decided that they did not care for life in Britain and chose to return to France (where most of them soon found themselves in German prison camps), Churchill's well-meant gesture was to a great extent wasted.

To the British people, however, the escape of the bulk of the BEF at Dunkirk was a miracle. To such an extent did their spirits rise, indeed, that Churchill found it necessary to sound a cautionary note. 'We must be very careful not to assign to this deliverance the attributes of a victory,' he said in his report to Parliament. 'Wars are not won by evacuations.' Yet the miracle of Dunkirk kept Britain in the war.

German Consolidation

In spite of stiffening resistance in places like Normandy, some of Hitler's Panzers turned west, moving with incredible speed to secure the Atlantic coast. Others sped south,

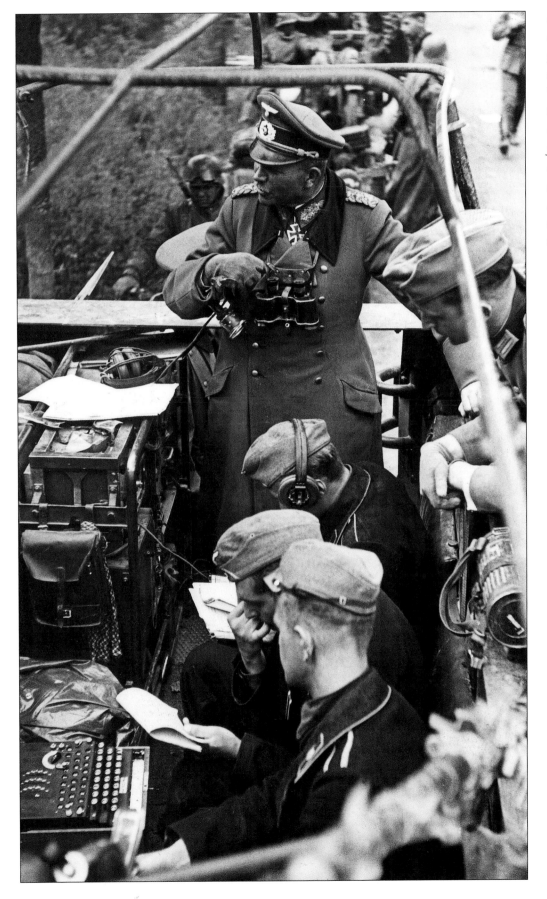

Left: Heinz Guderian, the architect of the German panzer force, led the spearhead of the Wehrmacht's advance. As with most German Generals, he led from the front, using a well-equipped communications half-track. Note the Enigma coding machine being used by the operator nearest the camera.

Right: Cut off by the rapid German advance, the bulk of the British Expeditionary Force retreated to the coast at Dunkirk. Most were saved by the Royal Navy in Operation Dynamo. Many were plucked off the beaches by an armada of small craft that had been pressed into service for the purpose.

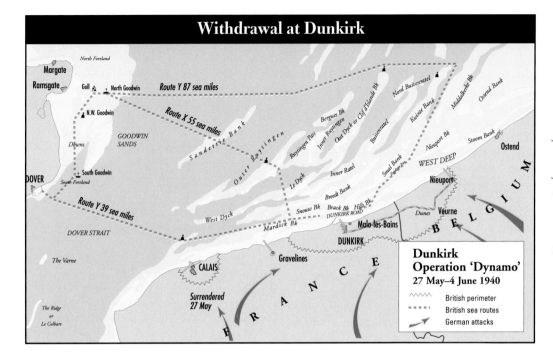

Withdrawal at Dunkirk

Margate
Ramsgate
North Foreland
Gull
North Goodwin
Route Y 87 sea miles
N.W. Goodwin
Route X 55 sea miles
GOODWIN SANDS
Downs
Sandettie Bank
Outer Ratyingen
Bergues Bk
Ruytingen Pass
Inner Ruytingen
Oost Dyck or Clif d'Islande Bk
Nord Buitennatel
Kwinte Bank
Middelkerke Bk
Ostend Bank
South Goodwin
South Foreland
DOVER
Buitenratel
Smal Bank
Zuydcote
WEST DEEP
Nieuport Bk
Stroom Bank
Ostend
Route Y 39 sea miles
Le Dyck
Inner Ratel
Nieuport
BELGIUM
West Dyck
Breedt Bank
Snouw Bk
Brack Bk
Hill Bk
Dunes
Veurne
DOVER STRAIT
Mardick Bk
DUNKIRK ROAD
Malo-les-Bains
The Varne
Gravelines
DUNKIRK
FRANCE
CALAIS
Surrendered 27 May
The Ridge or Le Colbart

Dunkirk Operation 'Dynamo'
27 May–4 June 1940

⌇⌇⌇⌇ British perimeter
▪▪▪▪ British sea routes
➤ German attacks

Left: In the nine days of Operation Dynamo, 338,226 French and British soldiers were taken off the beach by a fleet of over 900 vessels, ranging from cabin cruisers and trawlers to cross-channel ferries and destroyers. More than 50,000 vehicles were abandoned, and the evacuation was made possible only by a valiant rearguard action by 40,000 French troops.

completely bypassing the Maginot line, leaving more than 400,000 French troops bewildered and demoralized in their suddenly useless fortifications. Once the German army had occupied Dunkirk and the French coast as far west as Abbeville and the mouth of the Somme, there was nothing except Hitler's orders to stop them turning south and driving down into the body of France; as early as 29 May, the *Führer* had intimated to both Rundstedt and Bock that his next plans would be to 'settle the French army's account'. Britain could wait, or better still, come to terms. He was convinced that with Germany and its partners in control of Europe, the British would eventually have to make peace.

As a result, even before the Dunkirk evacuation was over, Bock had deputed his Eighteenth Army to clear up Belgium and press on westwards, and had directed the remainder of his Army Group B down to take position along the line of the Somme, alongside von Rundstedt's triumphant infantry and Panzer divisions closing up to the coast. By 5 June, the 10 Panzer divisions of both army groups had been redeployed into five armoured corps (three under Bock, two under Rundstedt), and that morning at dawn, preceded as usual by clouds of dive-bombers, two of them burst out of bridgeheads west of Amiens and drove for the Seine.

'The second great offensive is starting today with formidable new resources!' announced Hitler, while General Weygand, who had been recalled from the Levant to take command of the French army when it became obvious that Gamelin had lost control, appealed to his troops: 'May the thought of our afflicted country inspire in you an unflinching resolve to stand firm. The fate of your country and the future of our children depend on your firmness.' This was hardly the most inspiring message for troops in a desperate situation.

Nevertheless, French troops hurriedly assembled into 'hedgehogs' around what their commanders considered strategic nodal points and held back the flood for a few hours, destroying the leading Panzer formations as they came within range, and giving the German commanders pause for thought. 'The French are putting up strong opposition,' reported one of them. 'We are seeing a new French way of fighting.'

Right: The crew of a massive French Char B tank surrenders to German infantry. French tanks were not concentrated like those of the Wehrmacht: *they were distributed in penny packets among infantry formations.*

Opposite: A young German soldier poses for the camera in the advance towards Dunkirk. He is armed with a Kar-98 rifle and has a grenade tucked into his belt.

But in a very short time the 'hedgehogs' were being bypassed, and by 11 June Hoth's XV Panzer Corps controlled the Seine from Vernon to Le Havre. Two of Bock's Panzer corps, XXXIX and XLI, had passed the Chemins des Dames and were driving down between Rheims and the Aisne, and his Ninth Army was heading straight for Paris. The following day, Rommel's 7th Panzer Division reached St Valery and captured the western flank of the French Tenth Army, including the survivors of the British 51st Highland Division under General Fortune. Two days later, on 14 June, German troops drove into Paris, which was saved from damage by an 'open city' declaration from the French Government as it hastily left for Bordeaux.

It must be said that the spectacular advance of the German army was aided throughout by the dilatoriness and uncertainty of the French High Command. Under Gamelin, this had been a major factor in precipitating disaster, and under Weygand it showed little improvement. Even the 'hedgehog' formations were described by one French general as: 'only a last resort to enable these weak but brave troops to resist with honour before being overwhelmed'. Reynaud, the French premier, when asked on the evening of 7 June if hope was fading, replied, 'No, it can't be! And yet I know that the battle is lost!'

Some French divisions, nevertheless, defended their positions resolutely, especially on the eastern sector, where the 14th Infantry Division under General de Lattre de Tassigny held XLI Panzer Corps (and in one action took 800 prisoners). A little further west at Rethel the 2nd

Division for a whole day fought off every attack mounted against it. Instead of continuing to assault these positions, the Panzers found the space between and drove through to Rheims. Even at the lower levels of the French army, there seems to have been no understanding of the impracticability of static defence against strong and mobile armour. At one point, an armoured battle did take place, when a counterattack was put in by a formation of French heavy 'B' tanks – the strongest in the world at that time – which worried Guderian when he saw his anti-tank shells ricocheting 'off the thick plate of the French tanks'. The French armour drove north towards a small village called Perthes, where they rescued an infantry regiment that had been surrounded – only to find that they were surrounded themselves and out of petrol!

Everywhere else, though, the French divisions were overwhelmed or cut off and control from headquarters lost. As the Panzers cut deeper into the heart of France, and the grey-clad columns marching so cheerfully behind them occupied more villages and towns, French morale plummeted and the French army moved closer to disintegration.

The Fall of France

As early as 9 June, Weygand had stated, 'our armies are fighting the last possible defensive battle. If this attempt fails, they are doomed to rapid destruction.' Two days later, he moved his GHQ out of Paris to Briare on the Loire, where that evening the last of the Anglo-French conferences was held. Churchill arrived accompanied by Eden and Generals Ismay and Spears, while General Weygand was supported by Marshal Petain and attended – somewhat guardedly, one suspects – by Brigadier de Gaulle. Weygand opened the meeting with the declaration that 'the last line

CHURCHILL'S ORATORY

During his speech to Parliament following the British evacuation from Dunkirk, Winston Churchill delivered what was to become one of the most famous passages of rhetoric in British history:

'Even though large tracts of Europe and many old and famous States have fallen or may fall into the grip of the Gestapo and all the odious apparatus of Nazi rule, we shall not flag or fail. We shall go on to the end. We shall fight in France, we shall fight on the sea and oceans, we shall fight with growing confidence and growing strength in the air; we shall defend our island, whatever the cost may be. We shall fight on the beaches, we shall fight on the landing-grounds, we shall fight in the fields and in the streets, we shall fight in the hills; we shall never surrender; and even if, which I do not for a moment believe, this island or a large part of it were subjugated and starving, then our Empire beyond the seas, armed and guarded by the British Fleet, would carry on the struggle, until, in God's good time, the New World, with all its power and might, steps forth to the rescue and liberation of the Old.'

of defence has been overrun and all the reserves are used up. We are on a knife-edge, and don't know which way we will fall from one minute to the next.' When eventually the argument and discussions died away, he closed the conference with the warning: 'Once our disposition is upset, and that won't be long now, there is no hope of reforming it, because of our lack of reserves. In this case, I can see no way of preventing an invasion of the whole of France.'

'These three hours of discussions achieved nothing,' wrote de Gaulle later. 'I thought how empty this chatter was, because it was not directed towards the only viable solution; recovery across the sea.' This was indeed a solution that Weygand was to reject with venom. On the evening of the day Paris fell, Reynaud suggested that Weygand should follow the example of the Dutch chief of staff, and surrender to the Germans the army on metropolitan soil, while the Government went to North Africa with the whole of the French navy, whatever formations of the French air force could fly there, and every French soldier who could escape. From there, it could continue the struggle alongside Britain – and America and every other freedom-loving country as soon as they saw fit to join in. 'I rejected the proposal with indignation!' Weygand claimed later. 'I would never

Above: The Wehrmacht *was still largely equipped with light tanks in 1940, but significant numbers of larger and more capable Panzer IIIs and Panzer IVs were now making an appearance. The Panzer IV seen here was armed with a short-barrelled 7.5-cm (3in) cannon.*

*Above: The rapid
destruction of the French
Army left tens of
thousands of* Poilus *–
ordinary French
conscripts – without
leaders. Some tried to get
home: others wandered
aimlessly through the
ruins of France. Many
were rounded up and
taken into captivity by
the Germans.*

agree to inflicting such shame on our flag! This would have been the ultimate crime, damning and doing irreparable harm to the military honour of our nation....I cannot think of such an ignominious proposal without a shiver of disgust!'

What 'ignominy' Weygand saw in this proposal is difficult to understand, especially as only eight days later he was to order the remaining French army formations in and behind the Maginot Line, some 400,000 troops, to 'ask for a cessation of fighting, with war honours'. Under the French Code of Military Justice, the 'ultimate crime' is 'to surrender without having exhausted every means of defence', so the behaviour of the French C-in-C during June 1940 presents something of an enigma.

On 16 June, Reynaud resigned and Marshal Petain took his place, determined to obtain an armistice from the Germans as quickly as possible and to establish a form of government of which Hitler would approve. By 20 June, German troops were in Lyons and Grenoble in the south, along the Swiss border to the east and controlling the Biscay coast to the west as far south as Royan. Mussolini, who had declared war on both France and Britain 10 days earlier, was endeavouring furiously to prod his soldiers into crossing the Franco-Italian frontier and capturing Nice before the Germans got there.

They were prevented by the events of the following day. At 3.30 p.m. on 21 June, a French delegation headed by General Huntziger was led into the very railway carriage at Compiègne in which the 1918 Armistice had been signed. Hitler had arrived with an entourage including Göring, Keitel, Ribbentrop and Hess. He read the inscription at the museum of Compiègne, which condemned 'the criminal pride of the German Empire'. His face bore a look described as 'combining hatred, scorn, revenge, and triumph'. He did not stay beyond listening to the preamble of the terms, and then joked with his subordinates in a rare display of good humour.

Little negotiation took place, for Hitler knew very well that he had won, and any arguments which Huntziger might have put up had to be referred back to Petain, who tended to agree wholeheartedly with Hitler. Forever the shrewd politician, Hitler knew just how much to give. For appearances' sake, he had to let the French people convince themselves that French national pride had been salvaged even in defeat.

Armistice Signed

Article three of the Armistice acknowledged Petain's government as the government of all metropolitan France, as well as of her overseas territories. France was allowed to keep her empire and the illusion of her national sovereignty. The promise was also made that the French battle fleet in Toulon and other Mediterranean ports would remain there under French command. Hitler was very satisfied with this, for one of his main fears had been that the powerful French battleships might join the Royal Navy.

By 7 p.m. on 22 June, the Armistice had been signed, the limits of German occupation agreed. But the terms were a sham. Hitler wanted to punish France. No particular date was given for the release of the two million French soldiers in captivity. The Vichy army was to have no more than 100,000 men, and in a further echo of Versailles, the French people were to pay not only reparations to Germany, but also had to finance the occupation.

Hitler, usually uninterested in visiting the places that he had crushed, made an exception for Paris. The amateur architect visited the French capital during his trip, accompanied by Albert Speer and his favourite sculptor Arno Breker. The city seemed deserted – its population had fallen from three million to 800,000 in the exodus that accompanied the German advance. The *Führer* visited the Eiffel Tower, paid homage at Napoleon's tomb in the Hotel des Invalides, and commented on the ugliness of the Sacre Coeur. 'It would have pained me greatly if I had had to destroy Paris,' he later added. He marvelled at having laid low the arrogant and decadent French whose love of culture, he claimed, had so undermined her martial spirit.

The humiliation of France was complete. She had been betrayed by leaders who did not have the stomach for a fight. In Paris, as the posters and German radio broadcast the terms of the disgrace, the people wept. By contrast, the German public shared Hitler's joy, and the *Führer* enjoyed a Roman-style Triumph on his return to Berlin. The streets were strewn with flowers and lined with adoring crowds. They were celebrating the man that in seven years of struggle had transformed Germany. Little more than a pariah among nations in 1933, the Reich was now the master of Europe.

The German Administration

On 25 June, Marshal Petain announced over French radio, 'Honour is saved! We must now turn our efforts to the future. A new order is beginning!' Seventeen days later, he

Map, page 66: After the fall of Paris, France's defeat became a rout. German columns raced west, southwest and southeast. Within a week, they had reached the Brittany coast, the Spanish border, the Alpes Maritimes and the border with Switzerland.

'Under the deeply moving impression of the capitulation of France, I congratulate you and the whole German Wehrmacht on the mighty victory granted by God.'

Former Kaiser Wilhelm II, letter to Hitler, July 1940

Fall of France

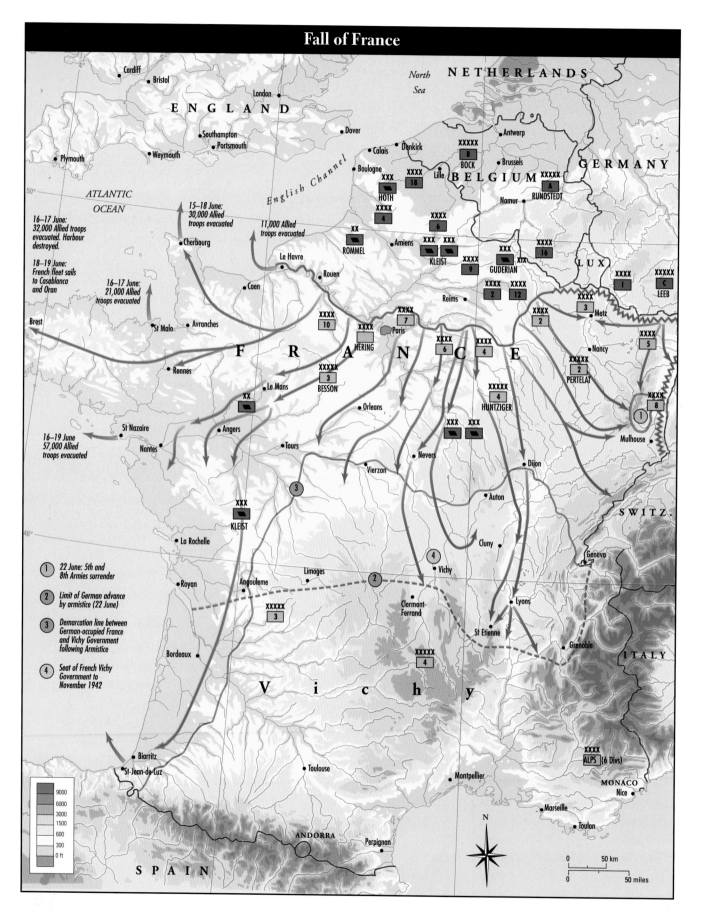

16–17 June:
32,000 Allied troops evacuated. Harbour destroyed.

18–19 June:
French fleet sails to Casablanca and Oran

16–17 June:
21,000 Allied troops evacuated

15–18 June:
30,000 Allied troops evacuated

11,000 Allied troops evacuated

16–19 June
57,000 Allied troops evacuated

1 22 June: 5th and 8th Armies surrender

2 Limit of German advance by armistice (22 June)

3 Demarcation line between German-occupied France and Vichy Government following Armistice

4 Seat of French Vichy Government to November 1942

indicated the form of the new order with an announcement of the 'First Bill of the Constitution', which opened: 'We, Philippe Petain Marshal of France, in accordance with the Constitutional Law of the 20th of July, hereby assume the functions of the Head of the French State.' The Republic was abolished; Parliament was dismissed.

Although many attempts were later made to blame her defeat on social causes which had sapped the morale of the rank and file of her army, it should be remembered that one of the aphorisms of France's most famous soldier, Napoleon Bonaparte, had been: 'There are no bad soldiers, only bad officers.'

Hitler had achieved such a complete and unexpectedly rapid victory over France that he could not immediately decide what to do with her. Paralyzed by his success, he lost out on bringing down Britain as well. For the moment, he was content to look at the white cliffs of Dover across the mere 32km (20 miles) of sea that separated them from Nazi Europe. Hitler never did develop any clearly defined long-term strategy for France. In the event, he treated it much as he did other occupied territories, looting the country to fuel the aims of his foreign policy elsewhere.

The Nazis quickly set about dismembering the French state. A small area of south-eastern France was allocated to the Italians, and a total exclusion zone around the Pas-de-Calais was established to protect the Reich from the area nearest England. Both of

Above: General von Briesen, military governor of Paris, takes the salute as the victorious Wehrmacht *parades down the Champs Elysees. The city fell on 14 June: France's new leader, General Petain, was to sue for an armistice a week later.*

Opposite: French North African troops peel potatoes in a German prisoner of war camp. These were some of the lucky ones: colonial troops captured by SS units, especially Africans from south of the Sahara or from West Africa, were considered to be subhuman and were often shot out of hand.

these zones were greatly extended after 1942. The rest of France was split between the 'zone occupée' and the 'zone libre', the latter to be controlled directly by the regime established at Vichy. Ordinary French people soon nicknamed the zones 'Zone O' and 'Zone NoNo'.

Hitler, always a pragmatist, was content to leave some part of France with a semblance of self-government. It suited his needs, as occupied territories were less of a drain on finances if they could govern themselves. Petain could rule in the south until the *Führer* determined otherwise. On the occasions that the two leaders met, Hitler could barely conceal his contempt for a man and a nation once great that had fallen so low.

The French spirit was so cowed by the German victory that in the early months of the occupation Hitler was able to maintain his grip on the country with a mere 30,000 troops – a ratio of just 1 German to every 1000 French citizens.

In Paris, the presence of the occupying power was quickly made evident when a vast Swastika was placed atop the Eiffel tower. The engineers doing the job had to climb the structure, the lifts having been sabotaged in a spirit of futile resistance by the departing French. And the legend *'Deutschland Siegt an allen Fronten'* – Germany Victorious on all Fronts – was placed on the Palais Bourbon in enormous letters 13m (43ft) high.

At the earliest opportunity, the German army staged a victory march down the Champs Élysées, and repeated the exercise every day until the liberation of Paris. The street signs were now in Gothic lettering, and everywhere was the presence of field-grey uniforms.

In just a few weeks, Norway, Denmark, Holland, Belgium and France had capitulated to the mightly *Wehrmacht*. Only Britain remained to oppose Hitler as master of Europe, and it was towards the British Isles that Hitler now turned his attention.

Britain Alone

France's collapse in June 1940 gave Hitler the victory he wanted most, since he blamed the French for the most vindictive terms of the Treaty of Versailles. However, the British, now led by Prime Minister Winston Churchill, adamantly refused to accept defeat.

The German high command knew that it was essential to keep Britain under pressure, initially from the air and then by the threat of a seaborne invasion. On July 16, Hitler issued Directive 16, ordering that plans for *Seelöwe* – Operation Sealion – be prepared, and engineers started converting large river barges into landing craft. There was a problem, however. Any force trying to cross the Channel would be at the mercy of the Royal Navy.

The first step in dealing with superior British sea power would be to win air superiority. The *Luftwaffe* was tasked with neutralizing the RAF. If the RAF could be eliminated, the *Luftwaffe* could, along with the *Kriegsmarine*, hold back the Royal Navy long enough for the German ground forces to be ferried across the Channel.

The *Luftwaffe* was the newest and most glamorous of Germany's combat arms. In 1939, Hermann Göring, creator of Hitler's air force, sent an order of the day to his men. 'I have done my best in the past few years' he said, 'to make our *Luftwaffe* the largest and most powerful in the world.' Within a year, that same *Luftwaffe* – which had not existed five years before – had spearheaded the all-conquering *Wehrmacht* as it rampaged its way to mastery of Europe. Only the stubborn British were holding out, but their defeat could only be a matter of time…

Air Supremacy

At the outbreak of war, the *Luftwaffe* comprised 302 *Staffeln* with 2370 operational crews and 2564 combat aircraft of all types. They were to enjoy considerable success in the first years of the war, and German aircrews were better trained and tactically superior to their opponents. As dawn broke on the morning of 1 September 1939, three Junkers Ju 87s of *Stukageschwader 1* came screaming down out of the sky, dropping bombs from a near vertical dive onto the Dirschau Bridge across the Vistula. Eleven minutes later, German Panzer divisions began pouring across the Polish frontier. Hitler's *Luftwaffe* had fired the opening shots of World War II.

Opposite: The crew of a Junkers Ju 88 prepares for a bombing mission over England. For the first time, the Luftwaffe *was to encounter an air force as determined, as well-equipped and as well organized as itself, and the Battle of Britain was to prove the first setback for Hitler's dreams of conquest.*

Above: A Heinkel He 111 passes over London's docks. The German decision to switch from attacking the Royal Air Force in favour of bombing cities gave the RAF a much needed respite.

The initial task for the 1600 aircraft of *Luftflottes 1* and *4* was to destroy the Polish air force. Air bases were heavily bombed by Heinkels and Dorniers, and obsolete Polish PZL fighters were hacked out of the sky by the *Luftwaffe's* Bf 109 fighters. Aerial opposition was wiped out within two days. The dive-bombers were tasked with attacking enemy troops and key communications targets. The Panzer formations used the Stukas as flying artillery, blasting any military opposition. In the process, the ugly crank-winged bombers spread fear and confusion amongst enemy troops and civilians.

By 9 September, German tanks were approaching Warsaw. Over the next week, while the capital held out, the *Wehrmacht* smashed what remained of Polish armed resistance, and then turned its attention on the city. Heavy artillery bombardment, followed by an aerial attack by the massed *Kampfgruppen*, left Warsaw in ruins, and the Poles capitulated on 27 September.

Although Britain and France had declared war on 3 September, there was little aerial activity over the cold winter of 1939/1940. Before the war, the British, like many others, believed that bombing alone could defeat Germany. However, although the *Luftwaffe* had been designed as an offensive weapon, German planners had not neglected the nation's defences. As a result, the RAF found the task to be far more difficult than expected.

The initial British raids in 1939 dropped only leaflets. Combat operations were limited to attacks on ports and coastal targets. In a daylight raid on Wilhelmshaven in 1939, 24 unescorted Wellington bombers were intercepted by radar-directed Messerschmitt Bf 109s, and 12 were shot down. This and similar experiences forced the RAF to switch to night operations.

In the spring, the *Luftwaffe* was again in action, supporting operations in Scandinavia. Close co-operation between land, sea and air elements saw the *Luftwaffe* transporting large numbers of troops in surprise air-landing assaults in Denmark and Norway, performing its customary close-support mission, and providing an anti-shipping strike force to counter the anticipated intervention by the Royal Navy.

The *Wehrmacht* launched its major assault in the west on 10 May 1940. Three entire Army Groups – 141 divisions – struck into France, Belgium and the Netherlands. *Luftwaffe* strength included 1100 medium bombers and 400 Stukas, escorted by 850 Bf

'Night gangsters! For this crime, I will exact a thousand-fold revenge!'

Adolf Hitler, after the RAF's first night bomber attack on shipyards at Bremen in 1940.

THE ORGANIZATION OF THE *LUFTWAFFE*

In September 1939, the *Luftwaffe* was organized into four *Luftflotten* (air fleets), but as the war progressed three more were added, including *Luftflotte Reich*, which was formed for the defence of Germany. Each *Luftflotte* had a strength of up to 1250 aircraft, grouped in a number of *Fliegerkorps*, or smaller *Fliegerdivisions*.

Both corps and division contained a number of *Geschwader* that equated roughly to an RAF Group or a USAF Wing. Each was divided into three *Gruppen*, in turn composed of three to four *Staffeln* (squadrons) of 12 aircraft. These were designated by type.

Kampfgeschwader operated the *Luftwaffe's* medium bombers. *Stukageschwader* were equipped with the dive-bombers that many Germans believed would be war-winning weapons. Later in the war, the *Stukageschwader* were superseded by *Schlachtgeschwader*, or ground-attack wings. Another new type of which much was expected was the *Zerstörer*, or destroyer. These heavy twin-engine fighters were flown by *Zerstörergeschwader*. *Jagdgeschwaders* flew single-engine fighters, and were tasked primarily with escorting the bombers.

Right: The shape of the Luftwaffe's daylight campaign against Britain was largely determined by the short range of the Messerschmitt Bf 109 fighter. Unescorted bombers had the range to reach most of the United Kingdom – but would have been chopped from the sky in huge numbers by British fighters. Escorted missions were limited to the south and southeast of England.

109s and 350 Bf 110 fighters. Five hundred transport aircraft and gliders were available for supply and airborne missions.

The attack followed the pattern set in Poland. The *Kampf-* and *Stukagruppen* struck opposing airfields at first light, and then ranged far into the enemy rear, hitting communications and transport targets. At the same time, small units of *Fallschirmjäger* dropped by parachute and glider to seize key river crossings. Most were successful, though fierce resistance meant that losses in the Junkers Ju 52 force were high.

Kampfgruppen were also deployed against enemy cities: the bombing of Rotterdam on 14 May destroyed the heart of the port, killing 1000 civilians and making more than 70,000 homeless. Air superiority was quickly established over the whole front. The Bf 109 was superior to the French Morane Saulnier MS 406 and the British Hawker Hurricane, and the German advantage in training and tactics was decisive. Even when Allied aircraft did get through the fighter cover, they encountered a storm of anti-aircraft fire from *Luftwaffe* flak units operating with the ground troops. On the afternoon of 14 May, Fairey Battle light bombers attacked the German pontoon bridges across the Meuse: 28 out of 37 aircraft were shot down.

Without fear of enemy attack, the *Luftwaffe's* dive-bombers were free to provide total support to the army. Whenever the Panzers encountered resistance on the ground, Stukas would be on the spot within minutes. The psychological effect of these screaming pinpoint attacks was considerable; by the end of the campaign, British and French troops were running almost as soon as they heard the distinctive sound of a Stuka's sirens. By the end of May, the British Expeditionary Force was pinned to the coast at Dunkirk, and it seemed only a matter of time before it was overwhelmed. Indeed, Hermann Göring claimed that the *Luftwaffe* could win the battle on its own, and Hitler ordered his Panzers to stop.

But for the first time in the war, the *Luftwaffe* could not win air superiority over a battlefield. Over Dunkirk, they encountered the Supermarine Spitfire, which the Royal Air Force had held back during the battle for France. Now the Messerschmitt pilots were engaging an aircraft at least as good as their own. The bombers and dive-bombers could no longer count on getting to their targets unscathed, and although they inflicted heavy damage on the evacuation force, their own losses were substantial. They could not prevent the evacuation: over 300,000 British troops escaped.

It was clear to the men on the front line that the Royal Air Force was going to be a formidable opponent in the weeks and months to come.

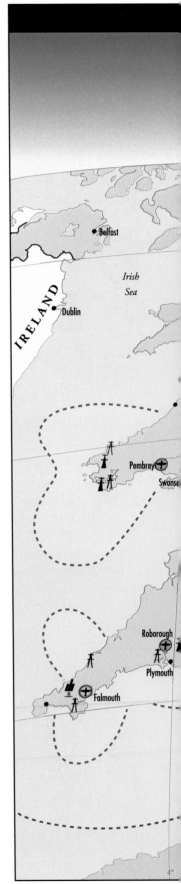

Battle of Britain

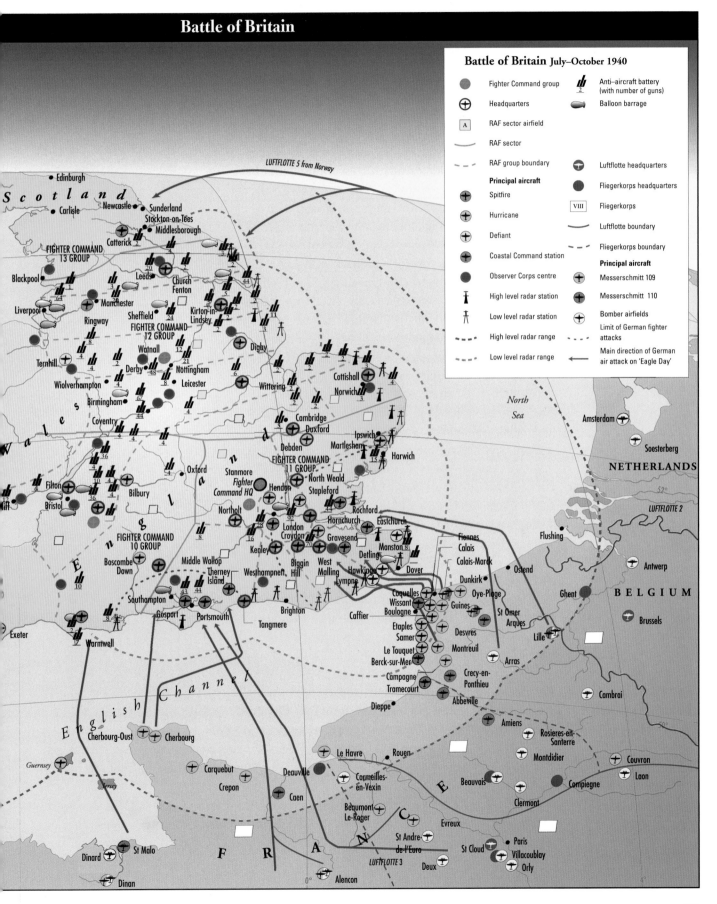

Battle of Britain July–October 1940

⬤ Fighter Command group	𝍔 Anti–aircraft battery (with number of guns)
⊕ Headquarters	🎈 Balloon barrage
A RAF sector airfield	
RAF sector	
RAF group boundary	✈ Luftflotte headquarters
Principal aircraft	⬤ Fliegerkorps headquarters
✈ Spitfire	VIII Fliegerkorps
✈ Hurricane	Luftflotte boundary
✈ Defiant	Fliegerkorps boundary
✈ Coastal Command station	**Principal aircraft**
⬤ Observer Corps centre	⊕ Messerschmitt 109
⊤ High level radar station	⊕ Messerschmitt 110
⊤ Low level radar station	⊕ Bomber airfields
High level radar range	Limit of German fighter attacks
Low level radar range	← Main direction of German air attack on 'Eagle Day'

LUFTFLOTTE 5 from Norway

Scotland

Edinburgh
Carlisle
Newcastle · Sunderland
Stockton-on-Tees
Middlesborough
Catterick
Hull

FIGHTER COMMAND 13 GROUP

Blackpool
Leeds
Church Fenton
Manchester
Liverpool
Ringway
Sheffield
Kirton-in-Lindsey
FIGHTER COMMAND 12 GROUP
Ternhill
Watnall
Digby
Derby
Nottingham
Wolverhampton
Leicester
Birmingham
Wittering
Coventry
Cottishall
Norwich
North Sea
England
Cambridge
Duxford
Ipswich
Martlesham
Harwich
Debden
Oxford
Stanmore Fighter Command HQ
FIGHTER COMMAND 11 GROUP
Hendon · North Weald
Stapleford
Rochford
Filton
Bilbury
Northolt
Hornchurch
Bristol
Eastchurch
London
Croydon
Gravesend
Manston
FIGHTER COMMAND 10 GROUP
Kenley
Detling
Fiennes
Calais
Calais-Marck
Flushing
Boscombe Down
Middle Wallop
Biggin Hill
West Malling
Dover
Dunkirk
Ostend
Amsterdam
Soesterberg
NETHERLANDS
LUFTFLOTTE 2
Therney Island
Westhampnett
Hawkinge
Lympne
Coquelles
Oye-Plage
Ghent
BELGIUM
Antwerp
Southampton
Brighton
Wissant
Guines
St Omer
Brussels
Gosport
Portsmouth
Tangmere
Caffier
Boulogne
Arques
Lille
Exeter
Warmwell
Etaples
Samer
Desvres
Arras
Montreuil
Le Touquet
Berck-sur-Mer
Crecy-en-Ponthieu
Campagne
Tramecourt
Abbeville
Cambrai
Dieppe
English Channel
Amiens
Rosieres-en-Santerre
Couvron
Guernsey
Cherbourg-Oust · Cherbourg
Le Havre
Rouen
Beauvais
Montdidier
Laon
Compiegne
Jersey
Carquebut
Crepon
Deauville
Cormeilles-én-Vexin
FRANCE
Clermont
Caen
Beaumont-Le-Roger
Evreux
Dinard · St Malo
St Andre-de-l'Eure
St Cloud
Paris
Villacoublay
Orly
Dinan
LUFTFLOTTE 3
Deux
Alencon

Right: Pilots of No 92 Squadron scramble for their fighters early in 1941. The squadron took part in the final stages of the Battle of Britain, but by this time they had switched to offensive operations over France.

The Attack on Britain

The main German air assault on the United Kingdom, which Churchill was to call the Battle of Britain, did not begin until 13 August 1940. However, as early as 30 June, Göring had issued 'General Directions for the Operation of the *Luftwaffe* against England'. These defined the *Luftwaffe's* primary targets as the Royal Air Force, its airfields and its supporting industries. On July 11, the *Reichsmarschall* announced that shipping in the Channel was to be attacked. However, as the Germans tried to intercept the British convoys, the RAF attacked the bombers, with the previously all-conquering Stuka proving especially vulnerable. In June and July, the *Luftwaffe* launched small-scale raids on England from airfields in France, Belgium, Holland and Scandinavia. These allowed the RAF to test their defensive measures before the main attack came in August and September. It was soon clear that the *Luftwaffe* had numerical superiority, but the RAF had some decisive advantages as well.

To fight the British, the Germans had amassed a force of 1260 medium bombers, about 320 dive-bombers, 800 single-engine and 280 twin-engine fighters and several hundred reconnaissance aircraft. *Luftwaffe* forces were divided into three air fleets. Field Marshal Albert Kesselring's *Luftflotte 2* was based in eastern France and the Low Countries, while Field Marshal Hugo Sperrle's *Luftflotte 3* operated from western France. Colonel-General Hans-Jurgen Stumpff's *Luftflotte 5* would attack across the North Sea from bases in Scandinavia.

Ranged against the *Luftwaffe* was RAF Fighter Command, led by Air Chief Marshal Sir Hugh Dowding. One Fighter Group was assigned to protect each of the major areas of the country. The southwest was covered by 10 Group; 11 Group under Air Vice Marshal Keith Park was closest to the enemy in the southeast; 12 Group commanded by Air Vice Marshal Trafford Leigh-Mallory was based in East Anglia and the Midlands; and 13 Group operated from the north and Scotland. Fighter Command had 900 fighters in the main operational area, of which Dowding could commit 600 to action.

The RAF were supported by the Chain Home belt of radar stations. Even though it had been invented only five years before, British radar could detect high-flying aircraft deep over northern France. Low-level intruders were picked up only at about 35km (22 miles) – the width of the Straits of Dover. A sophisticated system of ground control allowed the British to make best use of their resources. Primed with radar information,

'Let us therefore brace ourselves to our duties, and so bear ourselves that, if the British Empire and its Commonwealth last for a thousand years, men will say, "this was their finest hour".'

Winston Churchill, 18 June 1940

the sector control stations allowed RAF fighters to be scrambled early and vectored to attack the *Luftwaffe* before it had reached its targets.

Engines of War

In the Messerschmitt Bf 109, the Germans had an excellent single-seat fighter. Very fast, agile, with a good climb and dive performance, its only major drawback was its range, which limited it to escort missions over southeast England. Going as far as London meant that its pilots had only a few minutes of combat time before having to turn for

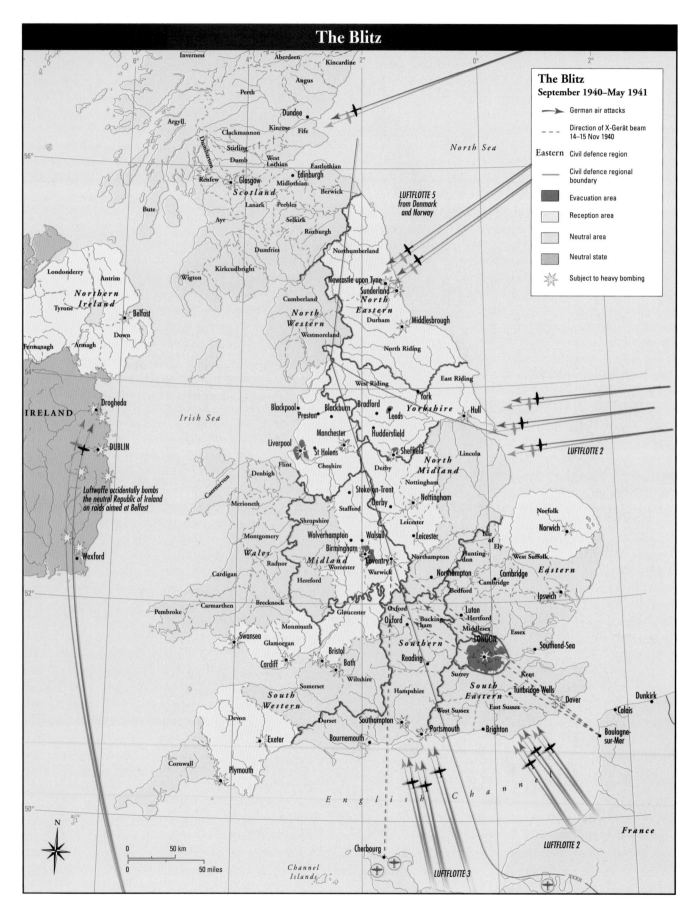

The Blitz

The Blitz
September 1940–May 1941

→ German air attacks

- - - Direction of X-Gerät beam
14–15 Nov 1940

Eastern Civil defence region

Civil defence regional
boundary

Evacuation area

Reception area

Neutral area

Neutral state

✦ Subject to heavy bombing

North Sea

LUFTFLOTTE 5
*from Denmark
and Norway*

LUFTFLOTTE 2

Inverness
Aberdeen
Kincardine
Angus
Perth
Dundee
Kinrose
Clackmannon
Fife
Stirling
West Lothian
Dumb
Eastlothian
Edinburgh
Renfew
Glasgow
Midlothian
Berwick
Scotland
Lanark
Peebles
Selkirk
Bute
Ayr
Roxburgh
Dumfries
Kirkcudbright
Wigton

Londonderry
Antrim
Northern Ireland
Tyrone
Belfast
Fermanagh
Armagh
Down

IRELAND
Drogheda
DUBLIN

*Luftwaffe accidentally bombs
the neutral Republic of Ireland
on raids aimed at Belfast*

Wexford

Irish Sea

Northumberland
Newcastle upon Tyne
Sunderland
North Eastern
Cumberland
Durham
Middlesbrough
Westmoreland
North Western
North Riding
North Western
West Riding
East Riding
York
Yorkshire
Hull
Blackpool
Blackburn
Bradford
Preston
Leeds
Liverpool
Manchester
Huddersfield
St Helens
Sheffield
Cheshire
Lincoln
Flint
Derby
North Midland
Denbigh
Stoke-on-Trent
Nottingham
Caernarvon
Derby
Merioneth
Stafford
Leicester
Shropshire
Norfolk
Montgomery
Wolverhampton
Walsall
Leicester
Norwich
Wales
Radnor
Birmingham
Midland
Worcester
Coventry
Northampton
Huntingdon
Isle of Ely
West Suffolk
Cambridge
Eastern
Cardigan
Hereford
Warwick
Northampton
Cambridge
Ipswich
Pembroke
Carmarthen
Brecknock
Gloucester
Oxford
Bedford
Luton
Hertford
Buckingham
Middlesex
Essex
Monmouth
Oxford
LONDON
Swansea
Glamorgan
Southern
Reading
Southend-Sea
Bristol
Surrey
Kent
Somerset
Bath
Wiltshire
South Western
Hampshire
Tunbridge Wells
South Eastern
Dover
Devon
Dorset
West Sussex
East Sussex
Exeter
Southampton
Portsmouth
Brighton
Bournemouth
Cornwall
Plymouth

Dunkirk
Calais
Boulogne-sur-Mer

English Channel

France

N

0 50 km
0 50 miles

Cherbourg

LUFTFLOTTE 3

LUFTFLOTTE 2

Channel Islands

home. The Messerschmitt Bf 110 *Zerstörer* was big, fast, and had the long range its smaller sibling lacked. It also had a formidable armament packed in its nose – four machine guns and two 20mm (0.79in) cannon. But it was no match for the faster and more manoeuvrable Hurricanes and Spitfires. The Junkers Ju 87 Stuka had been a battle winner in Spain, Poland and France, earning an awesome reputation. However, in combat against high-performance fighters it proved to be horribly vulnerable. Slow and cumbersome in flight, it was hacked out of the sky in large numbers by the RAF.

Left: Once Adolf Hitler cancelled the planned invasion of the United Kingdom, the British Army could concentrate on re-equipping and training for the day when they returned to Europe. These infantrymen mounted in a Bren-gun carrier are in the middle of a 24-hour gasmask exercise.

Opposite: Defeat in the Battle of Britain meant that the Luftwaffe was forced to switch to night bombing operations. With less of a fighter threat than by day, bombers were able to mount raids from airfields in France, Holland, Denmark and Norway.

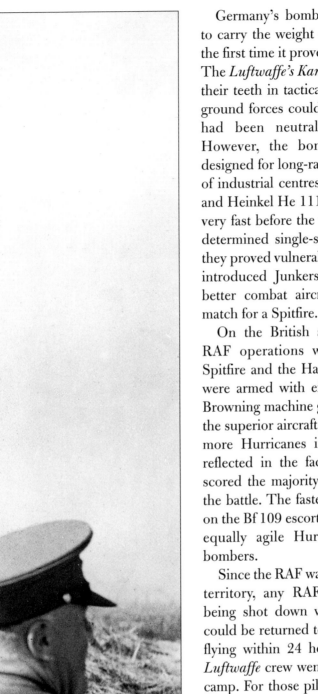

Germany's bomber fleet was intended to carry the weight of the air war, but for the first time it proved unequal to the task. The *Luftwaffe's Kampfgeschwader* had cut their teeth in tactical operations in which ground forces could capture airfields that had been neutralized by air attack. However, the bomber force was not designed for long-range strategic bombing of industrial centres. The Dornier Do 17 and Heinkel He 111 had been considered very fast before the war, but in the face of determined single-seat fighter opposition they proved vulnerable. The more recently introduced Junkers Ju 88 was a much better combat aircraft, but was still no match for a Spitfire.

On the British side, the mainstay of RAF operations was the Supermarine Spitfire and the Hawker Hurricane. Both were armed with eight 7.7mm (0.303in) Browning machine guns. The Spitfire was the superior aircraft, though there were far more Hurricanes in service – which is reflected in the fact that the Hurricane scored the majority of the RAF's kills in the battle. The faster Spitfires would take on the Bf 109 escorts, while the slower but equally agile Hurricanes attacked the bombers.

Since the RAF was operating over home territory, any RAF pilot who survived being shot down without serious injury could be returned to his squadron and be flying within 24 hours or less. Downed *Luftwaffe* crew went straight to the POW camp. For those pilots who landed in the English Channel, high-speed launches and seaplanes operating from Britain or German-occupied France ran competing rescue missions.

On 19 July, Hitler directed a speech in the Reichstag at Britain. Dubbed 'The Last Appeal to Reason', he said 'If we do pursue the struggle, it will end with the complete destruction of one of the two combatants. Mr Churchill may believe that

Opposite: Prime Minister Winston Churchill visits Britain's coastal defences. Without the heavy equipment and artillery abandoned in France, how they would have stood up to a German Panzer attack is questionable. Fortunately, neither the Luftwaffe *nor the* Kriegsmarine *had the ability to deliver or protect an invasion force from the RAF or the Royal Navy.*

'The gratitude of every home in our Islands goes out to the British airmen… Never in the field of human conflict was so much owed by so many to so few.'

Winston Churchill, 21 August 1940

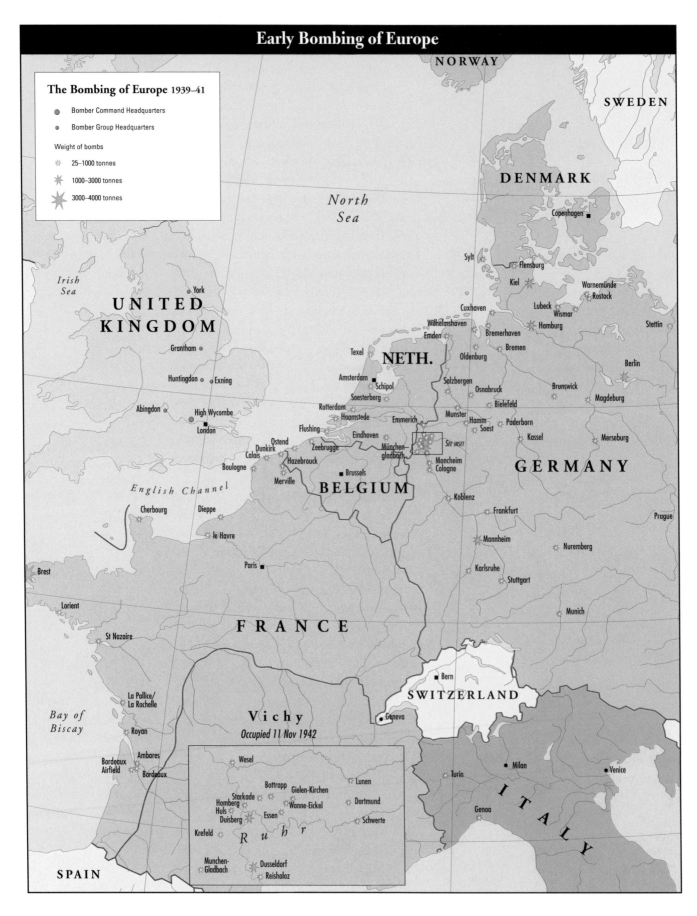

Early Bombing of Europe

The Bombing of Europe 1939–41

● Bomber Command Headquarters

● Bomber Group Headquarters

Weight of bombs

✳ 25–1000 tonnes

✳ 1000–3000 tonnes

✸ 3000–4000 tonnes

NORWAY

SWEDEN

DENMARK

Copenhagen

Sylt

Flensburg

Kiel

Warnemünde

Rostock

North Sea

Cuxhaven

Lubeck

Wismar

Stettin

Wilhelmshaven

Bremerhaven

Hamburg

Emden

Bremen

Irish Sea

York

Texel

Oldenburg

Berlin

UNITED KINGDOM

Amsterdam

NETH.

Salzbergen

Osnabruck

Brunswick

Magdeburg

Grantham

Schipol

Bielefeld

Huntingdon

Exning

Soesterberg

Rotterdam

Munster

Paderborn

Kassel

Merseburg

Abingdon

Haamstede

Emmerich

Hamm

High Wycombe

Flushing

Eindhoven

Soest

London

Ostend

Zeebrugge

München-gladbach

SEE INSET

Dunkirk

Moncheim

Prague

Calais

Hazebrouck

Cologne

Boulogne

Brussels

Koblenz

Merville

BELGIUM

GERMANY

Frankfurt

English Channel

Mannheim

Nuremberg

Cherbourg

Dieppe

Karlsruhe

le Havre

Stuttgart

Brest

Paris

FRANCE

Munich

Lorient

St Nazaire

SWITZERLAND

Bay of Biscay

Bern

La Pallice/La Rochelle

Geneva

Vichy

Royan

Occupied 11 Nov 1942

Ambares

Turin

Milan

Venice

Bordeaux Airfield

Bordeaux

Wesel

Genoa

ITALY

Lunen

Krefeld

Bottrapp

Gielen-Kirchen

Starkade

Homberg

Wanne-Eickel

Dortmund

Huls

Essen

Duisberg

Schwerte

Ruhr

SPAIN

Munchen-Gladbach

Dusseldorf

Reishaloz

it will be Germany. I know it will be England'. Since this drew no positive response from the British Government, orders were given to launch a major air assault against the RAF on *Adlertag* – Eagle Day, 12 August.

The Battle Begins

Among the German targets was the important radar station at Ventnor on the Isle of Wight, which was put out of action. On the 13th, the weather was poor and though some squadrons took off, the planned massed assault was called off. It was not until the 15th that the three *Luftflotten* attacked in concert, putting 2000 aircraft over Britain in an afternoon.

Luftflotte 5 launched 169 bombers from Aalborg in Denmark and Stavanger in Norway against Scotland and the northeast of England. Operating beyond the range of single-seat fighters, they were escorted by twin-engine Messerschmitt Bf 110 *Zerstörers*. No match for Spitfires or Hurricanes, the 110s proved unequal to the task, and the bombers suffered badly at the hands of 12 and 13 Groups. Sixteen bombers and seven Bf 110s were shot down. Without adequate fighter protection, *Luftflotte 5* was to play little further part in the battle.

Raids of between 100 and 150 aircraft from *Luftflottes 2* and *3* crossed the Channel all through the afternoon of 15 August. If *Luftwaffe* crews did not know they were in a serious fight, then the events of 'Black Thursday' convinced them. The British lost 34 fighters that day, but 75 German aircraft did not return. During the air operations, both the RAF and the *Luftwaffe* overestimated their victories – understandable in the confusion of a dogfight, when two pilots might both claim the same aircraft as a 'kill'. The huge figures of enemy losses were undoubtedly good for morale, but were not the basis for sound planning.

Similarly, bomb damage to airfields, which could look spectacular in aerial photographs, was often relatively superficial. *Luftwaffe* planners took such intelligence at

Opposite: The Royal Air Force was the only means of striking back at Germany that Britain had. Early daylight raids were savagely mauled: forced to fly by night, the RAF mounted numerous small raids. However, the accuracy of the bombing was abysmal.

Below: No match for British single-seat fighters, the Messerschmitt Bf 110 heavy fighter was used as a fighter bomber in the later stages of the Battle of Britain, but it found its true métier later in the war, as a night fighter.

face value, however, and thought that the RAF was hurting more than in fact it was. The Germans believed that the RAF now had only 300 front-line aircraft, and the *Luftwaffe* commanders decided to go all out to destroy Fighter Command once and for all.

Small groups of bombers flew to Britain as bait to draw up the RAF fighters. As Spitfires, Hurricanes and Bf 109s battled through the summer skies, more bombers slipped through to hit key airfields at Biggin Hill, Hornchurch, North Weald and West Malling. RAF losses started to climb. However, just as they were close to achieving their operational goal, the Germans switched their attacks to British cities.

The Blitz

Why the *Luftwaffe* took the pressure off the RAF is still disputed. The high command may have been convinced that they had broken the back of the RAF. Alternatively, a night raid by the RAF on Berlin on August 25 – timed to coincide with a visit by Soviet Foreign Minister Molotov – might have enraged Hitler and prompted retaliation.

The RAF raid was itself a reaction to a lost *Luftwaffe* bomber, which had jettisoned its payload over the East End of London. However, the Berlin raid was not an isolated incident: the RAF mounted small-scale raids over Germany all through the period. The largest involved 169 twin-engine bombers sent to Berlin on 8 November 1940, during which 21 aircraft were lost. In a military sense, the British raids had little effect. Hitting a target at night was almost impossible with the technology of the time, and the November raid killed only 11 on the ground.

For whatever the reason, German air attacks against British cities began with daylight raids on London on 7 September. Carried out by 300 bombers with 600 escorting fighters, these initially enjoyed considerable success, causing huge fires around the London docks. On 15 September, the *Luftwaffe* abandoned its usual practice of sending diversionary attacks to confuse radar and ground controllers – possibly believing that the RAF was a spent force. But the RAF was waiting.

The respite from direct attacks on its airfields had allowed the RAF to replenish its fighter strength in the south. The raids on London gave 11 Group in particular more time to get fighters aloft. Park was able to get paired squadrons into the air, and Leigh Mallory's 12 Group formed even larger formations in what were known as 'Big Wing' attacks. The *Luftwaffe* was met by massed fighters, and by the close of the day had lost 60 aircraft. Total *Luftwaffe* losses since 7 September totalled 175, all caused by a force that German pilots had been told was beaten. Two days later. Hitler postponed Operation Sealion indefinitely, as he turned his attention towards the Soviet Union.

The *Luftwaffe* switched to night raids. Up to 400 bombers attacked London each night until mid-November, weather permitting. Contrary to pre-war theories about air power, the raids, known to the citizens of the UK as the Blitz, did not cause panic in the civilian population, nor did they break the national will. There was a lull in midwinter, though the raiders returned in the New Year. In a series of raids lasting until May, *Luftwaffe* bombers also attacked Liverpool, Birmingham, Plymouth and Bristol.

Intensification

Between 19 February and 12 May 1941, the *Luftwaffe* intensified attacks against London and the Channel ports. In some raids, they employed 700 bombers, though others involved single fighter-bombers. These would fly fast and low across the Channel, keeping beneath the British radar cover.

Opposite: Victims of German bombers are pulled from the wreckage of their home during the Blitz. Attacks on populated areas were designed to wear down civilian resistance: in fact, they heightened community spirit and made ordinary civilians more determined than ever to do their bit to win the war.

'Then whose bombs are these that we are sheltering from?'

Reputedly said by Soviet Foreign Commissar Molotov during an air raid on Berlin in November 1940, on being informed by German Foreign Minister Ribbentrop that Britain was defeated.

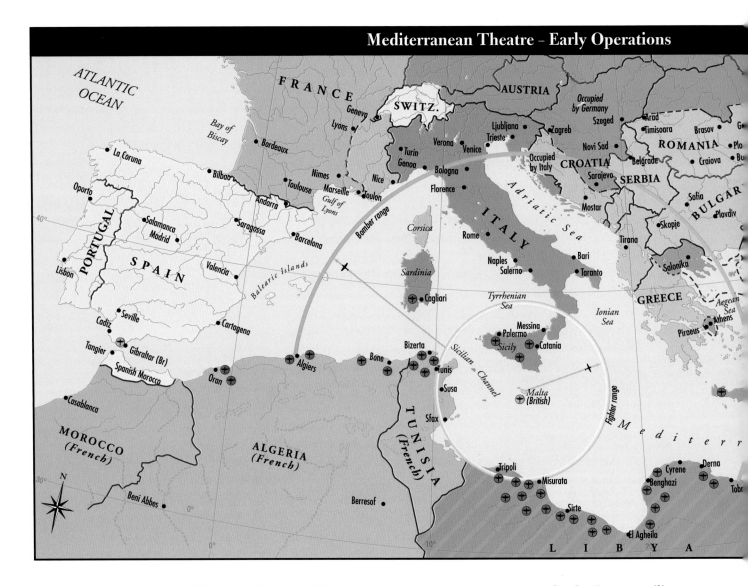

Mediterranean Theatre – Early Operations

Above: The war in the Mediterranean was dominated by lines of communication: Axis troops in North Africa could be supported from Italy only a short distance across the Mediterranean. The British had much longer and more vulnerable supply routes, but these were anchored by key bases at Gibraltar, Malta and Alexandria.

The intensification of the bombing was to some extent a cover for the German military redeployment eastwards: by 21 May, the *Luftwaffe* had shifted 90 per cent of its forces to eastern Germany, occupied Poland and East Prussia, ready for operations against the USSR. During its attacks on Britain in 1940 and 1941, the *Luftwaffe* dropped 49,359 tonnes (54,420 tons) of bombs and incendiaries. Most raids were against area targets, killing 40,000 people and injuring 86,000. Two million homes were destroyed, of which 60 per cent were in London. Exact air losses are still disputed, but the best estimates are that the *Luftwaffe* lost 1294 aircraft between 10 July and 31 October 1940, while the British lost 788. During the night Blitz, the *Luftwaffe* lost a further 600 bombers, though many of these were due to flying accidents in bad weather. However, by 1941 the RAF had become a formidable enemy even at night, with twin-engine radar-equipped night-fighters supplemented by radar-controlled searchlights and anti-aircraft guns on the ground.

Taking the War to Germany

The Battle of Britain was the first major setback for Germany's armed forces. Even though the British were gravely weakened, they remained implacably opposed to Hitler and the Nazis, and would provide one of the springboards by which Germany would

The Mediterranean
Late 1942

Under German or Axis occupation

Allied to Germany

Italian territory

Under Italian occupation

Allied or under Allied occupation

French, under Vichy control

Axis occupied

Neutral countries

Allied convoy route

Axis convoy route

Allied airfield

Axis airfield

ultimately be defeated. In the meantime, however, the only way Britain could strike at Germany was from the air, and the RAF continued its night bombing raids over the German homeland.

Initially targeted against key industrial and communications targets, RAF crews found that accurate navigation and bombing by night was almost impossible – so much so in fact, that bombers were simply instructed to bomb towns and cities. Aircrew returned with reports of large fires burning and immense damage done, but neutral news reports out of Germany were painting a different picture.

To assess the effectiveness of the campaign, D.M. Butt of the War Cabinet Secretariat was asked to examine over 600 operational photos, comparing them with crew claims and Bomber Command assessments. The Butt report, released in August 1941, was devastating. Many bombers were not finding the correct target – some were not even bombing the right towns. Only one bomber in three was getting within 8km (5 miles) of its target and over the vital Ruhr industrial area, which was often covered in haze, only one in ten. On moonless nights, the ratio fell to one in fifteen. These poor results had come at the cost of 700 British bombers destroyed and thousands of aircrew killed or captured.

Clearly something would have to be done. It would not be until the appointment of Air Marshal Arthur Harris as the head of Bomber Command in 1942 that the bomber campaign began to receive added impetus, greatly helped by the introduction into service of powerful new four-engine bombers.

The Mediterranean Theatre

Although the bomber campaign was the only way that Britain could strike directly at the Third Reich, British forces were also very active in the Mediterranean. The main threat to the British there came from the powerful Italian Fleet. Mussolini had declared war on Britain and France on 10 June 1940. On 9 July, the British Mediterranean Fleet was preparing to escort two convoys to Malta, while the Italian Fleet was returning to Italy after covering a supply convoy to Benghazi. The two forces met off Calabria. In a confused action that started at about 3 p.m., the battleship *Warspite* hit the Italian battleship *Giulio Cesare* at a range of 23,764m (26,000 yards), the longest such hit in history. The drawn battle left neither side in control of the local seas.

Two months later, on 13 September 1940, the Italian Army under Marshal Graziani invaded Egypt from Libya. Pushing tentatively forward, the Italians made contact with British troops and settled down in a series of fortified positions around Sidi Barrani, while the British were centred on Mersa Matruh, about 121km (75 miles) further east. The Egyptian army held back from the conflict. Indeed, young nationalist officers, including

MALTA

In 1941/42, many officers of the German high command made a strong argument for a German assault on Malta, from which the RAF and Royal Navy inflicted unsustainable losses on the Italian convoys on which Rommel's army depended. German and Italian airborne forces were assembled and trained for Operation Hercules, and the island bombed by the *Luftwaffe* and the *Regia Aeronautica*.

Malta was the key to holding the Mediterranean, but the 250,000 Maltese and 20,000 British defenders were dependent on imported food and oil that had to run the gauntlet of Axis bombers. In September 1941, eight of nine merchant ships arrived in Malta, bringing 77,095 tonnes (85,000 tons) of supplies.

However, a February 1942 convoy of three ships from Alexandria could not get through. One month later, three cargo ships and an oiler attempted a resupply mission, a heavy Royal Navy escort managing to keep the Italian navy at bay. But German air attacks resulted in one of the cargo vessels sunk, and the tanker was destroyed within sight of the island. The two survivors reached Malta, but were sunk at their moorings just as unloading got under way. Under constant bombardment, Malta could support no submarines or bomber aircraft. Italian merchant ships enjoyed a welcome respite and Rommel's forces were replenished. Malta existed under a state of virtual siege until May 1943, during which time over 5000 Maltese civilians were either killed or wounded by the bombing.

Gamel Abdel Nasser and Anwar el Sadat, made clandestine contact with the Germans in the hope of ensuring Egyptian independence in the event of a British defeat.

While the two sides faced each other in North Africa, the British navy was establishing its dominance over the Mediterranean. On 11 November 1940, Admiral Cunningham's Mediterranean Fleet launched a surprise attack against the major Italian naval base at Taranto. Launched from the carrier HMS *Illustrious*, a force of just 21 antique Swordfish biplanes torpedoed and bombed the Italian fleet, sinking or badly damaging three battleships and two cruisers for the loss of just two aircraft. This strike gave the Royal Navy a decisive edge in the Mediterranean – and impressed the Japanese navy so much that it was to use the same technique on a much larger scale at Pearl Harbor just over a year later.

Britain's North African Offensive

In December 1940, the British finally acted against the Italians in Egypt. General Archibald Wavell unleashed the Western Desert Force, commanded by General Richard O'Connor, through a gap in the Italian chain of defences. O'Connor's force, numbering some 31,000 men, was outnumbered more than four to one. However, in a lightning campaign of mobility, the British leapfrogged each Italian position, reaching Bardia at the end of the year. By the beginning of February 1941, the British had reached Beda Fomm. In two months, O'Connor's men had advanced 805km (500 miles), taking 130,000 prisoners and

Opposite: A column of Indian troops from Wavell's Western Desert Force move through the town of Berna as part of General O'Connor's campaign to push the Italian army out of Cyrenacia.

effectively knocking out the Italian presence in Cyrenaica. However, a month later, they were facing a new challenge as the German Afrika Korps, sent to Africa to save Mussolini's forces, mounted its first attacks at El Agheila.

At the same time as the Western Desert Force was ripping through Italian Libya, another British campaign got under way against the Italians in East Africa. In a rapid offensive action, the British, under Generals Platt and Cunningham, mounted a two-pronged invasion of Somaliland and Eritrea, and by 4 April had captured Addis Ababa. On 18 May, the Italian forces under the Duke of Aosta surrendered.

Success on land in Africa was matched by further success at sea, though a new threat had emerged with the arrival of German fighters, dive-bombers and bombers on Sicily in February 1941. These aircraft quickly made the narrow seas between Italy and

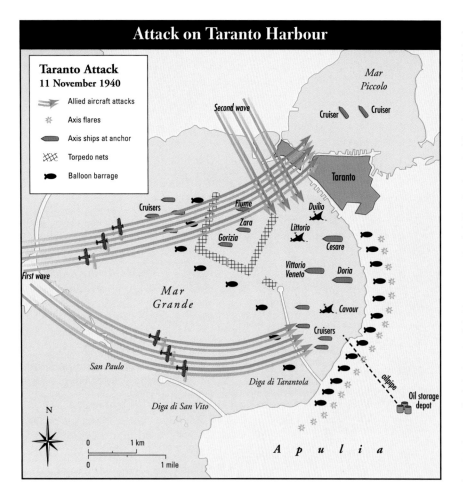

Attack on Taranto Harbour

Taranto Attack
11 November 1940

↗ Allied aircraft attacks
✳ Axis flares
▬ Axis ships at anchor
▨ Torpedo nets
⚫ Balloon barrage

Mar Piccolo

Cruiser Cruiser

Second wave

Taranto

Cruisers Fiume Duilio
Zara Littorio
Gorizia Cesare
Vittorio Veneto Doria
First wave
Mar Grande Cavour
Cruisers

San Paulo
oilpipe
Diga di Tarantola Oil storage depot
Diga di San Vito

N

0   1 km
0   1 mile

A p u l i a

Africa an extremely dangerous place for British shipping, and Malta came under intense bombardment.

Rising tensions in the Balkans led the British to send troops to Greece in March. In an attempt to intercept these movements, Admiral Angelo Iachino sortied with an Italian fleet of three battleships, eight cruisers and supporting elements. Harassed by the cruisers and aircraft carriers of Admiral Cunningham's Mediterranean fleet off Cape Matapan, the southernmost tip of mainland Greece, the powerful battleship *Vittorio Veneto* was damaged, as was the heavy cruiser *Pola*. The *Pola* had to be left behind, protected by the heavy cruisers *Zara*, *Fiume* and four destroyers.

At about 10 p.m. on 28 March, Admiral Cunningham with the battleships *Warspite*, *Valiant* and *Barham* closed with the three heavy

Above: On the night of 10 November 1940, a force of 21 obsolete Fairey Swordfish biplanes launched from HMS Illustrious ripped the heart out of the Italian fleet anchored at Taranto. The surprise attack gave the Royal Navy a moral advantage over the Italians, which was never to be challenged for the rest of the war.

Right: A flight of RAF Fairey Swordfish biplanes armed with torpedoes prepare to attack Italian shipping near Malta.

cruisers and their escorts. Opening fire with radar guidance at near point-blank range, the British sank five Italian vessels in a matter of minutes, including all three cruisers. The *Vittorio Veneto* and the rest of the Italian fleet did not offer battle, escaping into the darkness.

Kriegsmarine to the Rescue

In September 1941, with German supplies to Rommel's forces in North Africa being ravaged by British submarines and aircraft, the *Kriegsmarine* decided to send 25 U-Boats to bolster Mussolini's navy. Over the next two years, a total of 62 boats managed to run the gauntlet of the British-controlled straits of Gibraltar. Nine more were sunk while attempting the passage, while 10 had to abort their missions due to damage. Those that got into the Mediterranean quickly had an effect. On 13 November 1941, *U-81* under *Kapitanleutnant* Guggenberger torpedoed the aircraft carrier *Ark Royal* not far from Gibraltar. Initial damage did not seem serious, but progressive flooding eventually sank the ship, for the loss of only one life.

The veteran battleship HMS *Barham* was not so lucky. She was torpedoed by *Oberleutnant* Freiherr von Tiesenhausen's *U-331* on 25 November while hunting for an Italian supply convoy off the Egyptian/Libyan coast. Hit three times, the old vessel rolled over and exploded, taking 862 of her crew with her.

The German U-boats in the Mediterranean sank 95 Allied merchantmen totalling 407,429 tonnes (449,206 tons), as well 24 major Royal Navy warships, including the carrier HMS *Eagle*, four cruisers and 12 destroyers. However, none was to return to Germany: all 62 U-Boats were sunk in action or scuttled by their crews after their Italian bases were overrun.

Below: British superiority in the Mediterranean was sealed on 28 March 1941, when Admiral Cunningham's Mediterranean Fleet smashed an Italian heavy cruiser force off the southern tip of Greece, and forced the battleship Vittorio Veneto *to run for home.*

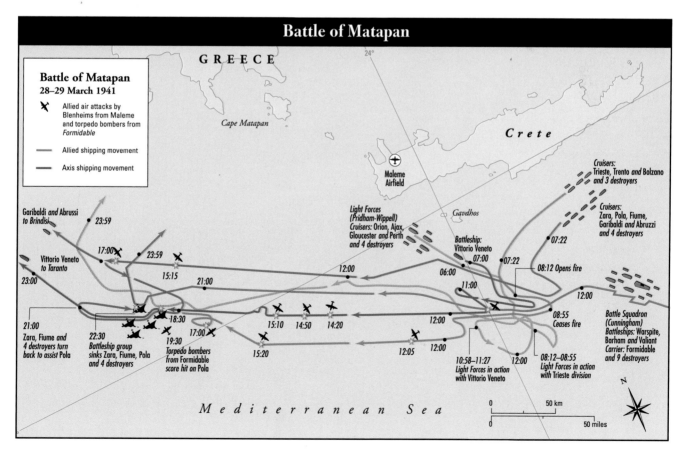

War at Sea

Ranging far out into the Atlantic and preying on sea-borne British trade, the *Kriegsmarine's* U-boat fleet was the biggest threat to Britain's survival during World War II. In 1939, half the food eaten in the United Kingdom came from overseas. Two-thirds of the raw materials required by Britain's war industries were imported too. If the German navy could stop this flow of goods by sinking Allied merchant ships, Hitler might win the war. However, like Napoleon before him, Hitler did not understand the importance of sea power.

The *Führer's* attitude to the navy was succinctly expressed in 1936. 'The Navy,' he asked. 'What need have we of that? I cannot conceive of a European war that will hang in the balance because of a few ships.' Nevertheless, as part of Germany's massive rearmaments programme in the 1930s, Hitler sponsored the development of the now famous 'Z plan'. The scheme to build a massive surface and underwater fleet of very modern design was due for completion in 1944.

The Atlantic Lifeline

At the outbreak of war, some 3000 ocean-going merchant ships flew the British flag and another 1000 coasters plied the waters around the UK: a combined total of 17.5 million tonnes (19.3 million tons) of shipping. In home waters and in the North Atlantic, the ships were organized into convoys, typically protected by four to six escorts armed with depth-charges. Heavier units from the Home Fleet were also assigned as distant escorts when intelligence was received of the possible presence of German warships.

The seaborne lifeline was vital. Without it, Britain could not even feed its population, let alone manufacture weapons, and it would be impossible to fight a war if the flow of imports stopped. However, the *Kriegsmarine,* not expecting to fight until the middle of the 1940s, was woefully unprepared to take advantage of Britain's vulnerability. Unable to face the British fleet to fleet, Germany had to resort to a campaign of commerce raiding.

The *'Deutschland'* class heavy cruisers, known as 'pocket battleships' because of their powerful 28cm (11in) guns, were Nazi Germany's first major warships. Purpose-

Opposite: The crew of a Type VII U-boat enjoy a rare meal in the open air. U-boat crews would spend many weeks on operational patrol, in the cramped confines of their submarine.

designed for commerce raiding, their diesel engines gave them excellent endurance. KMS *Admiral Scheer* and KMS *Graf Spee* had been sent out into the Atlantic before the outbreak of war, ready to go into action immediately war was declared. Both achieved some success, snapping up merchantmen sailing unescorted in the central and south Atlantic. *Scheer's* five-month raid sank 16 ships totalling 100,000 tonnes (110,254 tons).

However, operating alone made the pocket battleships vulnerable to concentrations of force made by the much more powerful Royal Navy, and *Graf Spee* was chased down by a cruiser squadron in the South Atlantic and was scuttled in the River Plate in December 1939. The *Kriegsmarine's* newer heavy warships were less suited to raiding operations. The 'Hipper' class heavy cruisers used high-pressure steam propulsion, and their notoriously high fuel consumption limited their range. Even so, the *Admiral Hipper* made a relatively successful cruise in February 1941, intercepting a convoy off West Africa and sinking seven ships totalling 27,210 tonnes (30,000 tons).

Too lightly armed to take on a real battleship, the battlecruisers *Scharnhorst* and *Gneisenau* had an indifferent war after their early success in sinking the carrier HMS *Glorious* during the Norway campaign. They largely failed in their attempts to harry British convoys in the North Atlantic, since the Royal Navy was assigning old 'R' class and 'Queen Elizabeth' class battleships to escort convoys.

The *Bismarck*

The *Kriegsmarine* did have one asset which could make a difference, however, and that was the powerful battleship *Bismarck*.

KMS *Bismarck* was launched by the Iron Chancellor's great grand-daughter on 14 February 1939. From completion to destruction, the huge battleship lasted only nine months, eight of which were spent on training. When she slipped out of the Baltic on 20 May 1941, escorted by the heavy cruiser *Prinz Eugen*, her mission was to disrupt the British supply line in the Atlantic. The Royal Navy was very conscious of the threat, and detailed

Right: In the early stages of the Battle of the Atlantic, German submarine attacks were concentrated on the approaches to the British Isles. Boats were small and few in number, and they had to make the long and perilous voyage around the North of Scotland to reach the Western Approaches.

Battle of the Atlantic I
September 1939–May 1940

—— Border of Pan-American Neutrality Zone (1939)

—— Extent of air escort cover

▭ Major convoy routes

• Allied merchant ships sunk by U-boats

⚓ U-boats sunk

▭ Territory under Allied control

▭ Territory under Axis control

▭ Neutral territory

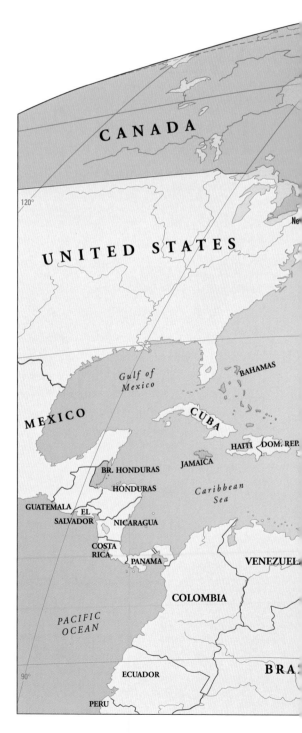

considerable resources to neutralize her. Initially shadowed by the cruisers *Suffolk* and *Norfolk*, the German squadron was intercepted off Iceland by the powerful battlecruiser HMS *Hood* and the new battleship HMS *Prince of Wales*.

The engagement was a disaster for the Royal Navy. The *Hood* was hit by a shell from *Bismarck's* main armament and exploded and sank, taking with her all but three of her

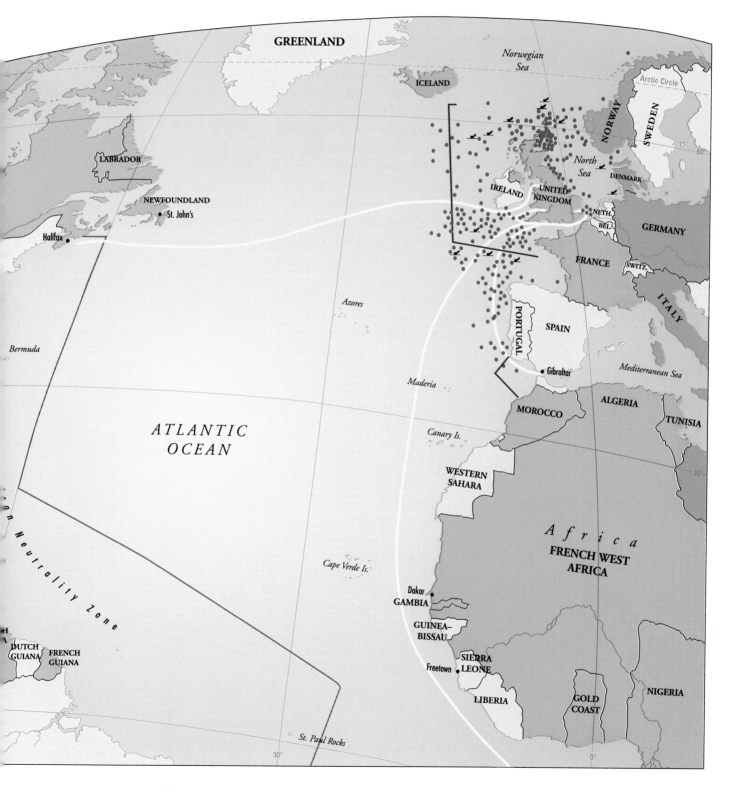

crew, and *Prince of Wales* was damaged and had to withdraw. No more serious blow was made by German warships to the British navy in the whole of World War II.

Bismarck's damage appeared minimal. She had been hit below the waterline, marginally decreasing her speed, and she was losing fuel. Admiral Lütjens, the German commander, ordered *Bismarck* and *Prinz Eugen* to proceed independently to Brest, where they would join the *Scharnhorst* and *Gneisenau*. In retrospect, Lütjens should have returned to Norwegian waters, perhaps polishing off the *Prince of Wales* on the way. He could then have waited until the *Bismarck's* sister ship *Tirpitz* was completed. The two massive battleships could then have tried to break out into the Atlantic again.

Although Lütjens succeeded in shaking off the shadowing British cruisers, the battleship was sighted again by a Catalina flying-boat on the morning of 26 May. By then, she was so far from the British Home Fleet that only a carrier strike could touch her before she reached friendly air cover. Launched from HMS *Ark Royal*, a strike by 15 Swordfish disabled the *Bismarck's* steering gear.

Unable to steer, the *Bismarck* was attacked on the morning of 27 May by the battleships HMS *Rodney* and HMS *King George V*. Within an hour, the German ship had been battered into ruin by 35.5cm (14in) and 40cm (16in) shells. The heavy cruiser *Devonshire* was then called in to administer the *coup de grâce*. After taking three torpedoes, the *Bismarck* sank by the stern, taking Admiral Lütjens and most of her complement of 2192 men to the bottom.

The U-boat War
The *Kriegsmarine* used armed merchant cruisers to much greater effect. These vessels were designed to look like ordinary merchantmen, but their sheep's clothing concealed

Below: To extend the operational range of its U-Boats, the Kriegsmarine *deployed* Milchcows: *large transport boats with extra fuel, supplies and torpedoes, which could be used to replenish U-boats far out in the Atlantic.*

very heavy weaponry. In terms of numbers of vessels sunk, their effect was not large, and they never threatened Allied command of the seas. But their activities did spread alarm, and forced the Royal Navy to devote considerable resources to tracking them down. They achieved most of their successes in distant waters before the end of 1941.

Whilst the activities of the *Kriegsmarine's* surface raiders made good copy for the propaganda machine, the German navy was never able to concentrate its capital ships to make a decisive difference, and the piecemeal operations of those raiders had little more than nuisance value.

In marked contrast to the surface fleet, the *Kriegsmarine's* U-boat force was a much more dangerous threat. The *Kriegsmarine's* submarine supremo, Admiral Karl Dönitz, well understood his priorities. He reckoned that a fleet of around 250 or even 300 submarines would be necessary to do the job. Hitler's pre-war 'Z-plan', the insanely ambitious Nazi naval construction programme, actually planned for such a fleet to be operational by 1943. But at the same time, the *Kriegsmarine* was to have two squadrons of giant battleships, bigger than any other warships in the world.

THE FOCKE-WULF FW 200 CONDOR

The Allied convoys had more to worry about than being shadowed by U-boats. There was what Winston Churchill called 'the Scourge of the Atlantic' – the Focke-Wulf Fw 200 Condor, which was the first demonstration of the value of air power in the Atlantic. The Fw 200s of *Kampfgeschwader 40* flew a giant loop from their base near Bordeaux in France, out over the convoy routes to their northern bases in Norway, doing the same trip in reverse the following day.

The idea was that once the Fw 200s found a convoy, the big aircraft were used as orbiting beacons. By transmitting continuously, they provided course data both to the high command and for the packs of U-boats, which could home in on their transmissions. Condors were fragile and vulnerable to fighters, but the British had been too hard-pressed for many a month to spare carriers or even catapult-launched aircraft to beat off the bombers.

The Condors did more than spot convoys for the U-boats, however. They also bombed stragglers and independently sailing merchantmen. In the first two months of 1941 alone, they sank 46 ships totalling 152,215 tonnes (167,822 tons) – the U-boats had themselves had only sunk 60. Only the continued disagreement and distrust between the *Kriegsmarine* and the *Luftwaffe* prevented a development that could have been catastrophic for the British.

The high command's obsession with battleships delayed the submarine-building programme, and was, in the view of Dönitz, irrelevant. He believed that only submarines offered a realistic prospect of blockading Britain.

Dönitz had learned his trade in U-boats during World War I. The Imperial German Navy was the first to make extensive use of submarines in attacking an enemy's trade, and in spite of the fairly primitive nature of the boats of the time, it achieved considerable success. U-boats wreaked havoc on British trade in the Mediterranean, and the unrestricted submarine warfare of 1917 and 1918 came within a whisker of bringing Britain to its knees. It was a major reason why Germany was denied a submarine force under the terms of the Treaty of Versailles after the war.

In spite of the ban, Germany set up clandestine U-boat design offices in Holland in 1922 and in Berlin in 1927. In 1932, months before Hitler's rise to power, the Weimar government approved a naval building plan that included 16 U-boats. The rise of the Nazis accelerated the navy's plans. In 1935, Hermann Göring announced Germany's intent to rearm, repudiating the Treaty of Versailles. Hitler managed to push through an

Anglo-German naval agreement, which allowed naval construction up to a ceiling of 45 per cent of the Royal Navy. Curiously, since the British had painful experience of what submarines could do, the agreement also allowed Germany to match the Royal Navy's submarine force, ton for ton.

Dönitz was given command of Germany's first post-war submarine flotilla that year and set about training a new U-boat fleet that could succeed where his generation had – by a narrow margin – failed. Once in charge of the German submarine force, he was able to define the types of boat best suited to near and distant operations as well as the number.

One requirement identified was for a coastal submarine, and the Type II went quickly into production. Type II U-boats proved to be handy and manoeuvrable, and could crash-dive in 25 seconds. Their profile and lively handling earned them the nickname of 'canoe'. But their small size and weapons load were handicaps in an open-ocean conflict, and construction ceased in 1941.

The majority of U-boats that fought the Battle of the Atlantic were Type VIIs. Like the Type II, the Type VII was originally designed for Finland and built in 1930. They were built in huge numbers, more than 800 being completed by the end of the war. Although intended for ocean operations, size was limited to allow the maximum number of boats to be built within treaty limits. This had the added advantage of making them agile and quick to dive.

As with most submarines of the period, the Type VII was powered by diesel engines on the surface and used battery-driven electric motors underwater. Under diesel drive, a Type VII could reach around 17.5 knots – more than enough to run rings around a slow-moving convoy. Underwater it could not do much more than 5 knots, and could sustain that speed for only a few hours. The Type VII carried between 11 and 14 torpedoes. Early boats also had a deck gun, but later in the war this was often exchanged for an increasingly heavy anti-aircraft gun fit.

Right: The introduction of larger, longer-ranged boats and of Milchcow *supply submarines in 1940 and 1941 saw U-Boat sinkings extend further out into the Atlantic and south as far as the coast of West Africa.*

Battle of the Atlantic II
June 1940–March 1941

— Pan-American Neutrality Zone

— Extent of air escort cover

- - Extent of surface escort cover

☐ Major convoy routes

· Allied merchant ships sunk by U-boats

⚓ U-boats sunk

▨ Territory under Allied control

▨ Territory under Axis control

▨ Territory under Vichy government (unoccupied France)

☐ Neutral territory

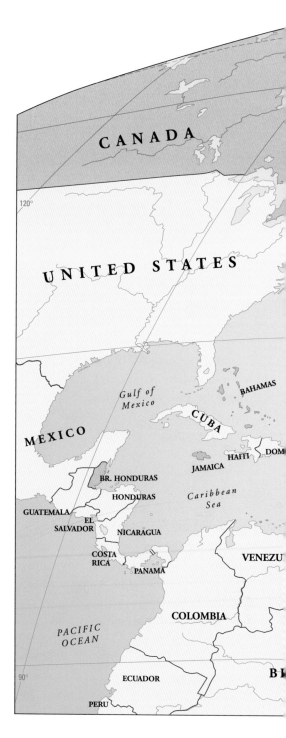

The larger Type IX class was designed for ocean warfare. Early Type IXs had enough range to operate in the southern hemisphere, mounting long patrols into the South Atlantic. Later versions with increased range could reach the Indian Ocean and even the Pacific without refuelling. Habitability was improved for these long-duration operations, and the number of torpedoes carried, at 22, was about 50 per cent more than those of a

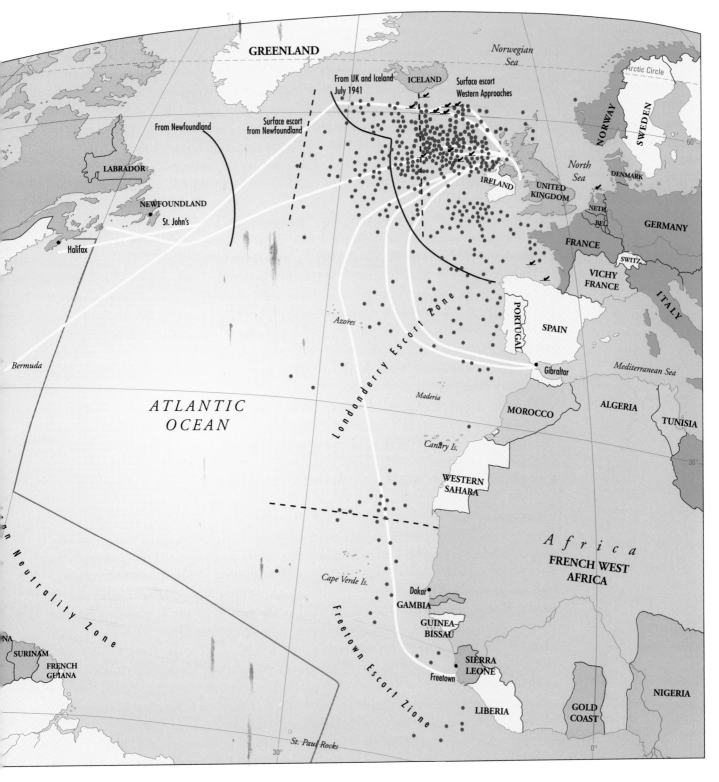

'As far as the Navy is concerned, obviously it is in no way very adequately equipped for the great struggle with Great Britain... the submarine arm is still much too weak to have any decisive effect on the war.'

Grand Admiral Erich Raeder, Kriegsmarine C-in-C, 1939

Type VII. Even so, crews preferred the smaller boats, since they could crash-dive more quickly and were quicker to manoeuvre under water. The big Type IX took up to 40 seconds to submerge in an emergency, leaving it vulnerable to air attack much longer.

Hunting the British

As late as the summer of 1939, Hitler was telling the German navy that there was little danger of war. Dönitz had only 46 operational submarines, of which more than half were the coastal 'ducks' – Type IIs – primarily used for training.

For the first eight months of the war, U-boat activity against Britain's vital supply lines was small – and was almost entirely directed against the few ships that sailed independently rather than in convoy. Indeed, during the Norwegian campaign, all U-boats were withdrawn from the Atlantic for operations in the North Sea.

That was about to change. Between the wars, Dönitz had developed theoretical group attack tactics. Once in control of Hitler's U-boats, he tested the concept of the 'wolf pack': co-ordinated strikes by groups of submarines far out into the ocean. Another technique Dönitz advocated was one he had learned in World War I: the most effective attacks were made by night on the surface. In 1939, he published a book, describing these methods – how the small silhouette of a submarine would be hard to see at night, and how the surfaced submarine of the 1930s enjoyed a considerably higher speed than the average merchant ship. No-one in Britain appears to have noticed.

The declared war zone first extended about 800km (497 miles) west of Ireland. In the first months of the war, pickings were rich amongst merchantmen returning individually to the UK. U-boat commanders had a healthy respect for British destroyers, whose Asdic underwater sound systems could detect the range and bearing of a submerged submarine. But there were never enough of them, and a frantic building programme undertaken to replace them with sloops and corvettes would take years to reach peak production.

The shortage of escorts on the major routes between the UK and Canada saw convoys escorted through only 15° longitude from either end. Empty ships could only be escorted to a line some 500km (311 miles) west of Ireland, where the escort would meet a heavily laden convoy coming home. In the middle of the Atlantic, the convoys were on their own. Thus began what U-boat commanders were to call the first 'Happy Time'.

Crisis in the Convoys

Early qualms about attacking liners were long gone. Merchant ships were escorted, armed and given instructions to ram on opportunity, so the *Kriegsmarine* considered that an unrestricted sinking policy was legally justified. Admiral Dönitz warned that ships of any nation entering the war zone would be subject to attack, whether belligerent or neutral. The crippling loss of Allied shipping in the early years of the war at sea was out of all proportion to the number of submarines causing that loss. There were rarely more than a dozen at sea at any one time.

After the fall of France, a higher proportion of the U-boat force was operational in the mid-Atlantic. They no longer had to make the long passage across the North Sea and around Scotland: the boats were now based in vast reinforced-concrete submarine pens on the Atlantic coast of France. From there, they could reach their patrol waters more quickly, and could stay on station longer. The shorter journey was not without risk. To reach the shipping lanes, they had to cross the Bay of Biscay. Travelling on the surface to get into action as quickly as possible, they ran the gauntlet of British long-range aircraft, often submerging by day to hide

A bigger threat came from Berlin. Building programmes were still skewed to large warships – U-boats, no matter how successful, were a lower priority. As a result, losses of U-boats exceeded commissioning so that, as late as February 1941, only 22 boats were actually operational. In July and August 1940, 27 Italian boats arrived in Bordeaux. But the Italian boats were of unsuitable design and national temperaments clashed. In the first two months, the Italians sank just one ship, while the German boats sank 80.

Allied Airbases in Canada and on the British west coast enabled RAF Coastal Command to maintain anti-submarine patrols at either end of a convoy's journey. But not in the middle. Once a convoy reached the 'Atlantic gap', it was on its own. In an attempt to evade the marauding wolfpacks, British convoys were routed as far north as possible as they crossed the Atlantic. Convoys also followed zig-zag routes, radical changes of course in the night being designed to lose shadowing U-boats.

Operational control of the U-boat fleet was maintained from Wilhelmshaven, though Dönitz also had a forward headquarters at Kerneval, overlooking Lorient on the coast of Brittany. The *Kriegsmarine* kept tight control of its boats, maintaining regular radio contact.

Without the threat of aerial attack during the day, the U-boats could assemble in lines up to 20km (12 miles) apart. Positioned across likely convoy routes, they assembled into

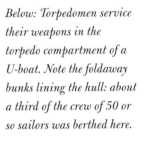

Below: Torpedomen service their weapons in the torpedo compartment of a U-boat. Note the foldaway bunks lining the hull: about a third of the crew of 50 or so sailors was berthed here.

informal groups often named after pirates, famous battles, areas of Germany or characters from Norse mythology. More than one pack could operate at a time; convoy SC 52 out of Nova Scotia was driven back to port by 20 boats from wolfpacks *Mordbrenner*, *Reisswolf* and *Schlagtod*.

Once a convoy was located, Dönitz assigned one or two U-boats as 'shadowers'. These followed the convoy, reporting its course and speed to U-boat HQ. Position reports were sent to operational boats in the Atlantic, and the wolf pack gathered for the kill. The procedure generated a lot of radio traffic, which would eventually contribute to the submarines' defeat, but until the codes were broken and direction-finding equipment perfected, Dönitz's system worked very effectively.

The first attacks were made underwater, but ace skippers quickly learned that night surface attacks were more effective, trusting to their low silhouette to avoid detection and to the U-boat's ability to outpace most escorts. More cautious skippers remained submerged and fired fans of torpedoes at the columns of merchant ships.

In the early days of the war, convoys were only lightly escorted. The first boats to attack, drew off the escorts, leaving later arrivals, often attacking from a wide arc, a free run in on the hapless merchantmen. Curiously, a U-boat became easier to detect when it submerged. These were the days before effective radar had been widely deployed aboard escorts, but they all had ASDIC detection gear, which used sound waves to search for submerged boats.

Convoy SC 7

One of the most destructive attacks occurred when the convoy SC 7 was targeted by a 'wolf pack' including 'aces' Kretschmer, Schepke, Endrass and Frauenheim. Convoy SC 7, consisting of 34 ships, left Nova Scotia on 5 October 1940 with a single sloop in attendance. By the 16th, it was 800km (498 miles) west of Ireland, where it was met by another sloop and one of the new 'Flower' class corvettes. Also in attendance was one lone U-boat,

Right: Through 1941, the most profitable operating area for the U-Boat was in the mid-Atlantic gap: the stretch of the ocean south of Iceland that was beyond the range of air cover where convoys were at their most vulnerable.

Battle of the Atlantic III
April–December 1941

— Limit of US merchant responsibility from April

— Extent of air escort cover

– – Limit of surface escort from April

Major convoy routes

• Allied merchant ships sunk by U-boats

⌐ U-boats sunk

Territory under Allied control

Territory under Axis control

Territory under Vichy government (unoccupied France)

Neutral territory

which promptly signalled all relevant details to headquarters and then, in bright moonlight, torpedoed two of the transports and slipped away. In their inexperience, the escorts stayed behind to pick up survivors. The convoy steamed on unescorted until the

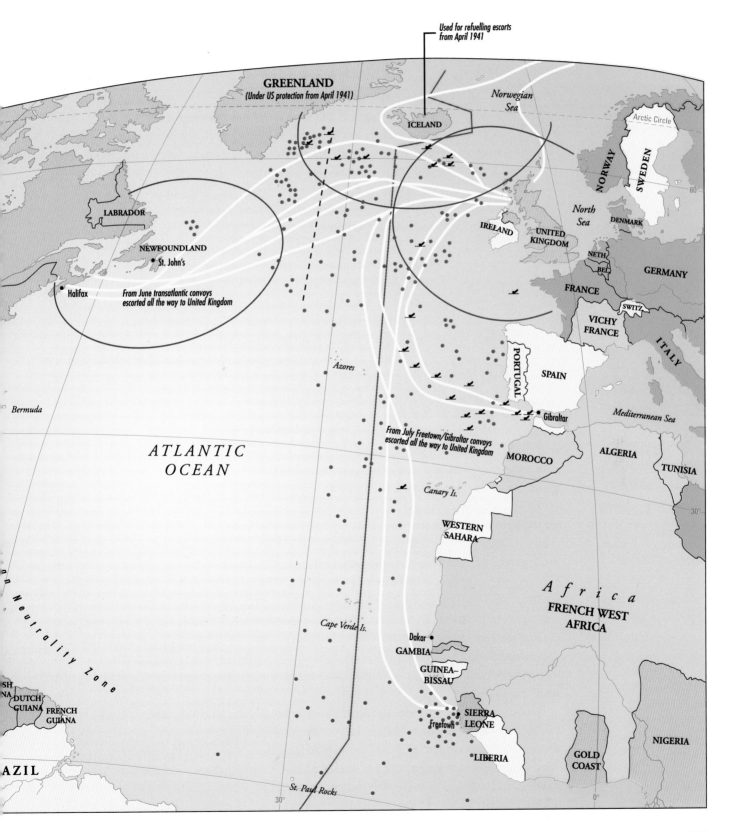

Above: The primary weapon of Allied convoy escorts was the depth charge. Once an enemy submarine was forced to submerge, its speed and endurance was cut drastically, and it became vulnerable to patterns of depth charges laid from the stern of destroyers and corvettes.

following evening, when another U-boat damaged a third transport. By nightfall on 18 October, two sloops and a corvette were shepherding the remaining 31 ships. Just over the horizon was waiting a patrol line of six U-boats, whose commanders knew exactly where and when their quarry would arrive. Two of these commanders were the acknowledged aces, Joachim Schepke of *U-100* and Otto Kretschmer of *U-99*.

They struck just after midnight and a night of chaos and confusion followed. It was filled with death and destruction for the unfortunate convoy – and high excitement and triumph for the U-boat crews. All around, ships were burning, blowing up, sinking. Some settled slowly and wearily, the frigid waters lapping higher and higher until the final lurch; others broke in half, with one section sticking upright out of the water until the imprisoned air leaked out and it went down with a rush and a gulp. The steamship *Sedgepool*, with her bow blown off, knifed down into the sea like a U-boat doing a crash dive, propeller still whirling high in the air.

The escorts could do little but pick up survivors. Their Asdic was useless – the U-boats had attacked on the surface – and radar to replace it had not yet been fitted. By morning, the convoy had disintegrated and of the original 34 ships only 12 reached port – and that was only because word had reached Kretschmer and his comrades that yet another convoy, HX 79, was close behind and ripe for their attention. Of the 49 ships of this convoy, the U-boats sank 12 and damaged two more.

Allied Countermeasures

The U-boat war was not all one-sided. If a U-boat was detected, a deadly game of cat and mouse would follow in which the submarine, with its low underwater speed and limited submerged range, was at a distinct disadvantage. The crew listened as the 'ping' of enemy sonar echoed around them. If full speed on the electric motors and rapid alterations in course failed to shake the pursuer, they could try to escape by stealth, but all too often the U-boat men would hear the awful express train sound of a destroyer passing overhead to drop depth charges. The thunderous detonations of the explosive devices reverberated through the submarine. A near miss could smash dials, crack open valves and plunge the boat into darkness.

Bold skippers would take the boat down through the pre-war safety depth of 50m (164ft), the hull creaking as the pressure increased, down to and even beyond the normal maximum permissible depth of 150m (492ft). To escape from a particularly accurate depth-charging attack in 1939, Otto Kretschmer dived *U-99* beyond 210m (698ft). His gamble paid off because early-war British depth charges had a maximum depth setting of 150m (492ft). If the U-boat men were lucky, the escorts would lose contact or be compelled to abandon the attack and rush to head off an attack on another part of the convoy, at which point and the submarine could slink away.

The effect of such an attack was often to leave the U-boat a long way astern of the convoy. As long as the boat was not too seriously damaged, it would creep up to periscope depth after an hour or two. Catching the convoy again would be impossible while submerged, so captains would bring their boats back to the surface as soon as possible, using the U-boat's superior surface speed to regain contact, ready to renew its attack the following night. Once out of torpedoes, a U-boat commander would often be instructed to continue to shadow the convoy, sending position reports for the benefits of fresher boats arriving on the scene, before receiving the order to return.

Early in the war, boats spent a good proportion of their time on the surface. However, the biggest danger to any U-boat was that of surprise attack from the air, and as the war progressed more and more commanders would submerge by day when in range of Allied air bases. Even so, many were caught by surprise.

A well-trained crew could submerge a Type VII boat in 20 seconds, the bridge lookouts hurling themselves down the ladder. Minor injuries were frequent, and terrible mistakes sometimes occurred. The first watch officer of *U-451*, accidentally left on the bridge when the boat crash-dived to escape a British aircraft, was rescued by a British warship. The submarine and the rest of the crew were never seen again.

U-boat losses exceeded new production throughout 1940, and by January 1941 there were just 22 boats operational: fewer than the number available in September 1939. Even so, from July 1940 until the worsening winter weather – and more numerous escort vessels – began to have effect, the U-boats had a clear run. They sank 520 ships totalling 2.17 million tonnes (2.4 million tons) by December 1940. They could have sunk considerably more, but German torpedoes were not reliable, and would not become so until late 1941.

Changing Fortunes

The Battle of the Atlantic changed dramatically in December 1941, when Hitler declared war on the United States. Dönitz had anticipated his chief's decision, sending five Type IX boats to the US coast 48 hours before the declaration. But Dönitz's men now had a new challenge: they would have to sink merchant ships faster than the world's most powerful economy could build them. For a brief period – the second 'Happy Time' – they did. Slow American reactions to the U-boat threat left merchantmen sailing individually without escort, and until a proper convoy system was established the U-boats wreaked havoc on America's eastern seaboard. Once the US Navy set up a proper convoy system, the

THE ATLANTIC ACES

The U-boat 'aces' were the new heroes of the Nazi pantheon: young, aggressive skippers prepared to attack on the surface and close to point-blank range before firing their torpedoes. The top three, Kretschmer, Luth and Topp, sank 121 ships totalling 623,109 tonnes (687,000 tons) between them. As with fighter pilots, it was the small number of aces who inflicted most of the damage. Ace status required a score of 45,350 tonnes (50,000 tons), later increased to 90,700 tonnes (100,000 tons) and was recognized by the award of the *Ritterkreuz* (Knight's Cross). As triumphant captains returned to port, their crews were awarded medals too, on the dockside by Dönitz in person. He would continue to greet his men as they made port, through the 'happy time' and into the grim months of 1943, when losses soared to unsustainable levels. Dönitz was an inspiration to the U-boat men, his praise desired, his anger dreaded.

'The enemy holds every trump card, covering all areas with long-range air patrols and using location methods against which we still have no warning... The enemy knows all our secrets and we know none of his.'

Grand Admiral Karl Dönitz

Type IXs moved down to the Caribbean and the Gulf of Mexico, where they wreaked havoc among the vital tanker traffic coming out of Texas and Venezuela.

Yet even though the picture looked black for the Allies, the tide was on the turn. In December 1940, convoy losses had reached such proportions that defeat through starvation threatened Britain. Only immediate and drastic measures could avert catastrophe. More escorts were needed, guarding more closely controlled convoys, with better detecting equipment. Fortunately, these measures were taken – just in time.

A year later, with the danger of German invasion past, fast escort destroyers could be released from home waters. Smaller escort vessels were coming off the slips at an increasing rate. Most significant of all, British scientists had made a major breakthrough: a practical and effective airborne radar that would allow surfaced U-boats to be detected, day or night, whatever the weather. The 'Happy Time' was coming to an end.

That was difficult to see at the time. The massacre of Allied merchant shipping in 1941 had been frightening. But 1942 was worse: 1664 ships – nearly 7.26 million tonnes (8 million tons) – were sunk. And U-boat operational strength was rising fast: from 91 boats in January to 212 in December. As Churchill was to write, 'The U-boat campaign of 1942 was our worst evil.'

After the war, Churchill claimed that the only thing that had really worried him was the Battle of the Atlantic. The genuine fears of the Government and the Royal Navy, the universal impact of rationing, and horror stories like the massacre of convoy SC 7 created an enduring impression.

But the picture is misleading. For every convoy decimated like SC 7, many others reached Britain without serious loss. By December 1941, the British had sailed some 900 convoys, and of 12,000 inbound ships, the U-boats had sunk less than 300. Also, by this time the best of the pre-war trained U-boat men were at the bottom of the Atlantic in the shattered hulls of their 'iron coffins'. Few aces enjoyed their glory for long. Prien and Schepke had been killed in March, and Kretschmer had been captured.

Despite some notable setbacks, most convoys still managed to cross with little incident. During 1941, close cover became possible for the whole crossing, not least because of the crucial expansion of the Royal Canadian Navy. A sustained air offensive against transiting U-boats in the Bay of Biscay also produced an excellent return. Having contacted a convoy, submarines were now also likely to find an escort carrier providing local air cover to keep them down, while cruising escort groups quickly reinforced the close escort at the onset of any threat.

The Allied Victory

The climax of the campaign came in March 1943. The Allies lost more than 453,000 tonnes (500,000 tons) of shipping in that month alone, but from then on it was the U-boats which suffered. Between May and August, 98 new boats were commissioned – but 123 were lost. Each represented a trained crew perished or prisoner.

Despite the horrendous loss rate, and in the face of Allied efforts to disrupt the German building programme by bombing, total U-boat strength remained well over 400 until the end of hostilities. But their North Atlantic success rate declined dramatically: 463 ships were sunk in 1943 but only 132 in 1944. The Allied victory in the Battle of the Atlantic was, arguably, the single most important campaign victory of the western war. It was a close-run thing; even though only one in three U-boats actually sank an Allied vessel, their operations cost the Allies some 13 million tonnes (14.3 million tons) of

Left: U-Boat crews were young, dedicated and courageous. They had to be: by 1943, Allied countermeasures were becoming increasingly effective and U-Boat losses were soaring. The 'Happy Times' were far in the past, and the average sailor in submarines stood about one chance in nine of surviving to the end of the war.

shipping. U-boats also accounted for 158 British warships and 27 from the US Navy.

However, whatever the losses the Allies suffered, the U-boats suffered in kind. Being a U-boat crewman was probably the most dangerous occupation of the war. More than 1100 boats were built between 1935 and 1945, of which 863 sailed on operational patrols. A total of 754 boats were lost in action: 27,000 U-boat crewmen died, a casualty rate of 85 per cent. A further 5000 were taken prisoner. People sent to concentration camps had a better chance of survival than these doomed warriors of the Reich.

The Balkans and Crete

The last thing that Adolf Hitler wanted in the spring of 1941 was a war in the Balkans, since his mind was full of the forthcoming invasion of Russia. However, his ally, Italian dictator Mussolini, was in serious trouble, and German troops and aircraft were needed to prevent catastrophe.

Unfortunately for his plans, the *Führer* got more than he bargained for. Yugoslavia's stand against the Nazis was rewarded with invasion, and initially, the *Wehrmacht* seemed to be unstoppable. But the German foray into the Balkans became more extensive as the Greeks doggedly resisted conquest, and before long a ferocious partisan war was diverting resources badly needed elsewhere. This was exacerbated by British attempts to intervene (though these proved unsuccessful) and German paratroopers went on to seize Crete, inflicting another defeat on the British Empire.

The Balkans Flashpoint

Much of the blame for the Balkans war was Mussolini's. The Italian leader had originally been the dominant figure in European fascism. However, as the Nazis consolidated their grip on Germany, he was rapidly being surpassed by his German rival. Jealous of Hitler's military triumphs, which confirmed Germany as the senior partner in the Axis alliance, *Il Duce* resolved to carve out his own place in the sun.

Past military adventures had been restricted to targets unable to resist and with no friends to intervene. Libya, Abyssinia and Albania were incorporated into his latter day Roman Empire. This was achieved at the minor cost of international censure from the toothless League of Nations. Depicted by cartoonists as the opportunist jackal to the Nazi lion, Mussolini waited until the defeat of France was certain before declaring war, but unlike the triumphant *Wehrmacht,* the Italian Army suffered a humiliating setback as the French held the invaders back in the south of the country. Mussolini decided to go for what he believed would be an easier target and launched an invasion of his own, deliberately not informing Hitler until his armies were on the move.

On 28 October 1940, Italy invaded Greece. Unfortunately for Mussolini, the Greek army was a very different prospect from the ill-equipped African tribesmen that his armies had defeated in the 1930s. Not only did the Italian invasion break down that

Opposite: Adolf Hitler and Benito Mussolini were the acknowledged leaders of European Fascism. Il Duce *was one of the few men the* Führer *respected and would continue to respect to the end of his life. This was in spite of the fact that the Italian leader's adventurism drew the* Wehrmacht *into conflicts Germany did not want.*

Opposite: The German campaign in the Balkans proceeded rapidly, in spite of the rugged terrain which characterized the region. Yugoslavia fell quickly, followed by Greece. However, an easy victory was not followed by an easy occupation: the partisan war that followed was as fierce and uncompromising as any in history.

winter, but a Greek counteroffensive in December drove the invaders back into Albania and back another 80km (50 miles) for good measure. Mussolini's invasion of Greece infuriated Hitler. The German dictator was annoyed with the blatant disregard of his stated opinions on the subject, and with its effect upon his own long-term plans. It soon became obvious, however, that Hitler could not leave Mussolini to collapse into defeat. Pulling him out of trouble would necessarily be a military, not a political, matter.

The German Involvement

Hitler had already laid plans for a drive down through Bulgaria to occupy the northeast coast of the Aegean. This was intended to secure the southern flank of his planned onslaught on Soviet Russia. The operation was codenamed *Marita*, and it also made provision for dealing with Greek resistance. If the Government in Athens could not be persuaded to accept German occupation of the north, the operation also included plans for the conquest of the whole of mainland Greece, should that become necessary.

But Hitler had hoped that the bonds between his own dictatorship and that of the Greek ruler, General Metaxas, would be sufficient to avoid actual battle. Hitler wanted a peaceful occupation, similar to those already in place in Romania and Hungary, and intended for Bulgaria. He also hoped for a peaceful solution to the problem posed by Yugoslavia. Even before the war started, Germany had arranged to take Yugoslavia's entire production of copper, plus substantial quantities of lead and zinc, in return for supplies of aircraft and guns. Hitler summoned the Yugoslav foreign minister to Berchtesgaden on 27 November 1940 to suggest that Yugoslavia place herself unreservedly upon the side of the Axis.

The *Wehrmacht* had been funnelling troops into Hungary and Romania – allied to Germany by treaty – since the autumn of 1940. By February 1941, more than 650,000 were in place, primarily to secure the southern flank of the invasion of the USSR, which at that time was planned for May.

When it became necessary to take action against the Greeks, who were putting up a stiff fight against the Italians, Hitler bullied the Bulgarians and Yugoslavs into signing the Tripartite Pact. This allowed Field Marshal List's 12th Army to cross their borders on its way to Greece.

Bulgaria was forced to allow the *Wehrmacht* free passage, and German forces began to assemble opposite the 'Metaxas Line' defences that separated these ancient enemies. But an assault through Bulgaria would restrict the invasion to a relatively narrow front, which the Greeks were well prepared to resist. More Nazi browbeating secured permission from the Yugoslav Government for German forces to cross their territory to attack Greece.

British troops were already landing in Greece. Bolstered by two Commonwealth infantry divisions, an armoured brigade and RAF Hurricanes, the Greeks prepared to meet the threatened invasion. On 19 March, Hitler gave Yugoslavia five days in which to agree to neutrality and the demilitarization of the Adriatic coast. Hitler made it quite obvious that if the Yugoslavs failed to sign, life would become increasingly difficult in the very near future. On 25 March, the Yugoslav foreign minister signed the pact at a ceremony so lacking in the festive spirit that even Hitler likened it to a funeral.

Hitler's plans were disrupted with 48 hours. Hardline Serb officers organized a military coup in the name of the young King Peter, overthrowing his uncle, the Regent Prince Paul. When news of the coup reached Hitler, he thought at first that it was a joke. But amusement soon vanished, replaced by fury. He interrupted a meeting of *Wehrmacht*

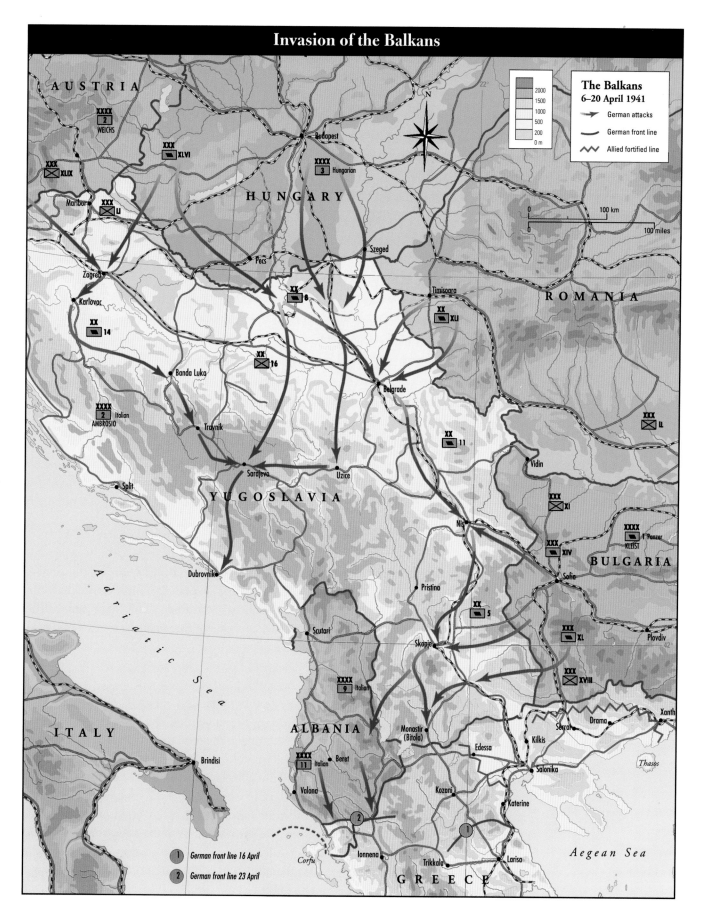

Invasion of the Balkans

The Balkans
6–20 April 1941

2000	
1500	
1000	
500	
200	
0 m	

→ German attacks
⌒ German front line
〰 Allied fortified line

N

22°

0   100 km
0   100 miles

46°

AUSTRIA

XXXX
2
WEICHS

XXX
XLVI

XXX
XLIX

Maribor

XXX
LI

HUNGARY

Budapest

XXXX
3 Hungarian

Szeged

Pecs

XX
8

ROMANIA

Timisoara

XX
XLI

Zagreb

Karlovac

XX
14

XX
16

Banda Luka

Belgrade

XXX
IL

XXXX
2 Italian
AMBROSIO

Travnik

XX
11

Vidin

Sarajevo

Uzice

YUGOSLAVIA

Split

XXX
XI

Nis

XXX
XIV

Dubrovnik

Pristina

BULGARIA

XXXX
1 Panzer
KLEIST

Sofia

Scutari

XXX
XL

Plovdiv

42°

Skopje

XXX
XVIII

XXXX
9 Italian

ALBANIA

Monastir
(Bitola)

Xanth

Serrai

Drama

Edessa

Kilkis

ITALY

Brindisi

Kozani

Salonika

Thasos

XXXX
11 Italian Beret

Valona

Katerine

(2)

(1)

Aegean Sea

Corfu

Ionnena

Trikkala

Larisa

GREECE

① German front line 16 April
② German front line 23 April

111

Above: Hungarian officers look on as members of a reconnaissance unit, part of the elite SS Das Reich *division, pass through Budapest on their way to the Yugoslav border. Das Reich had moved from the south of France to take part in the Balkan operation.*

commanders. Within hours, they had received new and unequivocal orders – there was to be no misunderstanding of the form Operation *Strafgericht* (Punishment) was to take. 'The *Führer* is determined...to make all preparations for the destruction of Yugoslavia, militarily and as a national unit....Politically it is especially important that the blow against Yugoslavia is carried out with pitiless harshness....The main task of the *Luftwaffe* is to start as early as possible...and to destroy the capital city, Belgrade, in waves of attack.'

The Assault on Yugoslavia

Spearheaded by *Luftwaffe* bomber and dive-bomber attacks, General Ewald von Kleist's XIV Panzer Corps attacked towards Belgrade. At the same time, the *Leibstandarte* 'Adolf Hitler', an elite brigade of the SS, and the 9th Panzer Division drove through Macedonia towards Skopje: the aim was to block any possible union of the Yugoslav and the Greek armies. The German onslaught began on Palm Sunday, 6 April 1941, with spectacular strikes by the *Luftwaffe*. The citizens of Belgrade were awakened by the noise of aircraft circling above them at 5.30 a.m. and within half an hour bombs were raining down on the railway station, the Royal Palace and the airfield at Zemun, where much of the Yugoslav air force was caught on the ground. For the whole of that day, the attack continued, until the centre of Belgrade was reduced to rubble. By the following evening, 17,000 people had been killed and fires continued to rage.

About 800km (500 miles) south, the menacing drone of approaching aircraft was heard in the Greek port of Piraeus. Soon afterwards, German bombers dropped mines at the harbour mouth. Then followed sticks of bombs that rained down across the shipping and warehouses along the harbour edge.

One of the victims was the SS *Glen Fraser*, anchored by the main quay. A bomb burst aboard her, and the 276 tonnes (250 tons) of explosives in her holds blew up with a shattering roar that devastated the port, and smashed doors and windows in Athens 12km (7 miles) away.

Back in Yugoslavia, the country splintered along its pre-1914 boundaries. Two Croatian divisions mutinied and a breakaway Croat republic welcomed the Germans into Zagreb while Belgrade burned. The Yugoslav Government requested an armistice on 14 April, and although Yugoslavia now fell under the iron grip of the Nazis, partisan forces would maintain a bloody campaign against the occupiers until the end of the war.

Fighting in Greece

The German attack on Greece was conceived as two main thrusts. A combined SS and armoured drive would turn south along the Albanian border, while List's Twelfth Army would attack though Macedonia, piercing or bypassing the Greek defensive lines. A smaller force was to make a series of landings on the Greek islands along the Turkish coast. The attack began on 6 April with the Twelfth Army advancing from Bulgaria with three corps. XXX and XLVIII Corps drove directly to the Aegean Sea, punching clean through the Greek defences. A British armoured brigade deployed in the north was ordered to fall back along the eastern coast. The German XL Corps included 5th Panzer Division and SS *Leibstandarte* Adolf Hitler. This force overran southern Yugoslavia to cross the Yugoslav-Greek frontier at Monastir on 10 April.

Air power was a decisive factor. The Greeks had no means to oppose the *Luftwaffe* and the British could not spare more than a token force of aircraft. Any attempt to move by day brought Stukas screaming out of the clear Mediterranean sky. Fighters joined in, and even bombers were used to strafe Allied road transport columns. It became so bad that drivers started to abandon their vehicles at the mere sound of aircraft approaching.

When Allied ground troops turned to fight, their positions were subjected to a hail of bombs. Communications broke

Below: The German invasion of Yugoslavia was supported by the Croatian Ustase movement, which created a breakaway fascist state in Croatia under the leadership of Ante Pavelic. Members of the Croatian Legion were to serve alongside the German Army in Russia.

down, artillery and anti-tank positions were knocked out, fuel and ammunition failed to arrive, and the wounded had to be left behind. At the same time, the Italian army launched a new offensive to coincide with Hitler's intervention. Their forces in Albania had been re-supplied and re-equipped, whereas the Greek logistic situation had not improved. Outgunned, out-numbered, and with the Germans pouring into northern Greece, the Greek army started to give way.

Hitler's Directive No.27 called for the encirclement of the Allied forces by a breakthrough in the direction of Larissa, the key road junction south of Mount Olympus. All north–south traffic east of the Pindus mountains came through this junction. With 5th Panzer Division charging down the roads and two German mountain divisions outflanking defensive positions in the valleys, the plan nearly succeeded in trapping the British.

By 12 April, the British commander General Wilson knew that the Germans were about to outflank him on the east. He ordered an evacuation southwards. By the 14th, those forces that had successfully disengaged were setting up defences along the line of the Aliakmon River and in the passes around Mount Olympus. They held the flood of German armour and infantry for four days while lorries full of exhausted men, trudging files of troops, and farm carts full of bewildered Greek families and their belongings fled

Opposite: The ancient pre-dreadnought Kilkis, *the former USS* Mississippi, *was bought by the Greek Navy from the USA in 1914. On 23 April 1941, during the German invasion of Greece, Kilkis was sunk at the Salamis naval base by German Junkers Ju 87 dive bombers.*

THE YUGOSLAV PARTISAN WAR

Following the Yugoslav armistice in April 1941, two separate groups of Serbs scattered into their barren mountains: *Chetniks*, loyal to the monarchy, and communist partisans dominated by Josip Broz, the guerrilla leader known as 'Tito'. The stage was set for an internecine war that would continue to the end of the 20th Century.

The German occupation of Yugoslavia opened a can of worms. In general, the Croats supported the Germans. Indeed Croatian *Ustase* nationalists conducted a genocidal campaign against the Serbs in Croatia and Bosnia. Some Serbs, led by local quisling General Nedic, also supported the Germans. Others – mostly pro-royalist fragments of the army and gendarmerie – took to the hills. Led by Draza Mihailovich, they adopted the old Serbian name of *Chetnik*, from *ceta*, or regiment. But the *Chetniks* were also deadly foes of the communist rebels led by Tito. The *Chetniks* offered to come over to the German side to fight the communists, while continuing to fight the Croatian fascists who were being supplied by the Germans. Internal rivalries were often more important than resisting the invaders. Serb fought Croat, *Chetnik* fought Communist, and Muslims, Catholics and Orthodox Christians killed each other with unbridled enthusiasm.

The communists were by far the most effective opposition to the Germans, and by the end of the war they claimed almost 200,000 men and women under arms. Although Tito himself was a Croat, he did more than any other Yugoslav to bring the war home to the Germans and their Croatian allies. Tito's partisan army won the support of the Western allies in preference to the unreliable Serbian *Chetniks*, since by their actions they tied down no less than 35 German divisions.

'As a base for air warfare against Great Britain in the Eastern Mediterranean, we must prepare to occupy the island of Crete; the Operation will be known as "Merkur".'

Adolf Hitler, War Directive 28, 25 April 1941

Above: German mountain infantrymen march through the dusty streets of Lamia, near the ancient battlefield of Thermopylae. The rugged terrain of Greece meant that the fitness of such elite troops was tested to the limit.

south. They were harried mercilessly by Stukas and machine-gunned by fighters. But the Allied positions were again being outflanked: German armour was driving for Ioannina and the Thessaly region to the west.

The British fell back to the ancient battlefield of Thermopylae on 18 April. British intelligence provided General Wilson with a stream of deciphered German signals that helped keep the withdrawal one step ahead of the advancing Germans, no mean trick given the mobility and tactical initiative of German commanders. On 19 April, Commonwealth troops were streaming back past Thermopylae, the rearguards digging in for yet another 'last stand': Already Royal Navy ships were evacuating base personnel from Piraeus. But 50,000 men could not be lifted from one port, so troops were sent south to keep open the bridge over the Corinth Canal and to guard the open beaches on the Peloponnesian coast, preparing for a Dunkirk-style evacuation.

The Greek commander, General Papagos, advised the King on 21 April that the Greek army could fight no more. To General Wilson he said that the British promise to fight alongside the Greeks had been faithfully kept, but now the time had come for them to go.

The rearguards at Thermopylae held on until 24 April, then slipped away; General Wilson left Athens on the morning of 26 April and crossed the Corinth Bridge, glad to know that he had been preceded by over 40,000 men. An orderly evacuation, however, was imperilled on the same day by a daring *coup de main*. German paratroops dropped nearby to capture the bridge, and German gliders landed in support. The bridge was blown even as the Germans raced over it searching for the charges – dropping them and the bridge neatly into the canal below.

For the next two days, only the *Luftwaffe* could harass the Commonwealth evacuation, and this they did, sinking one transport and two destroyers on the night of 26 April. But the Royal Navy carried on, lifting 21,000 men off five open beaches on the 27th.

Shortly after dawn on 28 April, 5th Panzer Division and the SS *Leibstandarte* crossed the Corinth Canal and drove south. The Panzers headed for Kalamata, where after a vicious fight it became obvious that no ships would be able to get in to rescue the 7000 Imperial troops still there. Many of these had fought in all the rearguards from the Vevi Gap southwards. The British and Commonwealth troops laid down their arms after exhausting their ammunition.

Athens Falls

German troops entered Athens on 27 April. Others embarked in commandeered local vessels to occupy the Ionian islands of Samothrace, Lesbos and Chios. However, in keeping with the strict timetable for Operation Barbarossa (the invasion of the Soviet Union), the bulk of the German invasion force began withdrawing in May, leaving Greece to be held by a mixture of German reserve units and Italians.

Greek losses in the brief campaign were almost 16,000 dead and missing and nearly a quarter of a million taken prisoner. Italy lost over 90,000 dead, wounded or missing. For Germany, the cost was nearly 5000 dead and wounded. The British lost nearly 4000 dead, wounded or missing and 9000 prisoners of war. But more importantly, 50,000 British and Commonwealth soldiers lived to fight another day, plucked from the Greek fishing ports and open beaches by the Royal Navy.

Many of the troops were evacuated to Crete. They assumed that the next stop would be Egypt and a welcome break from the war. What they did not know was that the Germans were planning to make the world's first full-sized airborne assault. The last battle for Greek territory was about to begin.

Airborne Operation

Crete lay to the south of Greece. It was a large island, 275km (171 miles) long and up to 48km (30 miles) wide. It had a good anchorage for warships at Suda Bay, and strategically located airstrips at Maleme, Retimo and Heraklion.

For Hitler and his planners, Crete presented a potential problem. Royal Navy warships based at Suda could control the Aegean and Ionian Seas. Should the RAF base bombers on Crete, they would be within range of the Romanian oil fields at Ploesti. Romanian oil was going to be vital to the success of Operation Barbarossa, the massive attack about to be launched against the Soviet Union. In German hands, those airfields would be invaluable for attacking British positions in Egypt or Libya, and ideal for harassing British shipping in the southern Mediterranean. Crete would have to be neutralized.

Such a task was easier said than done. Though the Axis powers enjoyed local air superiority, they did not command the sea. The Italian fleet had been severely mauled by

'We are determined to face the Axis by whatever means and sacrifices may be necessary. We shall do our duty to the end as devoted and loyal friends, even if we have to count only on our own forces.'

Greek communiqué following the German invasion

117

the Royal Navy and was in no position to support a major amphibious operation. However, British warships would not be a factor if the attack came from above, and it was decided to mount a major airborne assault. This was not without its risks. German paratroopers – *Fallschirmjäger* – had achieved great success in small-unit actions on the western front in 1940. But an airborne invasion was a whole order of magnitude greater.

Unlike most of the major combatants in World War II, whose airborne forces were part of the army, the elite German parachute and gliderborne troops were part of the *Luftwaffe*. Though this had some operational disadvantages when fighting alongside the *Wehrmacht*, it provided a unique bond between the transport pilots and ground-attack aircraft crews who supported the paratroopers in combat on the ground.

German intelligence about the island and garrison was patchy. They knew that there were about 6000 British and Greek troops stationed on Crete, but did not know that numbers had been swelled with 27,000 men who had been evacuated from Greece – though most had left their arms and equipment on the mainland. Almost all the troops lifted off the Peloponnesian beaches had been taken to Crete, thus releasing the ships for a quick return to pick up more of the hard-pressed British and Anzacs.

There were also some 400,000 Cretans who, though lacking military skills, would prove to be valiant supporters of the Allies. In addition, there were 14,000 Italians on the island, who had been taken prisoner in Albania. They all had to be fed, and now the only source of everything the island needed to exist, let alone to fight off an invader, was Egypt – the only supply route was across the Mediterranean from Alexandria.

Crete is dominated by a steep and narrow mountain range, which falls sharply to the sea along the south coast, but which

Above: Messerschmitt Bf 110s of Zerstörergeschwader (ZG) 26 patrol over the Greek coast. Although vulnerable to modern fighter opposition, the Bf 110 was used extensively over the Mediterranean.

in the north leaves three areas of flatter ground. The westernmost of these is around Canea and Suda Bay, and included the airfield at Maleme; the centre area is around Retimo and the most eastern area is around Heraklion, both with their own airfields.

The German plan of attack was the result of a compromise. Colonel-General Alexander Lohr of *Luftflotte 4* was in overall command of the operation. He favoured landings around Canea and Maleme in the west and a thrust eastward along the island. Commanding the paratroopers was Lieutenant-General Kurt Student, one of the founding fathers of the German airborne forces. He wanted landings at three points – Canea/Maleme, Retimo and Heraklion. The compromise was a two-phase attack, phase one consisting of a drop on Maleme/Canea on the morning of 20 May, with further drops on Retimo and Heraklion in the afternoon. These were the areas in which New

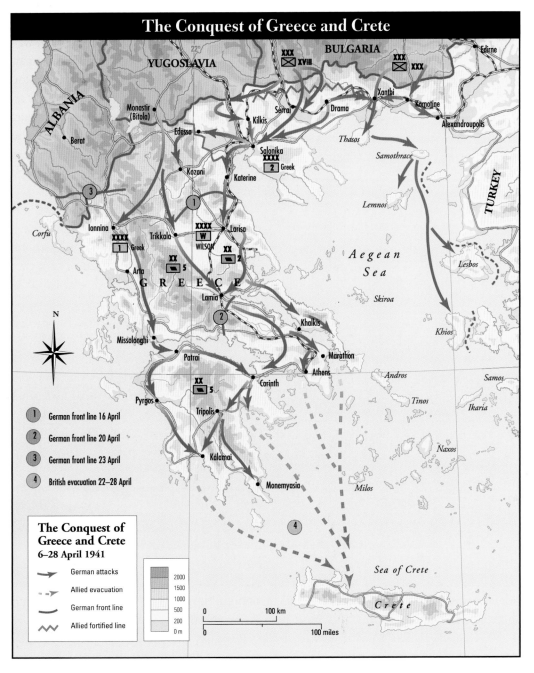

The Conquest of Greece and Crete

The Conquest of Greece and Crete
6–28 April 1941

1. German front line 16 April
2. German front line 20 April
3. German front line 23 April
4. British evacuation 22–28 April

German attacks
Allied evacuation
German front line
Allied fortified line

2000
1500
1000
500
200
0 m

0   100 km
0   100 miles

Zealander General Bernard Freyberg had concentrated his defence. There were two brigades around Maleme, supported by three Greek battalions. At Suda Bay, three battalions reinforced the 2000 men of the original garrison force. Three Australian and two Greek battalions were posted at Retimo. At Heraklion, he deployed another five battalions. In all, the defending force numbered around 40,000 troops by 7 May.

General Wavell, commander of British forces in the Middle East, helped as much as circumstances allowed. From his depots, he scraped 22 obsolete light tanks and infantry tanks, with some worn-out artillery in addition. The Allies on Crete trained, they dug defences – and they waited. The Germans were also preparing. The men, aircraft and equipment necessary for the assault were scattered through France, Germany and Greece. There was a lot of message traffic as the force was gathered, and as coded signals

Above: The German attack on Crete was the first major airborne invasion in history. Although ultimately successful, it came at great cost to the Luftwaffe *– close to half of the German air force's inventory of Ju-52s was destroyed.*

passed back and forth, they were intercepted. For years after the battle for Crete, the Allied cover story for their initial effective reaction to the airborne assault was to say that tactics had been based on a *Luftwaffe* manual captured during fighting in Holland in 1940. In fact, thanks to British success in decoding the German ULTRA signals, Freyberg knew the enemy plans almost as well as the German paratroopers who were about to land.

The main strike component of *Luftflotte 4* was General Student's *Fliegerkorps XI*. This comprised *Fliegerdivision 7* with a fighting strength of around 8000 men. Major-General Conrad commanded the transport element of the corps – nearly 500 Ju 52 trimotor transports and 72 DFS 230 gliders. Air support was provided by *Fliegerkorps VIII,* under the command of Lieutenant-General Freiherr von Richthofen. This comprised 180 fighters, over 200 dive-bombers and a similar number of medium bombers. Although almost exclusively a *Luftwaffe* operation, the invasion relied on the army for follow-up troops. These consisted of the 5th *Gebirgsjäger* division under Lieutenant-General Julius Ringel, whose three mountain rifle regiments and single motorcycle battalion were to be flown into action once the paratroopers had secured an airfield. Two further battalions of mountain troops would come by sea. Their vehicles, anti-aircraft guns, field artillery and support engineers were to be transported in two waves aboard Greek fishing boats, escorted by Italian motor torpedo boats.

The Attack on Crete

On each morning prior to the attack, German aircraft had been arriving overhead, either on reconnaissance or on the nuisance missions Allied troops called 'the morning hate'. However, at dawn on 20 May, the note and emphasis was entirely different. German fighters wove along the northern coastal strip between Maleme and Retimo. They strafed and shot up anything that moved. There were so many of them that to one startled observer there seemed to be a Messerschmitt or a Stuka for every human target.

Then, as men ducked into their trenches, a new note sounded – a prolonged buzz, like that of an approaching swarm of angry bees. As it got louder and louder, the New Zealanders around Maleme saw a huge fleet of transport planes come in towards them across the sea. As they arrived overhead, the sky blossomed with parachutes dangling men and containers. The battle for Crete had begun.

To the British and Commonwealth forces that were on the receiving end, the airborne attack on Crete was unlike anything ever seen before in war. Wearing high-laced rubber-soled boots and carrying sub-machine guns, the German paratroops in their zippered jump smocks could almost have come from another planet. This contrasted with the ordinary British soldier who still wore thick serge uniforms and leather gaiters, and who was armed with a bolt-action rifle dating from the 19th century. The first assault troops to arrive, the spearhead of Group West, were 500 glider troops delivered to the airfield at Maleme, followed by over 1800 paratroopers. The garrison reacted aggressively. Many Germans were killed as they floated down on their parachutes or as they struggled out of their harnesses. Some of the gliders crashed, killing their passengers. The Germans did, however, manage to achieve a foothold to the west of Maleme airfield and around Canea – but they were hard-pressed.

In the afternoon, the second wave of paratroops was dropped at Retimo and Heraklion. The fire coming up to meet them was just as devastating as at Maleme. This time, the paratroopers did not have the element of surprise. The survivors of the Retimo drop were reduced to two groups, besieged in a chapel and an olive oil factory.

At the *Luftwaffe* operational headquarters in Athens, Student decided that reinforcements should be committed to Group West only. A Ju 52 transport flown by Captain Kleye had managed to land at Maleme, albeit under small-arms fire, on the afternoon of the 20th. Reinforcing was risky, but was considered possible.

In the confusion of the battle, two understrength New Zealand battalions covering Maleme and Point 107 – the high ground closest to the airfield – were convinced that they were being outflanked. They pulled back on the night of the 20th. It was a move that would prove critical, since their withdrawal left Point 107 unoccupied. Fire from that high ground, which dominated the airfield, would have prevented its use for reinforcement.

Things were going even worse for the German seaborne attack. During the nights of 21 and 22 May, the Royal Navy intercepted and sank most of the seaborne elements of Ringel's mountain division. Three cruisers and a number of destroyers made short work of the fishing boats, and the glare of the searchlights and flashes of gunfire could be seen by the soldiers in Canea and Maleme less than 30km (19 miles) away.

At dawn on 21 May, German patrols discovered that Point 107 was undefended. With

Above: The British heavy cruiser HMS York *lies aground in Suda Bay, Crete. Damaged by an Italian explosive motor boat, she was later wrecked after being subject to numerous Luftwaffe attacks.*

Maleme airfield almost secure, the Germans piled on the pressure. Student committed his last reserve. On the 22nd, 1950 troops were landed and by the following day the total reached 3650. With reinforcements arriving, the paratroopers and men of the mountain division started to push eastwards to link up with their comrades at Canea. Under constant air attack, the Commonwealth garrison began to withdraw.

Withdrawal and Evacuation

General Freyberg, with victory snatched from his grasp, realized reluctantly that he would have to order the evacuation of Crete. The only viable port for the Royal Navy to evacuate troops from around Canea and Maleme was the tiny fishing point of Sphakia on the south coast. However, by now the Germans held the village of Galatas straddling the road south. On the 25th, two New Zealand companies were ordered to clear the village. The two companies found their numbers swelled by individuals and groups who were eager for revenge against the Germans. New Zealand, Australian and British troops who only a few days earlier had had the enemy on the run, were determined to prove they could do it again. Yelling a Maori *haka* and supported by two light tanks, the men charged into the village and drove the Germans out, clearing the road south.

On 26 May, General Freyberg ordered a general withdrawal over the mountains to the south coast and asked General Wavell to begin organization of an evacuation from the beaches at the village of Sfakia. On 28 May, the last rearguard action in the plains was fought. The long trudge over the White Mountains in progress, British commandos formed a perimeter across the ridges and ravines above Sfakia, through which the exhausted remnants of Freyberg's command made their painful way. All the time, the Germans were pushing southwards, and Stukas harassed the retreating soldiers.

The Royal Navy, with Narvik, Dunkirk and Greece behind them, were only too accustomed to the part in the drama that now occurred. They began taking troops off the beachhead on 27 May. Altogether, they lifted off over 16,000 men and took them back to Alexandria. *Luftwaffe* attacks wrought havoc during the evacuation. So high were Royal Navy losses – three cruisers and six destroyers sunk and 17 warships damaged – that the evacuation was abandoned on the 30th, leaving 5000 men to be taken prisoner.

At Heraklion, the Royal Navy was able to evacuate the garrison, but at Retimo, which had put up the most effective defence, they were all taken prisoner. Some of the men who had not been evacuated, evaded capture and a few of them managed to find craft to cross the 300km (186 miles) of water to North Africa. Others were evacuated by submarine. British and Commonwealth losses were 4000 killed, missing or wounded, with a further 11,000 captured. The Royal Navy lost 2000 men killed and nearly 200 wounded.

Occupation

When the fighting was over, unfounded rumours circulated that Cretan civilians had murdered German paratroopers. The Cretans suffered a harsh occupation, which began with the execution of 700 men whom the Germans regarded as *francs-tireurs* – civilian snipers. In four months, the occupation forces executed 1135 Cretans and destroyed four villages.

For the German airborne forces, it had been a Pyrrhic victory. Of the 8500 men dropped or landed by glider on Crete, 44 per cent were killed, the majority on the first day. As Churchill was later to put it, the 'very spearhead of the German lance' had been shattered. As for the price in aircraft, nearly half of the German transports had been destroyed. Losses were so high that Hitler came to a very similar conclusion as the British Prime Minister. Some days later, he decorated the more outstanding of the officers who had fought in Crete, then entertained them to lunch. Over coffee, he turned to Student and said: 'Of course, you know, General, that we shall never do another airborne operation. Crete proved that the days of parachute troops are over.'

With these words, the *Führer* ensured that the superbly-trained German *Fallschirmjäger* would no longer be used in airborne assaults, and would be expended as infantry. Hitler was proved wrong – as Allied forces were to show later in the war.

Apart from a few small operations, German paratroopers would never again be used on such a huge scale. They may have captured the island in May 1941, but Crete proved to be 'the grave of the German paratroop arm'.

Below: A wounded British soldier is helped by a comrade, following their capture after the fall of Crete. Over 11,000 British and Commonwealth troops were taken prisoner in the Greek campaign.

The Desert War

The war in North Africa began in earnest on 9 December 1940. Hitler watched, with caustic amusement, as Benito Mussolini tried to expand the Italian empire in North Africa. *Il Duce's* armies crept tentatively from Libya into Egypt. Then the British counterattacked. Italy was threatened with the annihilation of her forces and the total loss of her colonies. Germany would have to come to the rescue.

The Italian disaster threatened Fortress Europe. For his own security, Hitler felt that he had no option but to intervene on behalf of his ally. By the middle of February 1941, the first contingent of German support had reached Tripoli. It was not large – in fact, it consisted of one general and two staff officers – but the general was a man called Rommel.

Enter Rommel

As the commander of the 'Ghost' Division in France, Major-General Erwin Johannes Eugen Rommel had won a reputation as a brilliant commander. His orders were to stabilize the situation in North Africa. Rommel's force initially included only the 5th Light Division. For the moment, he was simply expected to stiffen Italian resistance. Perhaps, in due course, he would be given the resources to do more, but he was to await orders from above before contemplating offensive action.

Yet Rommel would not wait. Within days, he was planning a full-scale counterattack. With that would begin two years of cut-and-thrust battles between the Germans and British and Commonwealth forces. The battlefield was to be the Libyan desert, an area aptly described as a tactician's paradise and a quartermaster's nightmare.

Disobeying orders with a diligence that compels respect, Rommel moved the German 5th Light Division from Tripoli towards Agedabia on 24 March. There, on 3 April, Rommel set up his headquarters. He then cast aside all established principles of warfare by deliberately splitting the already tenuous forces at his disposal into three. He sent a mixed German and Italian force under Graf von Schwerin eastwards in a wide arc. While this passed through Giof el Matar and Tengeder towards Mechili, he directed the bulk of 5th Light to advance through Antelat and Msus. Rommel himself accompanied the armoured cars and light vehicles of the 3rd Reconnaissance Battalion to the north,

Opposite: British cavalrymen pose aboard their Vickers Light Tank on the Egyptian border with Libya. Commonwealth troops in North Africa were lightly equipped, but they were more than a match for the more numerous but poorly led Italian opponents.

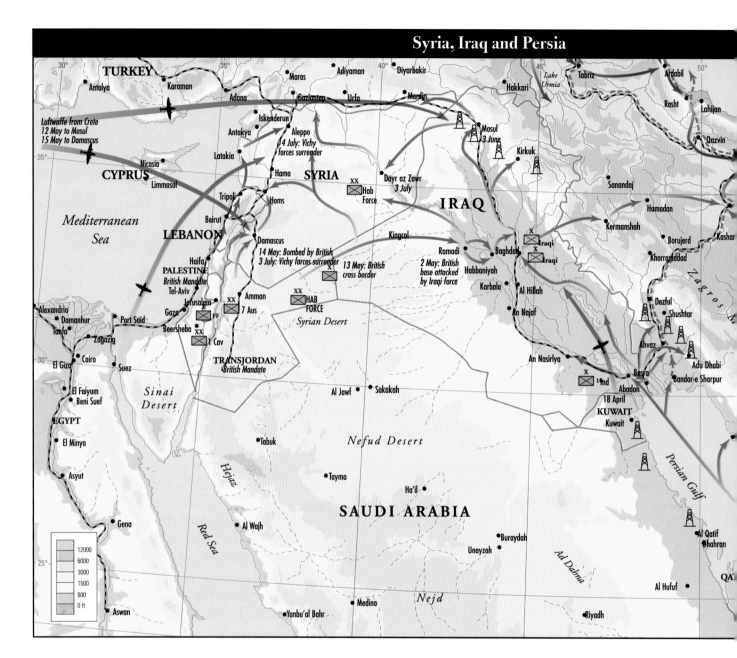

Syria, Iraq and Persia

Iraq, Syria and Persia
April–September 1941

→ Allied forces movements

→ Free French forces movements

→ Russian forces movements

✦ Allied bomber movements

✦ German bomber movements

--→ Allied supply routes

⛽ Oilfield

towards Suluch. Then, having heard rumours that the British were evacuating Benghazi, he ordered them to drive straight for the port. Here his troops were welcomed as conquering heroes. The *Afrika Korps* had come to liberate the Italian Empire in Cyrenaica, and the joy at seeing the advancing Germans appeared genuine. However, the wild enthusiasm exhibited by the inhabitants reminded one American observer of the jubilation with which the Australians had been received only a few months before. The desert taught the lessons of pragmatism.

Now free to manoeuvre in open desert, Rommel pushed his reinforcements forward. With numerical, and, more importantly, psychological advantage, the Germans surged east. The British were now in headlong retreat, being harried all the way by the Axis air forces, which enjoyed total control of the skies.

By 7 April, Rommel had captured Derna and isolated Mechili, and his reconnaissance units were probing eastwards south of Tobruk. Mechili fell to the Germans on the

morning of 8 April and the victorious Panzer troops encountered the all too familiar evidence of a broken enemy. All around was the detritus of a fleeing army – abandoned tanks, troop carriers and trucks, and, of course, the bodies of the fallen.

By the 9th, Rommel's reconnaissance units reached Bardia, with the Egyptian frontier, Halfaya Pass and Sollum just a few miles on. Some surviving British formations were scurrying past them towards the bases from which they had launched their own offensive only four months previously. But many had no opportunity to flee; large numbers were surrounded and others had already surrendered.

Rommel's headlong advance recovered all the territory lost by the Italians. He was soon talking to his staff about Egypt and the Suez Canal. But he would have to take into account the reactions of the Italians.

It is worth noting that the Axis forces in North Africa remained under Italian command until early 1943. At this time, Rommel was only a corps commander. The theatre commander in Africa was Italian, as were the majority of Rommel's troops. In that situation lay a problem. Italian units had dash and elan, but no endurance. Importantly, in the mobile warfare for which Rommel was so suited, their infantry divisions were not mechanized and so could rarely exploit the successes of German armour. All of the *Afrika Korps* units were mobile, and therefore the German infantry could keep pace with the Panzers and exploit the breaches made in the Allied lines.

Under Rommel's leadership, two Italian divisions, the *Ariete* armoured division and the *Trieste* motorized division, fought extremely well. The rest of the forces were of varying levels

Left: In addition to dealing with the primary theatre of operations in North Africa, the British Middle East Command was also responsible for campaigns against the Vichy French in Syria and for securing the vital Iraqi oilfields, threatened by a German-inspired uprising.

IRAQ UPRISING

In May 1941, the Germans added to General Wavell's problems in the Middle East by instigating an uprising in Iraq led by Rashid Ali, the Iraqi Prime Minister. Attacks at Basra and Habbaniyah threatened the supplies of oil vital to Britain's continued prosecution of the war. The Germans provided supplies and munitions, and set up an airbase at Mosul, in the north of the country. The British fought off the attacks, the airfield at Habbaniyah being defended by clerks and ground crew with support from hastily armed RAF trainers and transport aircraft. A small British relief column advanced from Palestine, and more reinforcements were sent from India. Taking the offensive, the British bombed the air base at Mosul and a ground column advanced on Baghdad, taking the city on 30 May.

To further add to the complications, the British also had to deal with the threat from 35,000 German-advised Vichy French troops in Syria. Churchill ordered Wavell to eliminate the threat. The hard-pressed commander managed to scrape together another 20,000 troops, who invaded Syria from Iraq and Palestine on 8 June. The British forces included Free French under General Georges Catroux. Damascus was captured on 21 June, and the Vichy forces surrendered on 12 July. Syria and Lebanon were transferred to Free French control, and most of the Vichy troops volunteered to join Catroux.

of mediocrity and when under pressure could be counted upon to fold like a house of cards. They did, however, prove reasonably effective if 'corsetted' at key points by intermingling with German units.

To consolidate and extend his gains, Rommel would need adequate reinforcement and supply. For this, he had to rely upon the Italian merchant navy. Here was another problem, because the Axis did not control the Mediterranean shipping lanes. The Royal Navy attacked Italian convoys with merciless professionalism. Cruiser and destroyer squadrons sortied from Egypt and submarines from the island of Malta, which lay conveniently astride the convoy routes. By the end of 1942, Italy had hardly a merchant ship left in service; the rest were on the bottom of the Mediterranean.

Facing the Germans

Rommel's forces reached the key port of Tobruk on 10 April 1941, but a hastily organized assault was beaten off by the Australian garrison. Rommel's offensive attracted the interest of the General Staff, which despatched Colonel-General Friederich Paulus to investigate. He was not impressed, describing Rommel as 'headstrong'. Paulus also worried that what had begun as a sideshow could become a major drain on resources just as the invasion of Russia was about to begin.

DESERT CONFLICT

The desert war was unusual in many respects. There were few cities and few obstacles to the rapid movement of mechanized forces. Armies required vast quantities of petrol and water. Supplies of fresh vegetables and fruit were scarce for both sides. Without enough water to drink, there was certainly none to be spared for washing. Occupation of oases was vital to both sides, and any fight over a water source was guaranteed to be hard.

More than in any other theatre, the desert war was fought by logistics. The length of the supply lines dictated the yo-yo nature of the North African campaign. The further from the supply port, the more difficult it was to sustain the advance. Conditions were not helped by the poor state of the roads – deeply rutted dust tracks in the summer and quagmires in winter. Consequently, there were never enough supplies. Rommel insisted on eating the same rations as his men, and his health steadily deteriorated as a result.

Yet the conventions of the desert war harked back to more civilized days. Rommel was a star in the Nazi propaganda machine, yet had no time for the ideology of the *untermensch*. There were no SS units in Africa, no *Einsatzgruppen*, and the civilian population, such as it was, consisted of Arab nomads, often well disposed to the Germans. Allied prisoners could expect reasonable treatment from their captors and did not starve even when the Germans themselves did not have enough.

Arguments about German offensive aims in Africa were rendered academic by a succession of British attacks. In May, General Wavell launched Operation Brevity, which was defeated. In June, the Allies tried again, this time reinforced with nearly 300 new tanks shipped from England. Operation Battleaxe showed Rommel and the *Afrika Korps* at their best. British armoured units tried to seek out and engage Rommel's armour in a tank-versus-tank battle. But the Germans made masterful use of their towed anti-tank guns, firing from well-concealed positions. They inflicted terrible losses before the Panzers wheeled in from the flank to finish the business. The *Luftwaffe's* 88mm (3.46in) anti-aircraft guns were pressed into service in a ground role since the army's standard 37mm (1.46in) weapon could not penetrate the British 'infantry' tanks, Matilda and Valentine. Ironically, the British had a similar weapon available, the equally high-velocity 93mm (3.7in) anti-aircraft gun, but lack of imagination and inter-service squabbling prevented them from using it the way the Germans employed their '88'.

In three days' fighting, known as the battle of Sollum by the Germans, the *Afrika Korps* demonstrated its superior leadership and vastly better staffwork. Wavell was sacked and replaced by General Auchinleck as Commander-in-Chief Middle East Command, who was pressed by London to renew the attack and relieve Tobruk, still besieged by the Axis forces. Both sides sent reinforcements, but Germany had little to spare as the invasion of the USSR was now in full swing. Rommel developed jaundice in August, but soldiered on, his forces now designated *Panzergruppe Afrika*.

Above: The smashing success of the Desert Force offensive in December 1941 left the British with a rich haul of captured Italian equipment. Here, a British Morris armoured car tows an Italian tankette.

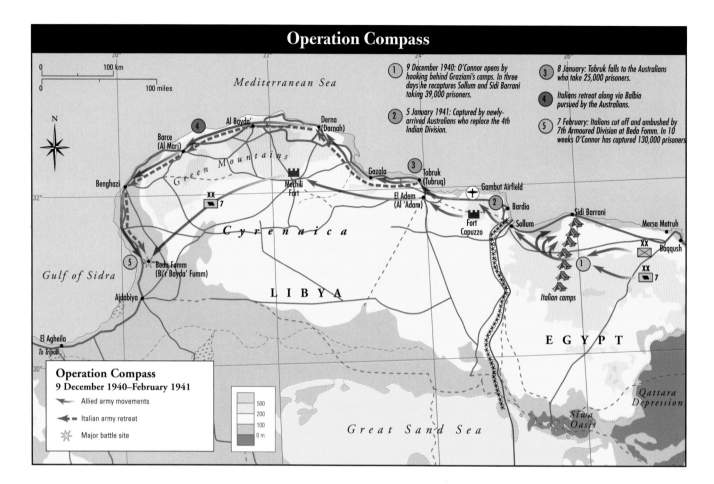

Operation Compass

1. 9 December 1940: O'Connor opens by hooking behind Graziani's camps. In three days he recaptures Sollum and Sidi Barrani taking 39,000 prisoners.

2. 5 January 1941: Captured by newly-arrived Australians who replace the 4th Indian Division.

3. 8 January: Tobruk falls to the Australians who take 25,000 prisoners.

4. Italians retreat along via Balbia pursued by the Australians.

5. 7 February: Italians cut off and ambushed by 7th Armoured Division at Beda Fomm. In 10 weeks O'Connor has captured 130,000 prisoners.

Operation Compass
9 December 1940–February 1941
- Allied army movements
- Italian army retreat
- Major battle site

Above: Operation Compass, the British offensive against the Italian army in North Africa, was a smashing success. Under the command of Major General Richard O'Connor, the outnumbered Desert Force advanced as far as Beda Fomm in little more than two months.

Tobruk was the key: by capturing the port, Rommel would get his supplies landed just behind the front, instead of having them driven across the hundreds of kilometres of coast road from Benghazi. Thanks to the ULTRA code-breakers, the British knew all about Rommel's plans for Tobruk. They deliberately staged their own offensive within days of the planned German assault. On 17 November, Rommel's signals staff reported 'complete English radio silence' – a sign of an impending attack. He ignored them, and ignored the first reports of a major British attack.

The British Eighth Army under Lieutenant-General Cunningham advanced to relieve Tobruk, its powerful tank force surging across the desert to find and destroy the German armour. On 19 November, the key airfield at Sidi Rezegh was overrun by British tanks. Rommel was reluctant to abandon his own attack on Tobruk, but when he reacted, he did so with his usual vigour. Fighting raged around Sidi Rezegh until 23 November, the combatants manoeuvring aggressively in the open terrain. There was no real front line. Both sides had headquarters units and supply columns taken by surprise by enemy tanks. Both sides also suffered heavily, but had only a hazy idea of their opponents' losses. In such a battle, psychological strength is a priceless asset. On 24 November, Rommel struck out behind the British, heading for the Egyptian frontier rather than staying to beat back the British assault along the coast road. It was a daring move, but it left the German commander out of touch with his own headquarters for several days. Cunningham, who had narrowly avoided capture in the chaotic battle, was sacked by Auchinleck. The British commander-in-chief placed his own chief of staff, Lieutenant-General Ritchie, in command of the Eighth Army.

Romme ... e wake of the
British ad ... on his own
initiative ... ed the 21st
Panzer Di ... as he raced
around th

Defeat an

Rommel a ... ious defence
line, and h ... Sirte. There,
in bad we ... Battle' as the
Germans ... d been from
there, nine ... ular advance
of the *Afri*

It seem ... cattered and
disorganiz ... erritory. But
as it would ... hary 1942, it
was comp ... he wags had
dubbed it,

Romme ... enemy radio
traffic. In J ... ounterattack.
The British ... o weakened
by their re

Below: Stretched by two months of hard fighting, the British were in no shape to resist Rommel's newly arrived Afrika Korps. Even as British troops were being evacuated from Crete, the Commonwealth force in North Africa was forced to give up the ground won during Operation Compass.

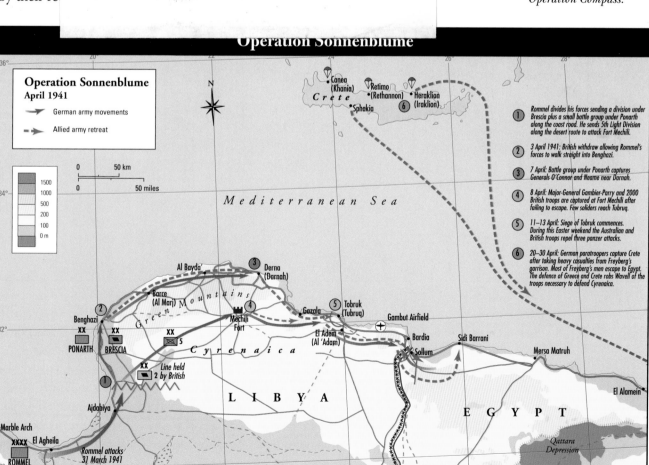

Operation Sonnenblume

Operation Sonnenblume
April 1941

→ German army movements
⇢ Allied army retreat

1500
1000
500
200
100
0 m

0   50 km
0   50 miles

Mediterranean Sea

Canea (Khania) — Retimo (Rethannon) — Heraklion (Iraklion)
Crete
Sphakia

1 Rommel divides his forces sending a division under Brescia plus a small battle group under Ponarth along the coast road. He sends 5th Light Division along the desert route to attack Fort Mechili.

2 3 April 1941: British withdraw allowing Rommel's forces to walk straight into Benghazi.

3 7 April: Battle group under Ponarth captures Generals O'Connor and Neame near Darnah.

4 8 April: Major-General Gambier-Parry and 2000 British troops are captured at Fort Mechili after failing to escape. Few soliders reach Tubruq.

5 11–13 April: Siege of Tobruk commences. During this Easter weekend the Australian and British troops repel three panzer attacks.

6 20–30 April: German paratroopers capture Crete after taking heavy casualties from Freyberg's garrison. Most of Freyberg's men escape to Egypt. The defence of Greece and Crete robs Wavell of the troops necessary to defend Cyrenaica.

Al Bayda'
Derna (Darnah)
Barce (Al Marj)
Green Mountains
Benghazi
XX PONARTH
XX BRESCIA
XX 5
Mechili Fort
Gazala
Tobruk (Tubruq)
Gambut Airfield
El Adem (Al 'Adam)
Bardia
Sidi Barrani
Sollum
Mersa Matruh
Cyrenaica
XX 2 Line held by British
El Alamein
L I B Y A
Ajdabiya
E G Y P T
Marble Arch
XXXX ROMMEL — El Agheila
Rommel attacks 31 March 1941
Qattara Depression

In contrast to the divided counsels of the British Eighth Army, Rommel was very much his own man. Theoretically subordinate to Army Command South-West and the Italian high command, he would ignore his German superiors. His Italian superiors learned of his plans only once their own formations were discovered to be on the move.

Both sides knew the Germans had landed over a hundred new tanks in North Africa. This was, as Rommel's chief of staff, Fritz Bayerlein, remarked, 'as good as a victory in battle'. Some of these new tanks were the up-gunned Mark IVs, better than anything the British could field. Rommel was not the man to allow men and material to stay idle if he could see a worthwhile purpose for their employment. On 21 January 1942, the Axis

forces caught the British by surprise, who were soon again in helter-skelter retreat.

By 10 February, weary, weatherworn, thirsty but triumphant, *Panzerarmee Afrika* under its remarkable leader was well back into Marmorica, with Tobruk – for so long their apparently unobtainable objective – again only 56km (35 miles) beyond their grasp.

In the meantime, Rommel's superior, Field Marshal Kesselring, advised against further precipitate action – at least until more men, more Panzers, more ammunition and especially more fuel were to hand. Even Rommel saw the wisdom of this, so for the moment only his reconnaissance units pressed much further forward than Tmimi. There they quickly found that Commonwealth troops had reassembled on a line running south from the Gazala inlet as far as the *Beau Geste*-style fort at Bir Hacheim. In the north and centre, they were in the process of building themselves defensive positions of considerable strength. Deep minefields bridged the gap down to Bir Hacheim. It was clear that *Panzerarmee Afrika* would need all its expertise to break through or to bypass these defences.

Both sides were engaged in a logistical race to assemble as powerful a force as possible for the next battle. However, Axis operations in the Mediterranean could not affect supplies being sent the long route around Africa, and by the spring of 1942 the first American supplies reached Egypt, including numbers of M3 medium tanks, known to the British as 'Lees' and 'Grants'. The M3 featured a 37mm (1.46in) gun in a turret plus a 75mm (2.95in) gun in the hull. The vehicle could not fight 'hull down', but it compared well to the thin-skinned British Cruiser tanks in widespread service and, being American, did not break down with the depressing regularity of so many British-built tanks.

Left: Much of the terrain in North Africa was perfect for armoured warfare – but by the same token, it provided unobstructed fire for anti-tank guns. Here a British 6-pdr crew go into action alongside a burned out Panzer III.

'To every man of us, Tobruk was a symbol of British resistance, and we were now going to finish with it for good.'

Erwin Rommel, June 1942

Objective: Tobruk

By mid-May, Rommel's battlefield reconnaissance teams detected signs that the British offensive was imminent. He was still outnumbered, but persuaded Kesselring to release many of his squadrons from the Malta operation, including dive-bombers and also

Messerschmitt Bf 109Fs, which were superior to any RAF fighters then in North Africa.

The British defences consisted of a succession of fortified camps, or 'boxes', occupied by infantry brigades with supporting artillery. Dug in behind barbed wire, with some 500,000 landmines surrounding them, they were designed to break up and channel the enemy attack. Behind these lines, the British armoured divisions waited, theoretically concentrated and ready to deliver a knock-out blow, but in reality scattered about the desert with confused command arrangements.

Rommel believed the British just did not understand the basic principles of war. In truth, his opponents grasped the theory; it was a failure of execution owing to the 'command by committee' syndrome that prevailed in the Eighth Army.

Rommel had visited Hitler in March and personally obtained permission for a new offensive. His objective was Tobruk. His orders were to go no further and to return the *Luftwaffe* squadrons to Sicily within a month. His own correspondence reveals greater ambition. He planned, even before the battle of Gazala, to break clean through to Egypt and the Suez canal, converting a hoped-for local success into a major strategic victory.

Rommel attacked on 26 May. Neither his plan nor that of the British survived first contact with the enemy. His feint at the centre of the British line failed to draw the British reserves; his predictable wide flanking manoeuvre was not intercepted by British tank divisions, which sat immobile while their commanders bickered.

General Cruewell, commander of the *Afrika Korps* (Rommel was by this time the commander of the entire *Panzerarmee*, of which the *Afrika Korps* was one element), was shot down in his light aircraft and captured. This occurred just as Kesselring was visiting

Below: Operation Crusader forced the Germans to retreat into Libya. In what was to become a characteristic of the Desert War, the back-and-forth nature of the conflict led to some troops giving it the nickname 'The Benghazi Handicap'.

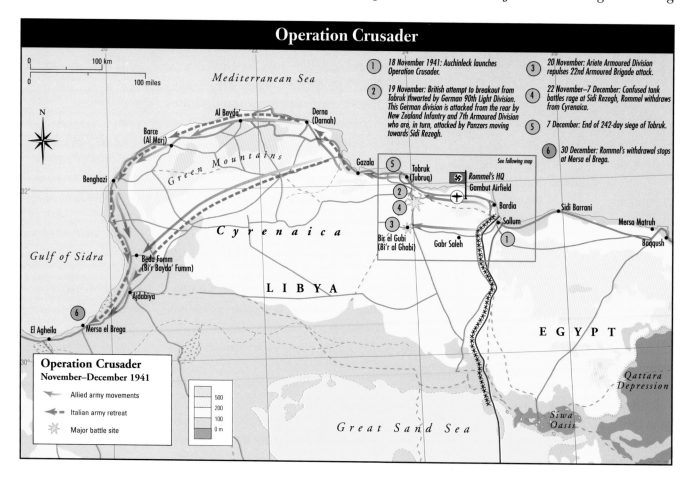

Operation Crusader

1 *18 November 1941: Auchinleck launches Operation Crusader.*

2 *19 November: British attempt to breakout from Tobruk thwarted by German 90th Light Division. This German division is attacked from the rear by New Zealand Infantry and 7th Armoured Division who are, in turn, attacked by Panzers moving towards Sidi Rezegh.*

3 *20 November: Ariete Armoured Division repulses 22nd Armoured Brigade attack.*

4 *22 November–7 December: Confused tank battles rage at Sidi Rezegh, Rommel withdraws from Cyrenaica.*

5 *7 December: End of 242-day siege of Tobruk.*

6 *30 December: Rommel's withdrawal stops at Mersa el Brega.*

Operation Crusader
November–December 1941

Allied army movements

Italian army retreat

Major battle site

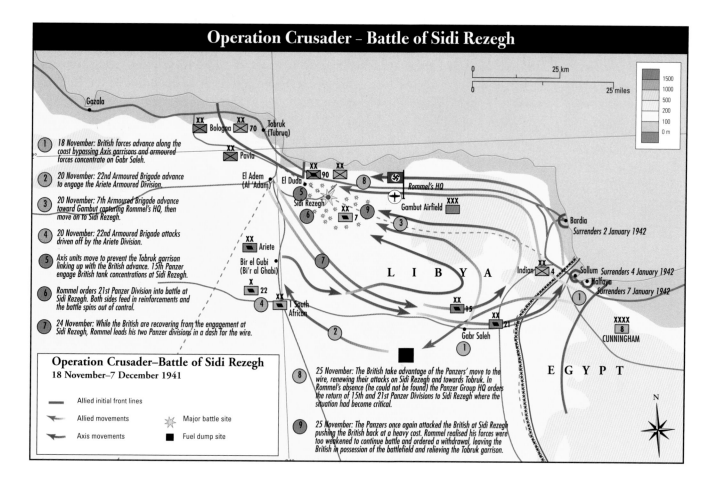

Operation Crusader – Battle of Sidi Rezegh

Gazala

XX Bologna XX 70 Tobruk (Tubruq)

XX Pavia

El Adem (Al 'Adam) El Duda XX 90 XX

(1) 18 November: British forces advance along the coast bypassing Axis garrisons and armoured forces concentrate on Gabr Saleh.

(2) 20 November: 22nd Armoured Brigade advance to engage the Ariete Armoured Division.

(3) 20 November: 7th Armoured Brigade advance toward Gambut capturing Rommel's HQ, then move on to Sidi Rezegh.

(4) 20 November: 22nd Armoured Brigade attacks driven off by the Ariete Division.

(5) Axis units move to prevent the Tobruk garrison linking up with the British advance. 15th Panzer engage British tank concentrations at Sidi Rezegh.

(6) Rommel orders 21st Panzer Division into battle at Sidi Rezegh. Both sides feed in reinforcements and the battle spins out of control.

(7) 24 November: While the British are recovering from the engagement at Sidi Rezegh, Rommel leads his two Panzer divisions in a dash for the wire.

Rommel's HQ

Sidi Rezegh (5)

(6) XX 7

Gambut Airfield XXX

Bardia
Surrenders 2 January 1942

XX Ariete

Bir el Gubi (Bi'r al Ghabi)

X 22

(4) XX 1 South African

L I B Y A

Indian XX 4 Sollum Surrenders 4 January 1942
Halfaya
Surrenders 7 January 1942

(7)

(2) (1)

XX 15

Gabr Saleh (1)

XX 21

XXXX 8
CUNNINGHAM

E G Y P T

Operation Crusader–Battle of Sidi Rezegh
18 November–7 December 1941

— Allied initial front lines

← Allied movements   ✳ Major battle site

← Axis movements   ■ Fuel dump site

(8) 25 November: The British take advantage of the Panzers' move to the wire, renewing their attacks on Sidi Rezegh and towards Tobruk. In Rommel's absence (he could not be found) the Panzer Group HQ orders the return of 15th and 21st Panzer Divisions to Sidi Rezegh where the situation had become critical.

(9) 25 November: The Panzers once again attacked the British at Sidi Rezegh pushing the British back at a heavy cost. Rommel realised his forces were too weakened to continue battle and ordered a withdrawal, leaving the British in possession of the battlefield and relieving the Tobruk garrison.

N

0 ___ 25 km
0 ___ 25 miles

1500 1000 500 200 100 0 m

the command post and the *Luftwaffe* Field Marshal (and former artilleryman) spent an enjoyable afternoon taking charge, as senior officer present, until Rommel arrived. For a commander often criticized for not paying regard to logistics, Rommel turned the tables on the British by personally organizing a night re-supply for 15th Panzer Division. His tanks had broken through the British lines, but found themselves surrounded. The British commanders believed they had him trapped.

It is one of the classic military maxims that commanders are beaten only when they themselves believe it. Rommel's confidence was supreme, as witnessed by a captured British officer who described him directing this most confused of battles. Hunched over a map in his command vehicle, headphones on, Rommel issued an endless succession of orders with quiet authority, his confidence, his grip on the battle in such dramatic contrast to the confusion on the other side.

There was no real front line. Situation maps showed a hideously complex intermingling of forces. Victory went to the man who believed he would win, defeat to commanders who, deep down, believed themselves and their system inferior. Fighting around the 'Knightsbridge' box, held by the Guards brigade, went in favour of the Germans. The southernmost anchor of the Allied line, the Free French position at Bir Hacheim, was attacked and taken after over a week of epic resistance. The British withdrew, their retreat taking on the appearance of a rout as Rommel threw every last man and every precious litre of petrol into the pursuit. Suddenly, Tobruk was under serious threat. Rommel attacked the southeastern quadrant of Tobruk's defences at 5.20 a.m. on the morning of 20 June. Unfortunately for the British, they were convinced

Above: Known to the Germans as 'The Winter Battle', Operation Crusader stopped Rommel's dash to the wire. Isolated at the end of long, vulnerable lines of communications, the Afrika Korps had to retreat back as far as the Gulf of Sirte.

that the attack, when it came, would be from the southwest. Most of the artillery and the entire 2nd South African Division were stationed in the western half of the fortress. In addition, most of the mines that had been used at Gazala had been taken from the defences at Tobruk, weakening the southeastern perimeter at the point where Rommel launched his assault. The German attack went like clockwork. Three hours after Kesselring's bombers had opened the offensive, the 15th Panzer Division punched through the British lines and fanned out. The Italian *Ariete* and *Trieste* divisions exploited the gaping breach in the defences. Once the Axis troops were through the perimeter, they were able to roll up the defences in true *Blitzkrieg* fashion.

The next day, to the astonishment and fury of the British and Commonwealth troops still defending doggedly, a huge white flag was hoisted above brigade headquarters. As it flapped open in the first morning breeze, a great moan of disappointment, anguish and misery welled up from all over the western half of the garrison. Defeat is bitter in any circumstances, but now, in the minds of thousands who were experiencing it, it was compounded by disgrace. Over 30,000 Allied prisoners were taken that day. As they moved off in file they passed a triumphant Rommel. Most probably did not recognize him. After all, which of their commanders would have shared the dangers of actual combat? The spoils were immense. Two thousand vehicles, 4535 tonnes (5000 tons) of supplies and 1814 tonnes (2000 tons) of fuel were given up. Rommel now calculated that nothing stood between him and ultimate victory.

The Collapse of the British

The capture of Tobruk brought exultation to the *Panzerarmee* and a field marshal's baton to Rommel. But there was to be no rest for either of them.

Rommel dismissed the news of his promotion with the comment that he would far rather have had another Panzer division. To the congratulations of his staff, he responded with the brusque order, 'All units will assemble and prepare for further advance.' For his eyes were now on the Egyptian frontier and the vast prize of the Nile Delta, the Suez Canal and all the horizons beyond. Rommel answered remonstrances from Kesselring and the Italian commanders by saying that the enemy were in such disarray that they would be able to offer little or no resistance to the swift and powerful drive he was about to launch. He added that, with the stores dumps of Tobruk now at his disposal, no critical shortage would impede his progress. As for previous plans and agreements, such overwhelming victory swept away the need for caution, a conclusion in which he was later supported by both Mussolini and Hitler.

By the evening of 22 June, the 90th Light Division was in Bardia and 21st Panzer was on its way to join it. By the following day, 15th Panzer and the *Ariete* Divisions were closing up to the Egyptian frontier to the south, shepherding the remains of Eighth Army before them. Rommel himself was examining another huge supply dump that 90th Light had seized at Fort Capuzzo, which contained particularly large quantities of fuel.

For the British, the *danse macabre* of military disaster continued. Orders failed to get through, reports were late and inaccurate, battalions had lost confidence in their brigade command and support battalions, the infantry distrusted the armour, the artillery and engineers withdrew into a world of their own. Men who would willingly give their lives for a worthwhile cause withdrew their loyalty and obedience from their leaders, who in their eyes were unworthy of their trust and more than likely to waste their efforts through incompetence.

Opposite: Under attack from Allied fire, crew members of a German 'eighty-eight' rush to load and respond. Although originally intended as an anti-aircraft weapon, the 88mm (3.5in) proved highly effective as an anti-tank gun.

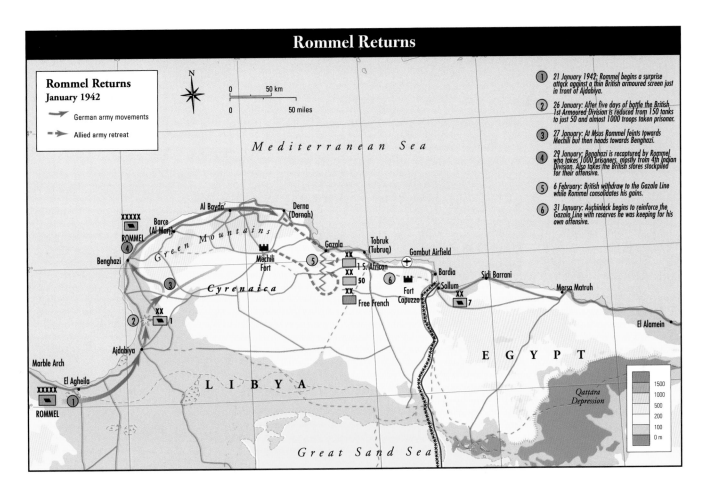

Rommel Returns

Rommel Returns
January 1942

→ German army movements
⇒ Allied army retreat

1. 21 January 1942: Rommel begins a surprise attack against a thin British armoured screen just in front of Ajdabiya.

2. 26 January: After five days of battle the British 1st Armoured Division is reduced from 150 tanks to just 50 and almost 1000 troops taken prisoner.

3. 27 January: At Msus Rommel feints towards Mechili but then heads towards Benghazi.

4. 29 January: Benghazi is recaptured by Rommel who takes 1000 prisoners, mostly from 4th Indian Division. Also takes the British stores stockpiled for their offensive.

5. 6 February: British withdraw to the Gazala Line while Rommel consolidates his gains.

6. 31 January: Auchinleck begins to reinforce the Gazala Line with reserves he was keeping for his own offensive.

A plan for holding the *Panzerarmee* south of Mersa Matruh failed miserably. By the time it had been demonstrably shattered, Auchinleck had taken a step which many people, including Churchill, thought he should have taken much earlier: he sacked General Ritchie and took command of the battle himself. In doing so, he effectively saddled Ritchie with the all the blame for the preceding disasters.

Logistical Success
Rommel seemed to have the upper hand, but in truth the Allies were winning the all-important logistics war. It now took three weeks to ferry Axis supplies by road from the port at Tripoli. The port at Tobruk was not yet serviceable, thanks to the demolition efforts of the retreating Royal Navy.

Malta was still under pressure, however. In July 1942, six heavily laden transports departed from Gibraltar, while 11 set out from Alexandria. They were escorted by a battleship, two carriers and four cruisers from Gibraltar with a further eight cruisers and numerous smaller escorts. Only two supply ships got through – six were sunk, three were badly damaged, five cruisers were badly damaged and four destroyers were sunk.

In August 1942, with Rommel knocking on the gates of Cairo, one last ditch attempt was made to get supplies and fuel through to Malta. Operation Pedestal saw 14 merchant ships escorted by two battleships, three carriers (one sunk), seven cruisers (two sunk) and 33 destroyers (one sunk). Nine freighters were sunk, but five arrived in Malta, including the badly damaged tanker *Ohio*. Yet by now Allied air reinforcements had relieved the pressure on Malta, and from July 1942 over a third of Axis shipping

Above: In January 1942, Rommel's eyes turned towards Tobruk. The capture of the port intact would allow supplies to be shipped much closer to the front lines, easing the Afrika Korp's critically stretched logistics efforts.

Opposite: The Luftwaffe attempted to resupply North Africa, but for all of its efforts its lift capacity could not match a single convoy of merchant ships. Additionally, the lumbering Ju 52s were vulnerable to Allied fighters based on Malta.

Above: South African troops engage in house-to-house fighting in Sollum, following the German assault on the town in June 1941.

dispatched from Italy ended up on the bottom of the Mediterranean. Allied air forces had built up a great store of British and American fighters, fighter-bombers and bombers. Although the number of British planes in the sky gave eager *Luftwaffe* aces like Joachim Marseille the opportunity to build up vast scores, the ceaseless air combat was inevitably a drain on resources of fuel and skilled airmen.

Rommel was also now to be deprived of his flying artillery, the Junkers Ju 87, which was a sitting duck when pitted against modern aircraft types. The *Luftwaffe* was being inexorably driven from the skies. The advantage to the British was not yet apparent. By the morning of 29 June, the Axis had passed Mersa Metruh and were driving along the coast road through Fuka and on to El Daba. The two Panzer divisions and *Ariete* were driving southwest towards El Quseir. Across the front of the German advance ran a desert track. It connected the impassable Qattara Depression to the south, with the newly

Left: The battle for Tobruk came to a head before dawn on 20 June 1942. Here, German assault troops wait for the start of a highly effective attack, which rolled up the outer defences in a single day.

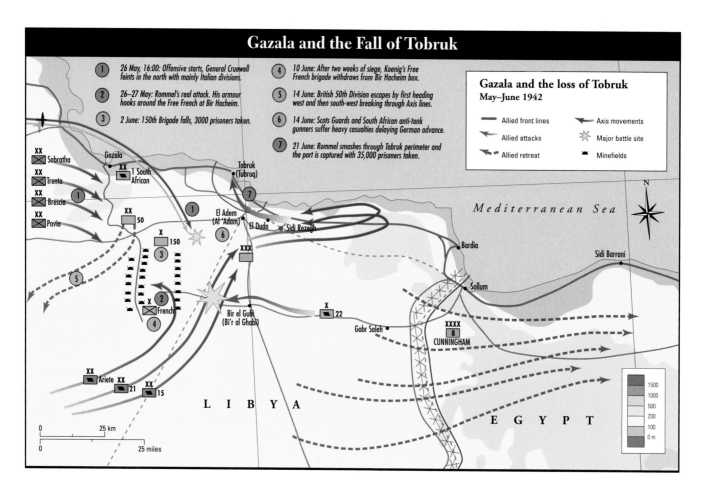

Gazala and the Fall of Tobruk

1 26 May, 16:00: Offensive starts, General Cruewell feints in the north with mainly Italian divisions.

2 26–27 May: Rommel's real attack. His armour hooks around the Free French at Bir Hacheim.

3 2 June: 150th Brigade falls, 3000 prisoners taken.

4 10 June: After two weeks of siege, Koenig's Free French brigade withdraws from Bir Hacheim box.

5 14 June: British 50th Division escapes by first heading west and then south-west breaking through Axis lines.

6 14 June: Scots Guards and South African anti-tank gunners suffer heavy casualties delaying German advance.

7 21 June: Rommel smashes through Tobruk perimeter and the port is captured with 35,000 prisoners taken.

Gazala and the loss of Tobruk
May–June 1942

Allied front lines — Axis movements
Allied attacks — Major battle site
Allied retreat — Minefields

Above: The fall of Tobruk and the subsequent drive eastwards by the Afrika Korps *saw the British collapse, with the remains of the Eighth Army being driven back towards the Egyptian border.*

Opposite: Erwin Rommel was a commander of great dash, whose exploits in North Africa won him a Field Marshal's baton. But even he could not drive his exhausted troops further against the massively reinforced British lines in Egypt.

created defence post around the little railway station of El Alamein, of which few people at that time had ever heard.

Rommel's orders were short and clear. There was no reason to believe that these new British defences would be any more difficult to smash than the countless others now to their rear. Although their commander did realize that his troops were exhausted after the tremendous efforts of the past four weeks, he called on them for one last supreme effort. But Rommel's iron will was not to be enough. The Axis had already experienced a succession of heavy bombing raids, against which the *Luftwaffe* could send only an occasional lone Bf 109. Late on the afternoon of 1 July, the men of the 90th Light suddenly found themselves under a barrage, the like of which none of them had ever experienced. Heavy guns, howitzers, light and medium field guns, mortars, anti-tank guns, all contributed to a storm of fire which shook even Rommel, who came hurrying up in an armoured car immediately. The extent of the opposition to 90th Light's advance became evident. Auchinleck had found a way of stopping Rommel at last.

Fighting continued for an intense three weeks, at the end of which Rommel had been pushed back only a mile. The battle had revealed with blinding clarity the lack of cooperation throughout the Eighth Army. Its general amateurism compared poorly with the professionalism of the *Afrika Korps*, and the necessity for complete reorganization and thorough training was obvious. The first battle at Alamein produced one success and one failure for each side. Auchinleck had halted Rommel's drive for the Nile – but the *Panzerarmee* was still in existence and no one could foretell when it would strike again, and whether or not it would succeed.

Right: British infantry advance across open ground at the battle of El Alamein. Despite German weakness, the British under Auchinleck could not force the Axis forces back at the first Battle of El Alamein.

'Now this is not the end. It is not even the beginning of the end. But it is, perhaps, the end of the beginning.'

Winston Churchill 10 November 1942, after victory at Alamein

A Change in Command

Here, for the moment, both sides were forced to pause. Until resupply could be achieved, there was a lull in the fighting. Weary soldiers were given the opportunity to relax in their trenches, and read mail from home. But everybody knew the quiet could not last.

On 30 August, Rommel attacked again, at Alam Halfa. The four days of battle that followed decided the desert war. This time, Rommel faced a new opponent. Auchinleck had appointed Lieutenant-General Bernard Law Montgomery to command the Eighth Army. The change in British fortunes at this time has often been ascribed, not least by Montgomery himself, to his assumption of command. But one man, no matter how influential, could not win a war on his own.

The RAF had control of the skies, and bombed German supply dumps and headquarters units with impunity. Rommel was sick, as were many of his 17,000 veterans, who had fought in North Africa without a break for well over a year. The British refused to play the old game. Their armour did not expend itself on suicidal charges into German anti-tank guns, but waited, with artillery and air support, for the Germans to come to them. The British displayed none of the unsteadiness Rommel scented earlier

Map, page 146: General Bernard L. Montgomery had taken command of the Eighth Army after the first Battle of Alamein. Determined to drive Rommel out of Africa, he decided to wait until he had built up an overwhelming material superiority before moving. Under an artillery barrage of World War I scale, he launched the attack on 23 October 1942.

Map, page 147: Montgomery's initial attacks served to tie down and weaken the enemy. He launched his main tank attack on 2 November, which Rommel counterattacked. Both sides lost large numbers of tanks, but Montgomery had plenty of replacements. Rommel had none. The Axis forces withdrew in defeat, and the Eighth Army began the long march that would drive the Germans out of Africa.

that summer. For the moment, his Plan Orient was on hold. This grandiose scheme, endorsed by the Reich Chancellery, had been conceived of as a great pincer movement. Whilst the *Wehrmacht* thrust down through the Caucasus, the *Afrika Korps* would seize Suez. Once the two forces linked up, there would be an opportunity to drive eastwards until they met the Japanese. But even if Plan Orient had once been practical, its time had long passed.

Rommel applied for leave. Fêted in Berlin, where he stayed with the Goebbels family, he disconcerted his stand-in General Stumme with the statement that he would return if the British attacked. And attack they would, even if they were taking their time about it. As Rommel confided to his staff, 'if I were Montgomery, we wouldn't still be here.'

The Battle of El Alamein

The second battle of El Alamein was to take place just as Rommel had feared. Montgomery had a deep aversion, learned on the western front during World War I, to squandering the lives of his troops. He resisted Churchill's demands for immediate action until everything was in place and victory assured.

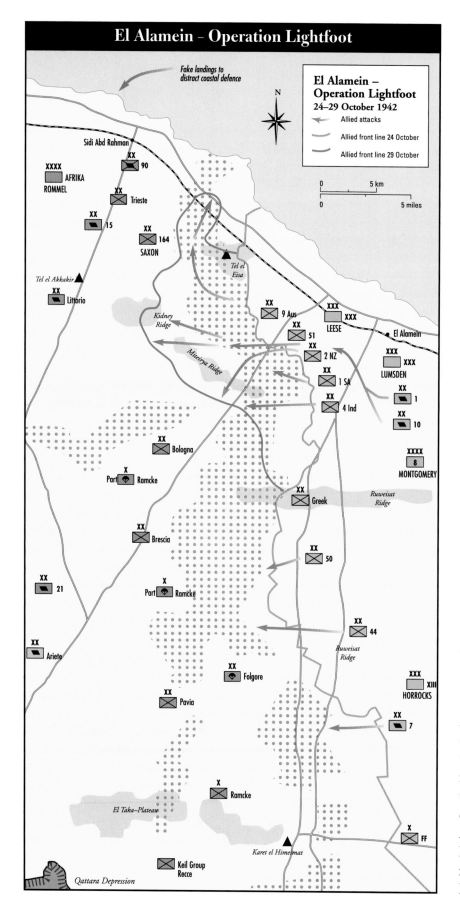

El Alamein – Operation Lightfoot

Fake landings to distract coastal defence

N

**El Alamein –
Operation Lightfoot
24–29 October 1942**

Allied attacks
Allied front line 24 October
Allied front line 29 October

0   5 km
0   5 miles

Sidi Abd Rahman

XXXX AFRIKA ROMMEL

XX 90

XX Trieste

XX 15

XX 164 SAXON

Tel el Akkakir

XX Littorio

Tel el Eisa

Kidney Ridge

Miteiya Ridge

XX 9 Aus

XXX LEESE **XXX**

El Alamein

XX 51

XX 2 NZ

XX 1 SA

XXX LUMSDEN **XXX**

XX 1

XX 4 Ind

XX 10

XXXX 8 MONTGOMERY

XX Bologna

X Part Ramcke

Ruweisat Ridge

XX Greek

XX Brescia

XX 50

XX 21

X Part Ramcke

XX 44

Ruweisat Ridge

XX Ariete

XX Folgore

XXX HORROCKS **XIII**

XX Pavia

XX 7

X Ramcke

El Taka–Plateau

Karet el Himeimat

X FF

XX Keil Group Recce

Qattara Depression

On 23 October 1942, with dominance of the air, a substantial advantage in both infantry and tanks and an artillery barrage organized on a scale not achieved by the British Army since 1918, Montgomery launched the sort of classic set-piece battle at which he excelled.

The next eight days saw an intensive series of actions taking place between the coast and Miteiya Ridge. Rommel, not calling the shots for once, had to release his reserves to contain the British attacks, and was further disadvantaged as the *Luftwaffe* had completely lost out in the air battle. As a result, German armour could not call on the close-support usually provided by the Stukas.

In the meantime, Montgomery, with an immense logistical advantage, prepared his armour for a further thrust. This was launched on 2 November. Although the initial British tank force of 100 machines was virtually annihilated by the Axis anti-tank guns, Rommel impetuously launched his own massed armour counterattack, in the hope of exploiting a weak position in the English line. He found no weakness, and the *Afrika Korps* was that day broken in its repeated charges against unyielding Allied gunnery. By dusk, Rommel's Panzer divisions had only 35 operational tanks between them.

Rommel quickly realized that the African dream was over, and the only choice left open, if he wanted to save the remnants of his once proud formations, was to quickly extricate them from the threatened envelopment by the British armour. Although they didn't know it, Montgomery's attack at El Alamein marked the beginning of the end for Hitler and the Nazis.

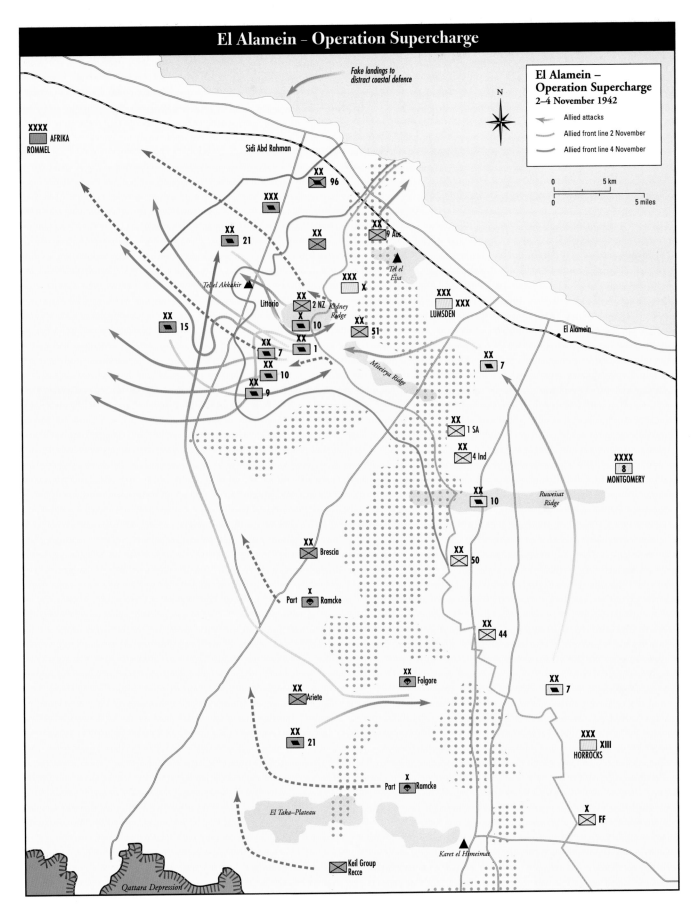

El Alamein – Operation Supercharge

**El Alamein –
Operation Supercharge**
2–4 November 1942

→ Allied attacks
Allied front line 2 November
Allied front line 4 November

0 — 5 km
0 — 5 miles

Fake landings to distract coastal defence

XXXX
AFRIKA
ROMMEL

Sidi Abd Rahman

XX 96

XXX

XX 21

XXX

XX 9 Aus

XXX X

Tel el Eisa

XXX
XXX
LUMSDEN

▲ *Tel el Akkakir*

Littorio

XX 2 NZ
Kidney Ridge

X
10

XX 51

XX 15

XX 7

XX 10

XX 9

Miteirya Ridge

XX 7

El Alamein

XX 1 SA

XX 4 Ind

XXXX
8
MONTGOMERY

XX 10
Ruweisat Ridge

XX Brescia

XX 50

X Part | Ramcke

XX 44

XX Folgore

XX 7

XX Ariete

XXX
XIII
HORROCKS

XX 21

X Part | Ramcke

X FF

El Taka–Plateau

▲ *Karet el Himeimat*

Keil Group
Recce

Qattara Depression

Operation Barbarossa

Adolf Hitler had long had plans for Russia. As early as August 1939, on the eve of the invasion of Poland, he said: 'I have sent my Death's Head formations eastwards. Poland will be depopulated and settled with Germans... the fate of Russia will be exactly the same.'

On 22 June 1941, Hitler launched the greatest invasion in military history – Operation Barbarossa. Three million German and Axis troops in three Army Groups attacked across the Russian border from the Baltic coast to the Romanian frontier. The Russians were taken by surprise. Stalin had been determined to do nothing that could provoke a German invasion until he had a chance to reorganize his own forces. Apparently unable to believe that Hitler would break their cynical alliance so soon, he saw to it that the USSR continued to deliver strategic materials to the Germans right up to the very night of the attack.

The *Luftwaffe* had been overflying Russian airbases for months before the invasion. Now the German air force scored the greatest victory in its history, wiping out the Red air force in a matter of days. Soviet bases were in the process of expansion, so many air regiments had their planes doubled up on the airstrips. Aircraft were packed together where a single bomb could destroy a whole squadron. If they got into the air, the Russians had neither the skill nor the aircraft to challenge the Messerschmitt Bf 109, and many German fighter pilots began to run up incredible numbers of victories.

Army Group Centre

Under the command of the icily aristocratic Field Marshal Fedor von Bock, Army Group Centre comprised two infantry armies and two Panzer Groups – in effect, tank armies – under Generals Hoth and Guderian. These were the armies whose commanders intended to reduce Napoleon's feat of arms of 129 years earlier to historical obscurity. They planned to reach Moscow in less than eight weeks, and to annihilate the Soviet army in the process.

In this hope, they were encouraged by Hitler, who had assured them, 'Before three months have passed, we shall witness a collapse in Russia, the like of which has never been seen in history. We have only to kick in the front door and the whole rotten Russian

Opposite: Operation Barbarossa, the German invasion of the Soviet Union, came as a surprise to Stalin, who had believed Hitler would adhere to the Soviet-German non-aggression pact. But anyone who had read Hitler's Mein Kampf *would have realized that Russia was the* Führer's *ultimate aim. It was Russia's vast steppes that would provide the* Lebensraum *which was a fundamental principle of the Nazi creed.*

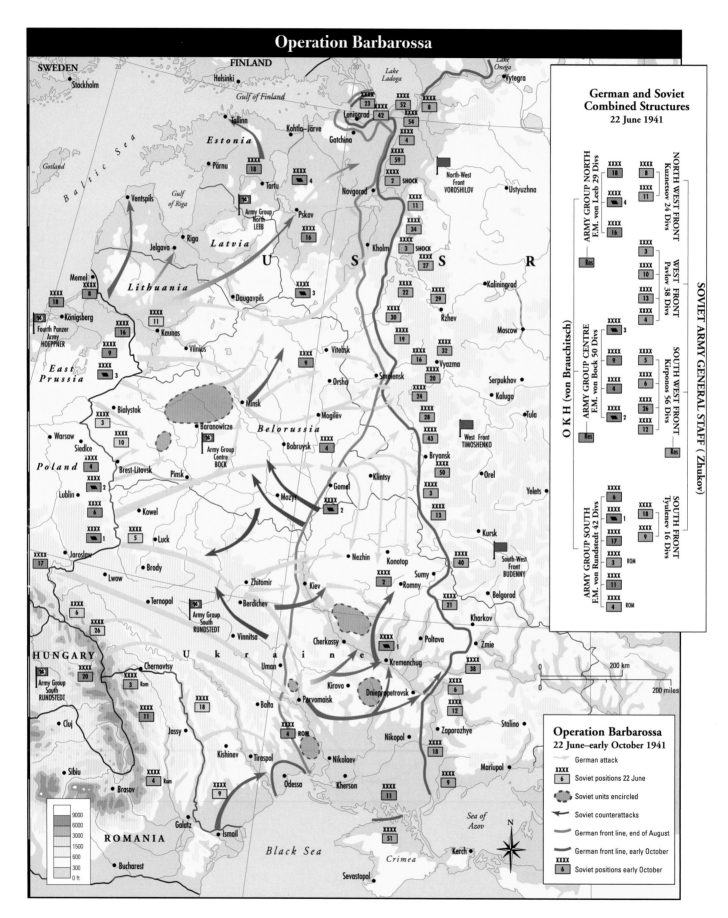

Operation Barbarossa

German and Soviet Combined Structures
22 June 1941

Operation Barbarossa
22 June–early October 1941

German attack

Soviet positions 22 June

Soviet units encircled

Soviet counterattacks

German front line, end of August

German front line, early October

Soviet positions early October

edifice will come tumbling down.' To Heinz Guderian, whose II Panzer Group included four Panzer divisions, this was the supreme moment of his military career. It was evident that he and Hoth between them commanded the most significant forces in the entire operation, and could well execute the most exciting and spectacular military feat of the century, perhaps of all history. And the first few days seemed to confirm the prospect.

Guderian's first task was to throw his Panzer Group across the River Bug on each side of the fortress of Brest-Litovsk, capture the fortress and then race with his armoured spearheads towards the city of Minsk. He would curve up to the city from the south to meet Hoth's spearheads coming down from the north. In this way, the Soviet front-line forces would be isolated in a huge cauldron. Once their supplies had run out, they would have little alternative but to surrender.

Above: German troops fight in the streets of Kiev. Caught by surprise, the Red Army could do little to halt the advance of the Wehrmacht, who swept through the ancient cities of the Ukraine and western Russia.

THE STATISTICS OF *BARBAROSSA*

To launch Operation *Barbarossa*, the Germans mobilized more than 150 divisions, including 19 Panzer divisions, which were supported by 1945 German aircraft and another 1000 Axis planes. They faced some three million men of the Red Army, which had another one million soldiers deployed across southern republics of the USSR and in the Far East, where they had recently beaten the Japanese in a series of border clashes. By the time the attack was launched in mid-June, enough fuel, ammunition and stores had been stockpiled to supply this vast force in a 600km (373-mile) advance. Half a million lorries waited in massed parks from East Prussia south as far as Romania, ready to rush those supplies forward on demand. To the modern mind, the only questionable, indeed alarming, figure to emerge from the tables of statistics is that for 'stabling': over 300,000 horses were to play an apparently essential part in this monumental military exercise.

Opposite: Three massive Army Groups struck on the morning of 22 June. Army Group North was directed at the Baltic States and Leningrad. Army Group South was to overrun the vast grainfields of the Ukraine. And Army Group Centre was poised like a spear to drive at Moscow, the heart of the Soviet Union.

'The war against Russia cannot be conducted in a chivalrous fashion. This struggle is one of ideologies and racial differences, and will have to be conducted with unprecedented, unmerciful and unrelenting harshness.'

Adolf Hitler, 1941

Right: Spearheading the German drive were 19 Panzer divisions. Using the panzers' mobility to the full, the Wehrmacht *surrounded and cut off huge numbers of Red Army troops before driving onwards across the seemingly endless steppes.*

By 24 June, only 60 hours after the launch of the attack, 17th Panzer Division was driving into Slonim, over 140km (87 miles) from the frontier and halfway to the Germans' first objective. Three days later, on the afternoon of 27 June, the leading tanks of the 17th Panzer Division drove into Minsk to meet the spearheads of Hoth's III Panzer Group, which had covered 350km (217 miles) in five days.

Behind them, they had left pockets of Soviet troops which, unlike most of the French army the year before, showed little inclination to lay down their arms and surrender. There were four of these pockets: the fortress at Brest-Litovsk, six divisions around Bialystok, six more at Volkovysk, and another 15 between Novogrudok and Minsk itself. The task of first containing and then destroying them was assigned to the German infantry of the Fourth and Ninth Armies.

The trouble was that the infantry, trudging stolidly after the Panzer divisions, were now quite a long way behind. The roads shown on the Barbarossa maps proved in the majority of cases to be little but dirt tracks, which were quickly reduced to calf-deep dust, through which it was impossible to move at more than 5km/h (3mph). There was also a problem with supply. A large proportion of the half million lorries that were supposed to be bringing supplies and reinforcements were of French origin, captured during the 1940 campaign. Many were not capable of carrying heavy loads across rough country, and spare parts were in short supply. Moreover, they

had already been driven halfway across Europe, and their useful mileage had been almost consumed.

Not surprisingly, arguments arose. Guderian and Hoth were convinced that they must immediately race further ahead, first to Smolensk and then to Moscow, confident that speed would prove the decisive factor in this campaign. On 1 July, in a burst of insubordination, the two Panzer commanders released units towards the next obstacle, the River Beresina. They were threatened with court martial for so doing by their immediate superior, General Günther von Kluge.

On the same day, Guderian's Panzers met the Soviet T-34 for the first time. A single tank blocked their advance for three hours, knocking out five Panzer IIIs. It was only removed when attacked from the rear by an 88mm (3.46in) flak gun. Fortunately for the Germans, no more T-34s were encountered in the area.

Pushing Forward

On 3 July, the order came for the next stage of the advance. From his unsanctioned bridgehead over the Beresina, Guderian launched the 18th Panzer Division towards the

River Dnieper, which was reached on 5 July. Here the division beat off a Soviet counter-attack and then waited until all three of the Panzer Group's corps were lined up along the river. It was not a safe position. Both flanks were exposed, the supply organization was becoming increasingly tenuous, and the support infantry was two weeks' hard marching behind them. No wonder Kluge remonstrated violently, and at first expressly forbade any attempt at further advance.

Yet every day that the Germans waited, the Soviet defences stiffened, and waiting too long would make the task of crossing the Dnieper become impossible for anything less than an army group. Eventually Kluge gave way. 'Your operations always hang by a thread!' he complained, but gave permission for the next stage. The next three weeks were occupied with the hardest fighting the Germans had yet experienced. For 10 days, II Panzer Group had three separate objectives to pursue. It was to bar the Soviet forces it had bypassed from escaping south or east. At the same time, it was to make contact with III Panzer Group fighting its way down from the northwest. Finally, it was to widen the German hold on the land east of Smolensk, turning it into a solid bridgehead for the final thrust towards Moscow.

Although advanced units of the 29th Motorized Division reached Smolensk on 16 July, fierce fighting still raged behind them, and there was as yet no sign of Hoth's III Panzer Group spearheads. On 29 July Hitler's adjutant, Colonel Schmundt, arrived at Guderian's headquarters, bringing with him Hitler's felicitations and the Oak Leaves to the Knight's Cross – Guderian was only the fifth man in the army to receive them. He also brought with him the first hint of changes of plan and emphasis.

Moscow was perhaps not so important after all. The rolling wheatlands of the Ukraine would provide the granary from which the ever-growing Axis armies could be fed. Moreover, down in that direction lay the Baku oilfields. Moscow could wait. Guderian for the moment must go no further east.

Army Group North

While Army Group Centre drove towards Moscow, Field Marshal von Leeb's Army Group North was aimed at the Baltic States and Leningrad. Group North consisted of two infantry armies containing 15 infantry divisions between them. The armoured punch was provided by IV Panzer Group, which comprised three Panzer divisions, three motorized infantry divisions and two infantry divisions. Three infantry divisions were held in support.

The fact that they had less of the *Wehrmacht's* mobile striking power than Army Group Centre was a matter of some irritation to von Leeb's staff – after all, they had further to go and, on paper, a much deeper enemy defence to penetrate. The differences did not extend to the two principals themselves. Leeb and von Bock were far too aristocratic to squabble – though they encouraged their subordinates to do so.

By midnight on 21/22 June, every unit was in position. At 3.05 on the morning of 22 June, Army Group North began the drive to Leningrad. The only early resistance encountered by the vital central thrust was quickly brushed aside, and by the evening of the first day the leading Panzers were 60km (37 miles) into Lithuania.

The 7th Panzer Division was racing along the main road from Kaunas to Daugavpils (Dvinsk) on the River Dvina. By the morning of the 26th, they had captured the two river bridges there. Counterattacks were beaten off, more Panzers came roaring in, and by the end of the day the city was firmly in German hands. The first objective of Army Group

Opposite: A flamethrower is used to sear the entrance to a Soviet bunker. Static Soviet positions such as these were rapidly cut off by the German armoured spearheads, and were then dealt with by the slower moving infantry that followed on foot.

Above: Dazed by the a massive artillery bombardment at Brest-Litovsk, a Soviet soldier surrenders to the Germans. Hundreds of thousands of captives were taken, but large numbers of Red Army men disappeared into the wilderness to continue the fight. These provided the nucleus of the partisan bands.

North – bridgeheads across the wide River Dvina, 300km (186 miles) from East Prussia – had been achieved in five days. On 2 July, the Panzer Group set out on the 250km (155-mile) race to the Ostrov/Pskov area. Ostrov was captured by the 1st Panzer Division on 4 July. The 6th Panzer Division smashed a way through the northern extension of the 'Stalin Line' on the same day, and three motorized divisions of the Panzer Group had crossed the old Latvian-Russian border opposite Opochka and were also driving up towards Pskov. When, on 5 July, the mass of Soviet tanks held to the east were thrown into a counterattack, German armour had been thoroughly reinforced. By the end of the second day, only the wrecks of 140 Soviet tanks lay between the Panzer divisions and Pskov itself.

A Fragmenting Advance

The Panzer Group's infantry could not keep up. The terrain encountered on the Soviet side of the border was so marshy and impenetrable that even the motorized infantry was reduced to the pace of the marching columns, and they were just clearing Daugavpils, over 100km (60 miles) back. Things moved more quickly to the west. The roads in Lithuania, Latvia and Estonia were so much better than those in Russia that the Eighteenth Army was moving almost as fast as the Panzers. By 7 July, 12 Soviet divisions had been destroyed, both Tallinn and Narva were under artillery fire and four divisions were driving towards the southern end of Lake Peipus.

To the commanders back in Germany – and to Hitler especially – the picture across the whole *Barbarossa* Front was one of increasing danger. Not only were the gaps opening between armour and infantry, they were also gaping widely between the army groups themselves. Even though the Soviet forces in these gaps ranged from confused to chaotic, they consisted of an apparently unlimited number of brave soldiers who seemed incapable of realizing when they were beaten.

Despite the anguished pleas of the Panzer commanders Reinhardt and Manstein, the idea of an immediate thrust into the heart of Leningrad would have to wait. Behind them, the infantry fought and marched, fought and marched again – and gradually their strength waned. Casualties were inevitably suffered, and battalions, regiments, even divisions had to be left behind to deal with pockets of resistance. Then in mid-July the orders came for units to be detached from the northern wing of Army Group Centre to fill the ominous gap between the two groups. The delay gave the Russian defenders the opportunity to strengthen their positions enormously. A German attack northwards was checked west of Lake Ilmen, largely by another immutable factor of warfare: after more than a month of constant fighting and forced marches, often in great heat, German infantrymen were suffering mounting exhaustion.

The assault ran into a Red Army counterattack. The storm of fire that erupted stunned both sides. Eventually, however, German training and efficiency prevailed. Four Panzer divisions broke through, and by 11 August were clear yet again for the drive on Leningrad – only to be held back by stiff Russian resistance.

Hitler now ordered Army Group Centre to release one of General Hoth's Panzer corps to help Army Group North. Driving up the west bank of the Volkhov, its leading tank units reached Ishora, only 17km (10 miles) from the centre of Leningrad. Its motorized infantry swung up to the east towards the River Neva and the shores of Lake Ladoga. The former capital of Russia was now surrounded.

It was not, however, yet occupied. The two leading divisions were soon enmeshed in a labyrinth of anti-tank ditches and straggling earthworks thrown up by the desperate Leningraders while the Germans had paused to regroup. By the evening of 10 September, German units had reached the Dugerdorf Heights, 10km (6 miles) southeast of the city. However, so many Panzers had been hit or had broken down that

Below: A Soviet KV-1 tank burns in a forest in Latvia. The Wehrmacht was unpleasantly surprised when it encountered the latest Soviet tanks such as the T-34 and the KV-1, since their armour was very effective at turning aside the projectiles fired by standard 37-mm (1.41in) anti-tank guns. Only the heavier 50mm (2in) shells could knock out these tanks.

Opposite: The Wehrmacht was welcomed like a liberator in some parts of the Soviet Union, but brutal German treatment of Russians and Ukrainians turned support into hatred. Moscow used German atrocities to great effect, and the Communist Party's propaganda presented the 'Great Patriotic War' as a struggle to liberate 'Mother Russia from Nazi oppression.

the momentum of attack had been dissipated. German infantry crept up on their left during the following day, entered the Leningrad suburbs of Slutsk and Pushkin, and in the evening occupied the Summer Palace of the Tsars at Krasnoye Selo. But the impetus had gone. By now, the lure of the wheatlands of the Ukraine and the Baku oilfields had taken complete control of Hitler's mind. Like Moscow, Leningrad must wait.

Army Group South

There is some irony in the fact that by August 1941 Hitler had decided that the southern front of Barbarossa was the most important, for in order to capture it Field Marshal Gerd von Rundstedt had originally been given command of the weakest Army Group. His most powerful forces were in the north: Sixth Army under Reichenau, I Panzer Group under Kleist and Seventeenth Army under Stulpnagel. In the south, driving out of Moldavia, a single German army was accompanied by two Romanian armies, a Hungarian army corps and an Italian army corps, all armed with obsolete equipment and with a bare minimum of artillery and vehicles.

The attack, however, made excellent progress from the start. The opposing Russian commander, General Kirponos, committed his forces piecemeal as they became available. They were all destroyed in turn, though this was not the end of early resistance. In their first powerful thrust, I Panzer Group had shouldered the Russian Fifth Army aside and into the Pripet Marshes, where neither German armour nor vehicles could follow. With the astonishing resilience typical of bypassed Soviet troops, the Fifth Army reorganized and in mid-July struck southwest from Korosten, towards the Soviet Sixth Army driving up from below Berdichev. German expertise and their skilful use of the 88mm (3.46in) flak gun in an anti-tank role broke this attempt to snap off the invading spearhead, but the Fifth Army then retreated back into the marshes. For the next six weeks, both Kleist and Reichenau were uncomfortably aware of the threat hanging over their shoulders.

The key German drive continued down between the Bug and the Dniester. The main Soviet forces, commanded by the flamboyant but incompetent Marshal Budenny and his political commissar Nikita Khrushchev, concentrated around two important centres – Kiev and Uman. Avoiding both by cutting between them, Kleist's Panzer Group with the Sixth Army in close attendance drove down the land bridge between the rivers, and part of Reichenau's forces headed west. There, they were joined first by Stulpnagel's divisions and then by Schobert's coming up from Moldavia.

The ground was much harder here than further north, so infantry could move more quickly. The Russian Sixth and Twelfth Armies and part of the Eighteenth were thus isolated between overwhelming forces. By 3 August, they had been sealed in, and by the 8th they were being subjected to heavy artillery fire from every side. Two days later, their resistance ceased. Some 20 Russian divisions had been annihilated and 103,000 prisoners taken.

Meanwhile, the two Romanian armies had marched along the coast and begun a siege of Odessa. Although it was to cost the Romanians dearly, the 64-day siege prevented the large Russian garrison from playing a part in the drama unfolding in the heart of the Ukraine. Here, the largest concentration of Red Army troops lay at Kiev and in the area immediately to the north. On Hitler's orders, Guderian's Panzer Group was now driving down from Army Group Centre to meet Kleist, thus cutting off three complete Russian armies and the remnants of at least two more.

Above: Ukrainian peasants dig anti-tank ditches as Army Groups Centre and South combine to encircle Kiev. Over 600,000 Red Army soldiers were captured in the huge battle that followed – but the campaign took up valuable time, delaying the crucial drive on Moscow planned for the autumn.

Guderian had not, in fact, immediately obeyed the *Führer* because his eyes – and ambition – were still focused on Moscow. On 4 August, Hitler travelled forward to Novo Borosow and talked to his senior commanders. For the moment, he was sufficiently impressed by the arguments of Bock and Guderian not to insist upon the abandonment of the drive on Moscow. During the next three weeks, however, his attitude hardened, and on 24 August in a solitary interview with Guderian, he ordered him to lead his entire Panzer Group down to assist in the occupation of the Ukraine. During the next two days, *Panzergruppe Guderian* (as it had been renamed as a sop to Guderian's feelings) swung its axis through 90° and headed south.

A Landmark Defeat

A new army group – the Bryansk Front – had been formed by the Red Army high command, or *Stavka*. It had the specific aim of attacking Guderian's flank as it moved south. This reflected the arrival from the Far East of General Zhukov, who was already exhibiting his uncanny gift for divining an enemy's plans. Unfortunately, Marshal Shaposhnikov, the Red Army chief of staff, believed that Moscow was still Guderian's objective. He thus ordered the most powerful elements of the Bryansk Front to stay in the north, so they were unavailable to attack Guderian. Nonetheless, two armies of the Bryansk Front under General Yeremenko moved forward on 30 August to attack Guderian's left flank. Lack of coordination and, more importantly, of air cover – the Red air force had by now been virtually annihilated – left them at the mercy of the Germans.

By 2 September, Bryansk Front was in tatters, and eight days later Stalin was receiving direct appeals from both Budenny and Khrushchev for permission for their still large but disintegrating forces to be allowed to escape through the rapidly narrowing gap between Kleist and Guderian. Stalin dismissed his old revolutionary comrade Budenny and appointed Marshal Timoshenko to preside over the ensuing debacle. During the remaining days that the gap was open, Stalin insisted through Shaposhnikov that all fronts, all armies, all divisions should stand fast where they were.

Guderian's Panzers met Kleist's at Lokhvitsa on 15 September. Infantry and guns from Second Army to the north and from Seventeenth Army to the south came up to harden the ring, and by the evening of the 17th, the biggest encirclement of the Barbarossa campaign – perhaps the biggest in history – had been formed.

That night, permission was at last given for the remnants of the Soviet armies to attempt to break out to the east, but most had too far to go and lacked the heavy mobile equipment to smash through the waiting German ring. Budenny and Khrushchev were flown out. Major-General Bagramyan brought out about 50 men, but Kirponos and most of the staffs of the Southwest Front and of the Fifth Army were killed as they tried to escape, or were rounded up and captured. With them into graves, or German prison camps of the most appalling nature, went nearly 500,000 Russian soldiers. In terms of numbers, this was the biggest military catastrophe in Russian history.

Guderian and Kleist were jubilant, Rundstedt modestly gratified that the greatest single success of German arms had been won by the army group under his command. In that atmosphere of heady euphoria, few remarked that for all their triumphs and all the ground won, something had been lost, and that was time. Kleist at least was aware that time was passing. With admirable speed, he drew his Panzer Group back south to the area around Dnepropetrovsk. On 30 September, it erupted from a bridgehead over the Samara at Novomoskovsk and drove down to the Sea of Azov, neatly trapping three Soviet armies while Eleventh Army, now under command of General von Manstein who had been moved down from the Leningrad front, drove eastwards along the coast. Another 106,000 prisoners were taken, together with 212 tanks and nearly 700 guns.

The Moscow Offensive

Rain, wind and the first snow flurries brought a hint of the white chaos that would soon engulf the whole Russian front. By the end of October, Kleist's Panzer Group was edging its way slowly into Rostov. Although they did not know it, they were also edging into a Soviet trap. The Soviets had at last learnt the effectiveness of the traditional Russian tactic of trading space for time. Many of the units threatened with encirclement at Kharkov had been allowed by Stalin to retreat. They were now being reformed into the Soviet Thirty-Seventh Army in the angle of the Donets Bend.

On 19 November, they began to move forward into Rostov, joined by shock troops of the Ninth Army. It was the first time in World War II that the Germans had to face a major enemy attack, prepared and launched after adequate organization. By 28 November, I Panzer Group had been squeezed out of Rostov, back through Taganrog to the line of the Mius River. One of the immediate results was Hitler's anger, followed by Rundstedt's resignation. Guderian and Bock were facing a similar situation in front of Moscow. On 6 September, Hitler decreed that Moscow would be the next objective. Army Group North's breakneck advance had come to a sudden stop as it entered the swampy forests that surrounded Leningrad. Its Panzer Group was assigned to Army Group Centre,

'An advance towards the Ukraine, the Donets Basin and the Crimean Peninsula will give Germany all the food and coal it needs....My Generals know nothing about the economic aspects of war!'

Adolf Hitler, after senior officers questioned the diversion of forces from the drive on Moscow to the Ukraine

Operation Typhoon

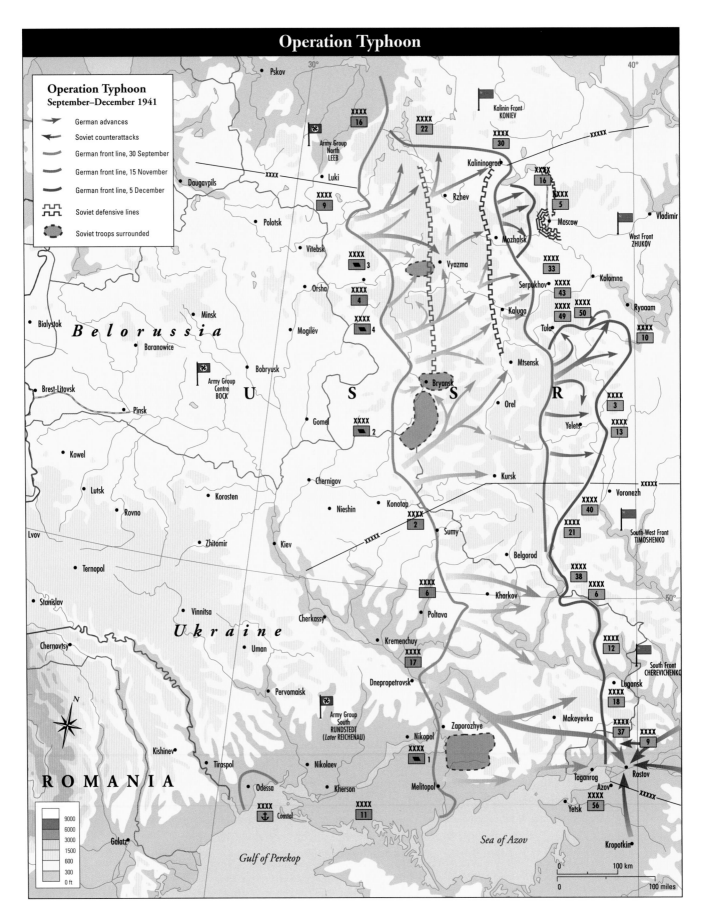

Operation Typhoon
September–December 1941

→ German advances

← Soviet counterattacks

German front line, 30 September

German front line, 15 November

German front line, 5 December

Soviet defensive lines

Soviet troops surrounded

Pskov

Army Group North LEEB

Luki

Daugavpils

Polotsk

Vitebsk

Orsha

Minsk

Baranowice

Mogilëv

Belorussia

Bobruysk

Army Group Centre BOCK

Brest-Litovsk

Pinsk

Gomel

Bialystok

Kowel

Lutsk

Rovno

Korosten

Chernigov

Nieshin

Konotap

Lvov

Zhitómir

Kiev

Ternopol

Stanislav

Vinnitsa

Cherkassy

Ukraine

Chernovtsy

Uman

Pervomaisk

Dnepropetrovsk

Army Group South RUNDSTEDT (*Later* REICHENAU)

Kishinev

Tiraspol

Nikolaev

Nikopol

Zaporozhye

Melitopol

ROMANIA

Odessa

Kherson

Coastal

Galatz

Gulf of Perekop

Sea of Azov

Kropotkin

Kalinin Front KONIEV

Kaliningrad

Rzhev

Mozhalsk

Vyazma

Moscow

Vladimir

West Front ZHUKOV

Serpukhov

Kaluga

Kolomna

Ryaaam

Tula

Mtsensk

Orel

Yelets

Kursk

Bryansk

Voronezh

South-West Front TIMOSHENKO

Sumy

Belgorod

Kharkov

Poltava

Kremenchuy

Lugansk

Makeyevka

Taganrog

Rostov

Azov

Yetsk

16

22

30

16

5

33

43

49

50

10

3

13

9

3

2

4

4

2

2

6

6

38

40

21

17

12

18

37

9

1

11

56

9000

6000

3000

1500

600

300

0 ft

0   100 km

0   100 miles

South Front CHEREVICHENKO

GERMAN SUPPLY FAILURES

The German supply network behind Operation Barbarossa had began to falter during the great advances of the summer of 1941. It proved impossible to sustain the front-line units using the primitive Russian rail and road network. The Russian railways used a wider track gauge than the German rail system, and it took longer than anticipated to convert them for use. It also did not help that the German logistics train had been filled out with captured vehicles from all over Europe. There were 2000 different vehicle types in service, with few interchangeable parts. Army Group Centre's spare parts inventory ran to over one million items. By early autumn, the *Luftwaffe* had been forced to ferry its own supplies forward in bombers – its fuel and other essential supplies were all held up in bottlenecks from Poland to the Smolensk–Moscow highway.

which now had three-quarters of Germany's tank forces at its disposal. In another giant battle of encirclement, Hoth and Hoepner's Panzers were to bypass Moscow to the north, while Guderian's Panzer Group would pass to the south. The tanks would link up east of Moscow, cutting the Soviet capital off from reinforcements and supplies.

Assigned the codename *Taifun* (Typhoon), the German drive on Moscow began on 2 October. The Russians had concentrated huge forces to bar the road to their capital, but these were smashed yet again. In two more great battles of encirclement, another 650,000 Russians were captured. The citizens of Moscow sensed which way the wind was blowing; party officials started burning documents and whole government departments were transferred east. Yet Stalin announced that he would be staying.

There were three reasons why the wily Soviet leader refused to abandon the Kremlin in late 1941. First there was the weather. On 6 October, German forces on the Moscow front awoke to find their tanks dusted with snow. Autumnal rains alternated with freezing nights, a seasonal phenomenon known to Russians as the *rasputitza* (literally the 'time without roads'). There were few metalled roads in the USSR. Most were wide dirt strips that now dissolved into a sticky quagmire, which even tanks were unable to cross. Germans on foot sank past the top of their jackboots. Airfields became unusable and the advance ground to a halt.

Stalin's second source of confidence came from his spy ring in Japan where, it was reported, Tojo's cabinet had definitely ruled out an attack on the USSR. Japan would attack America instead. The 750,000 Russian soldiers in the Far East were now available to reinforce the depleted forces fighting the Germans. Thirdly, the Red Army was replacing its staggering losses with unbelievable speed: 143 new divisions were mobilized between July and December, and 84 of the divisions destroyed in battle had been re-constituted.

Russia's Winter Ally

The *rasputitza* lasted for four weeks. Then, on 7 November, the temperature plunged and the liquid mud turned rock hard. The German advance began again with breakthroughs in the south as well as towards Moscow. At the end of the month, the 7th

Opposite: The headlong progress of the early advances slowed as Army Group Centre resumed the offensive against Moscow. Russian resistance had stiffened, but more ominously, the first signs of the ferocious Russian winter were appearing. From now on, the Wehrmacht *would have to fight the weather as well as the Red Army.*

Panzer Division established a bridgehead over the Volga canal. Its advance elements were soon within 20km (12 miles) of Moscow and in the cold, clear winter air the spires of the Kremlin were visible through binoculars.

Daytime temperatures around Moscow varied from -5 to -12°C (23 to 10.4°F) and the Germans found it increasingly difficult to keep fighting in the same uniforms they had worn through the baking heat of summer. Supplies of every kind were simply failing to arrive at the front, where battalions were reduced to a fraction of their authorized strength. Panzer divisions counted themselves lucky to have 50 tanks still running.

On 23 July General Halder, the army chief of staff, had reported to Hitler that the Soviet forces facing the *Wehrmacht* amounted to 93 divisions, of which 13 were armoured. Now, on 1 December his estimate had risen to 200 infantry divisions, 35 cavalry divisions and 40 armoured brigades, with at least another 70 mixed divisions deep inside Soviet territory. Eighteen divisions of excellently trained, well-equipped and warmly clothed long-service troops, with 1700 tanks and 1500 aircraft, were on their way to the Moscow front from the Far East. In early December, Stalin reviewed these Siberian divisions in Red Square. From the parade, they moved straight into the front line.

The Russians attacked on 5 December. The temperature plummeted to -15°C (5°F) and snow lay more than a metre thick in places. Unable to dig in properly, the undermanned German units were torn apart; the few serviceable German tanks were unable to manoeuvre in these conditions and the fuel was stuck hundreds of miles behind the front. The *Luftwaffe* was unable to help: its aircraft took an average of five hours to get airborne, even if the ground-crews kept fires lit under the engines to keep them from freezing. Russia's latest tanks, the T-34 and KV-1, had wide tracks and engines designed

Below: The first snows fell in early October, followed by rain, which turned the Russian countryside into one vast morass. When winter truly arrived in November, the Wehrmacht *found itself ill-equipped to deal with sub-zero temperatures, and soon frostbite was causing more casualties than enemy action.*

Left: Soviet cavalrymen enter a snow-bound village west of Moscow. Unlike the Germans, the Red Army was intimately familiar with 'General Winter', and its equipment was designed to operate with minimal maintenance in temperatures as low as -40°C below zero.

to keep running even in Arctic weather. Russian guns and small arms were similarly robust, built to function in snow or mud, and the Red Army's soldiers wore thickly insulated uniforms. The hitherto victorious German army fell apart. It had suffered some 750,000 casualties between June and December, and losses soared once the full fury of winter descended. The army reported over 100,000 frostbite cases in December alone. Frostbite caused more hospitalization than Russian guns. Hypothermia would soon be killing more. Now Russian attacks were forcing them out of their hard-won positions, causing the German commanders to look over their shoulders and seek safer defences to the rear. Hitler would have none of this. Haunted by the spectre of Napoleon's retreat from Moscow, he would not allow the *Wehrmacht* to turn its back, even momentarily, on

Right: Accompanied by light tanks, Soviet ski troops prepare to launch an attack north of Moscow in January 1942. The Red Army was much better prepared for the severe Russian winter, having adequate supplies of warm winter clothing, winter camouflage and skis. The German army, by contrast, often had to improvise winter camouflage from white sheets, and had limited cold weather clothing.

the Russian capital. 'Where would they retreat to?' he asked. 'Is it warmer 50km or 100km to the west?'

There would be no retreat. The German army would stand fast, just as it had in World War I. When his commanders protested, he sacked them. The most senior to go was Brauchitsch, the commander-in-chief. Also sacked were the two Army Group commanders, Leeb and Bock, and, just before Christmas, Guderian. Thirty-five corps or divisional commanders were likewise dismissed, and Hoepner, who had commanded the IV Panzer Group in the north, was cashiered, then called back into the army as a private. Only Rundstedt, for whom Hitler to the end had great respect, was allowed to resign. Hitler, the former corporal, now took personal charge of the war in the East.

Russian Resurgence

Opposite: Although German troops got to within sight of the Kremlin, they were driven back when the Soviets unleashed a major counteroffensive around Moscow with fresh Siberian divisions. Far from capturing Moscow, it was all the Wehrmacht could do to survive as they were driven backwards.

For a time, it seemed as though the all-conquering *Wehrmacht* might suffer the fate of Napoleon's Grand Army, melting away in the Russian winter. Only Hitler's iron determination stopped the headlong retreat and destruction of his hopes.

Yet even Hitler's demonic will could not alter the facts. Though vast tracts of the Soviet Union had been occupied, the ambitious plans of the summer had come to nothing. The Red Army had been crippled, but it had risen from the ashes. More numerous than before, formidably equipped, and led by a new generation of highly capable commanders, it would be a far tougher opponent in 1942. Moscow had not been taken, and neither had Leningrad. The oilfields of the Caucasus remained out of reach.

For the first time, the myth of the invincibility of the German army had been broken. Though few knew it at the time, the defeat at the gates of Moscow had undermined the very foundations of the Thousand Year Reich.

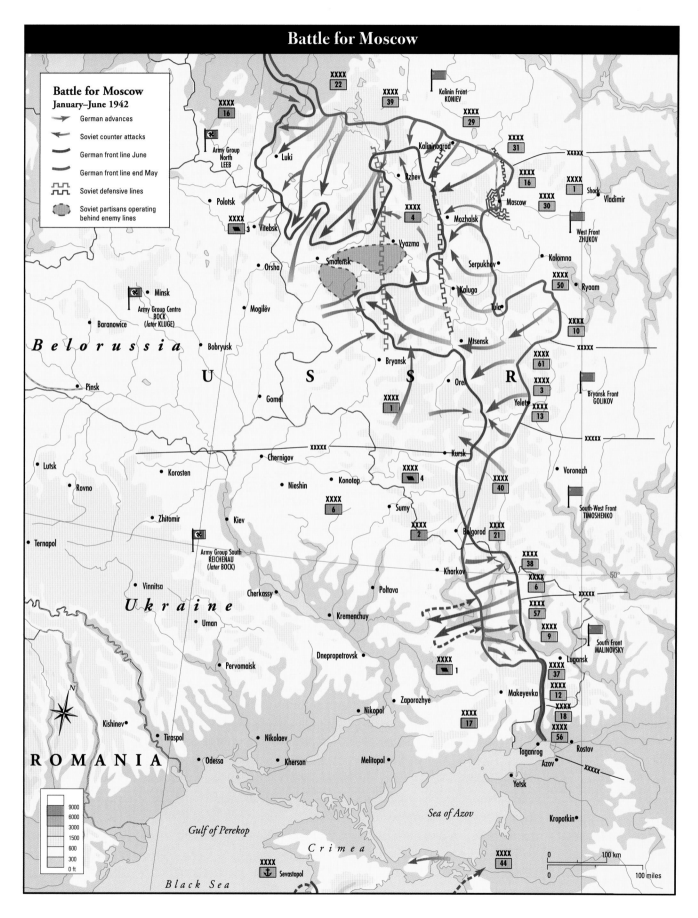

Battle for Moscow

Battle for Moscow
January–June 1942

→ German advances

← Soviet counter attacks

━ German front line June

━ German front line end May

⊓⊔ Soviet defensive lines

◖ Soviet partisans operating behind enemy lines

XXXX 22

XXXX 39

🚩 Kalinin Front KONIEV

XXXX 16

XXXX 29

XXXX 31

XXXXX

XXXX 16

XXXX 1 Shock

Vladimir

🚩 Army Group North LEEB

• Luki

Kaliningrad•

XXXX 4

Ryzhev

Moscow

XXXX 30

• Polotsk

XXXX 3 Vitebsk

• Mozhalsk

🚩 West Front ZHUKOV

Vyazma

• Serpukhov

• Kolomna

• Smolensk

• Orsha

• Kaluga

XXXX 50 • Ryaam

🚩 Minsk

Army Group Centre BOCK (*later* KLUGE)

• Mogilëv

Tula

XXXX 10

• Baranowice

• Bobryusk

• Mtsensk

XXXXX

B e l o r u s s i a

U   S   S

R

XXXX 61

• Pinsk

• Gomel

• Bryansk

• Orel

XXXX 3

XXXX 1

Yelets

🚩 Bryansk Front GOLIKOV

XXXX 13

• Lutsk

• Korosten

XXXXX

• Kursk

XXXXX

• Rovno

• Nieshin

• Konotop

XXXX 4

• Voronezh

• Zhitomir

XXXX 6

• Sumy

XXXX 40

🚩 South-West Front TIMOSHENKO

• Ternapol

🚩 Army Group South REICHENAU (*later* BOCK)

• Kiev

XXXX 2

• Belgorod

XXXX 21

• Vinnitsa

• Cherkassy

• Kharkov

• Poltava

XXXX 38

U k r a i n e

• Uman

• Kremenchuy

XXXX 6

XXXXX

50°

XXXX 57

• Pervomaisk

XXXX 9

🚩 South Front MALINOVSKY

N

• Dnepropetrovsk

XXXX 1

• Lugansk

XXXX 37

• Kishinev

• Zaporozhye

• Makeyevka

XXXX 12

XXXX 18

• Nikopol

XXXX 56

R O M A N I A

• Tiraspol

• Nikolaev

XXXX 17

• Melitopol

• Taganrog

Azov•

• Rostov

• Odessa

• Kherson

• Yetsk

XXXXX

9000
6000
3000
1500
600
300
0 ft

Sea of Azov

• Kropotkin

Gulf of Perekop

C r i m e a

0   100 km

0   100 miles

XXXX ⚓ 44

⚓ Sevastopol

Black Sea

167

Moscow to Stalingrad

The year 1942 did not start well for the *Wehrmacht*. Overextended in the great summer invasion of Russia, German armies had been checked for the first time in the last month of 1941.

Beaten back by fierce Soviet counterattacks from Leningrad to the Crimea, Hitler's War Machine was slowly freezing to a standstill. After being driven from the gates of Moscow, most of the generals who had made *Blitzkrieg* possible had been fired by the *Führer*. The former corporal had taken direct command of the armed forces. Hitler refused to consider the mere consolidation of 1941's huge territorial gains. He promised the German people that this year they would triumph.

Changed Priorities

Moscow was no longer the key: the massed Panzer and infantry formations were to drive southwestwards. They would seize the city of Stalingrad, a strategic city to be sure, but made even more important in Hitler's eyes because it was named after his hated rival, Joseph Stalin. From there, the Germans would be within striking distance of the real prize: the vital oilfields in the Caucasus.

The *Wehrmacht's* Panzers, however, were running short of fuel. Materially, Hitler's armies were dangerously depleted after the headlong advance of Operation Barbarossa, and losses from the fierce battles of the winter were far from being made good. Stalin also had something to prove. In January 1942, 12 German armies were locked in combat with 22 Soviet armies. On a front stretching from the Crimea to the Gulf of Finland, 141 divisions, including 11 from Axis allies, faced more than 300 Russian formations.

The very size of the war zone was in the *Wehrmacht's* favour. Stalin was trying not only to relieve Moscow and Leningrad, but also to destroy Army Group Centre. His generals knew what happened to commanders who failed, and Red Army offensives were launched all along the line. It was too much. Despite tattered uniforms stuffed with straw and newspaper, weapons that jammed in the arctic temperatures, and a grave lack of tanks or aircraft, the German army defended itself with extraordinary professionalism and courage. The fighting conditions were appalling, and favoured the Soviets, who were used to the rigours of the Russian winter. As the petrol froze in their fuel tanks, the

Opposite: Although the Wehrmacht *had suffered a considerable setback at the end of 1941, the spring of 1942 saw it return to its victorious ways. Reinforced and re-equipped, the German Army again took the offensive. This time, however, the target was no longer Moscow. Now its main thrust would be to the southwest – towards Stalingrad.*

Siege of Leningrad

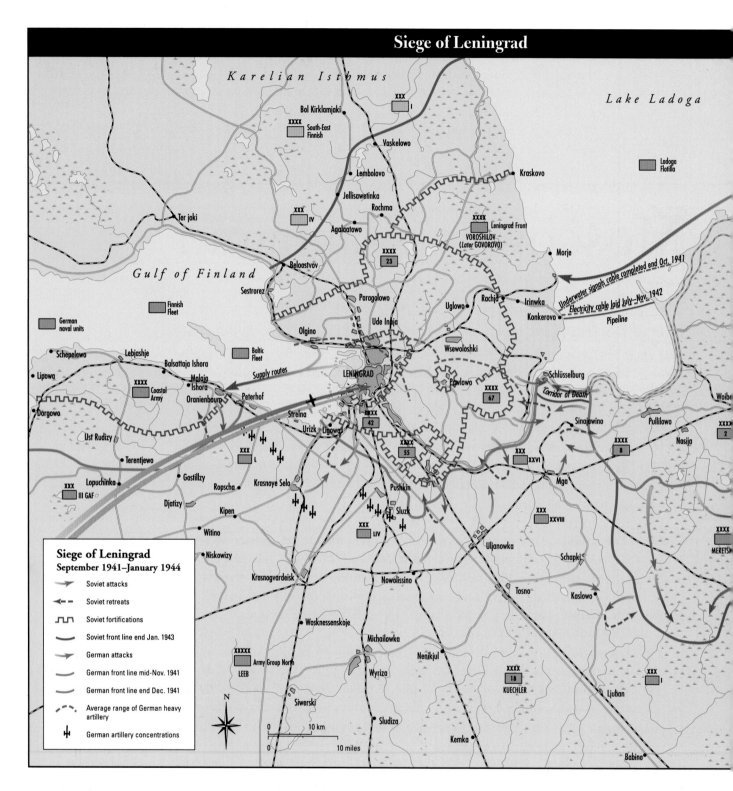

Siege of Leningrad
September 1941–January 1944

→ Soviet attacks

◄- - Soviet retreats

⊓⊔ Soviet fortifications

⌒ Soviet front line end Jan. 1943

➤ German attacks

⌒ German front line mid-Nov. 1941

⌒ German front line end Dec. 1941

⌒·⌒ Average range of German heavy artillery

⊢ German artillery concentrations

0   10 km

0   10 miles

N

Germans came to place greater reliance on horse-drawn transport. But as the winter drew on, they succeeded in stemming the Russian hordes. The stubborn German defence exposed the Red Army's lack of experience, its problems exacerbated by shortages of all kinds. By March, even Stalin had to admit that his great offensive was over.

Stalin's failure to relieve besieged Leningrad appeared to have doomed the city. Since Hitler had ordered that the cradle of the Bolshevik revolution be levelled, it seemed only a matter of time before it fell. Its population swollen to over three million by refugees flooding into the city, Leningrad was cut off by Germans to the south and to the north by the Finns, eager to avenge the Winter War.

Communist Party chiefs anxiously calculated their food reserves. On 1 November, they realized there was enough food for only another week. Winter was also approaching, and there was so little fuel that buildings could not be heated – electricity was rationed to an hour a day. What followed was the most appalling siege in history, a long drawn-out agony in which nearly a million men, women and children died of cold and slow starvation – three times the *total* war dead suffered by Britain or the USA in the whole of World War II. Only the barest of supplies reached the embattled population. Throughout the winter and into the spring, the Germans kept a relentless grip on the city, stopping all Soviet attempts to break through.

The Spring Thaw

The fluid fighting of early 1942 isolated numerous pockets of the invaders. The Soviet Northwest Front broke through in the Valdai hills, encircling several divisions in turn. In each case, the trapped German troops were clustered around an airfield. With the *Luftwaffe* flying in supplies, they continued to defend their perimeters until relief was at hand, or – in the case of General von Seydlitz's six divisions in the Demyansk pocket – broke out. Seydlitz's men took a month to battle their way to safety across the snow. Their epic escape was sustained by parachute drops and an iron determination never to surrender.

The spring thaw halted operations on both sides. The *rasputitza* turned the steel-hard ground into impenetrable rivers of mud. Nothing could move, and the Germans were given the chance to breathe again. With the *Wehrmacht* still less than 300km (186 miles) from Moscow – a distance the Panzer divisions could cover in a week – the Soviets concentrated their forces around the capital. It was the obvious military strategy, and it was wrong.

The *Wehrmacht's* high command calculated that over the entire Eastern Front the Germans had lost 376,000 men killed and wounded during the Soviet winter offensive. Nearly double that number had been lost from frostbite and sickness. At the beginning of April 1942, the German armies in the east were 625,000 men under strength.

However, they had inflicted over 400,000 casualties on their enemies, and many soldiers puzzled over the Red Army's ability to take such punishment. What the Soviets lacked in military skill, they seemed determined to make up for with fanatical – and often futile – bravery. Goebbels damned them as mindless automata, an enduring image that survived long after 1945. But in its counteroffensive the Red Army had learned the true nature of its opponents. The ordinary Russian soldier discovered that the most outlandish atrocity tales fed to them by the commissars were not so incredible after all.

In their retreat, the Germans had ruthlessly enforced a scorched earth policy. In village after village liberated by the Soviets, they uncovered grisly evidence of German

Opposite: Hitler confidently expected that his armies would soon take Leningrad, the spiritual home of Soviet communism. But the terrain favoured the defenders, and the assault soon lapsed into a siege, which would last for more than 900 days.

'We were disheartened when we discovered in the winter of 1941 that the beaten Russians seemed quite unaware that as a military force they had almost ceased to exist; indeed, their non-existent armies were providing ever tougher resistance.'

Guenther Blumentritt, Chief-of-Staff of the German Fourth Army

Summer supply route from 'lifeline' road

Novaya Ladoga

'Lifeline' road completed 6 December 1941

Kisselaja

Wolkow

XXXX 54

Tscherenzovo

Pcheva

Oskui

XXXX 4

Right: Dressed in winter camouflage, a Soviet infantryman waits in ambush in a birch forest on the Central Front, armed with a PPSh41s submachine gun. Although German equipment was generally well designed, it did not cope well with the Soviet winter. The standard German sub-machine gun, the MP40, often failed in snow and mud, and German troops often used captured PPSh41s. The PPSh41s was more crudely made, but could be relied on in almost any conditions.

atrocities. Buildings had been torched, livestock killed, women and children driven out into the snow to die – or summarily executed.

Many ordinary Russian peasants, brutalized by years of communist repression, had initially treated the Germans as liberators. However, any goodwill was quickly squandered by even greater German brutality. Large numbers of Russians took refuge in the forests and the steppes, where they joined the partisan armies fighting a no-quarter war with the occupiers.

For the coming campaigning season, Hitler needed to make good his losses, so he demanded his allies make up the numbers. Romania and Italy supplied half a million men in 1942. By German standards, they were poorly equipped and often badly trained, so they were mainly used to hold quiet sectors while the German formations led the attacks. By replacing German civilian labourers with slaves seized from Eastern Europe, by stripping battalions from divisions garrisoned in Western Europe, and by calling up the next year's conscription class a year early, the *Wehrmacht* was able to assemble 2.7 million men on the Russian front. This accretion of strength could not be repeated, so Hitler was betting everything on one roll of the die.

In material, too, the Germans were making considerable improvements, although even now the home economy was not on a total-war footing. The production of light tanks was halted and medium tanks were given heavier armour and bigger guns. The Panzer IV was equipped with a long-barrelled 75mm (2.95in) weapon, which had previously proved itself with the infantry in the anti-tank role. By so doing, the Germans to some extent overcame the nightmare posed by the appearance of superb Soviet T-34. At the same time, an increased number of cross-country vehicles allowed the *Panzergrenadier* infantry to follow more closely behind the tanks, and so exploit their successes. Thanks to the light armour and cannon fitted to their half-tracks, the troops were able to do some fighting without leaving their vehicles. Even so, it is important remember that the *Wehrmacht* still placed considerable reliance upon horse-drawn transport.

The German Summer Offensive

In Directive No.41, dated 5 April, Hitler stated: 'The enemy has suffered enormous losses of men and material. In attempting to exploit their apparent initial successes, they have exhausted during this winter the mass of their reserves, which were intended for later operations'. In this mistaken belief, Hitler set out his objectives for the

THE 'GUSTAV' RAILWAY GUN

Built originally to breach the Maginot Line, the 80cm (31.4in) 'Gustav' railway gun weighed over 1179 tonnes (1300 tons). It was carried by 25 special trains, and took up to six weeks to assemble on a prepared site. Over 1000 men under the control of a German army engineer unit dug through a small knoll to form a wide railway cutting, whose sides were raised to provide cover and protection for the gun. A further 500 men manned the weapon in action.

Gustav's shells weighed up to 10 tonnes (11 tons), and simply getting each shell and propellant charge to the breech was a major task requiring the use of lifting equipment. Projectile and charge then had to be rammed accurately and the whole barrel elevated to the correct firing angle. It all took time, and while the best firing rate was supposed to be one round every 15 minutes, in practice it was more like one shell per hour.

The gun had a maximum range of around 40km (25 miles), and all shots were observed by a special flight of Fiesler Storch spotter planes. At Sevastopol, one target after another was demolished by the gun, which pulverized Soviet coastal batteries, including the Molotov and Maxim Gorky forts, and the supposedly invulnerable underwater magazine beneath Severnaya Bay.

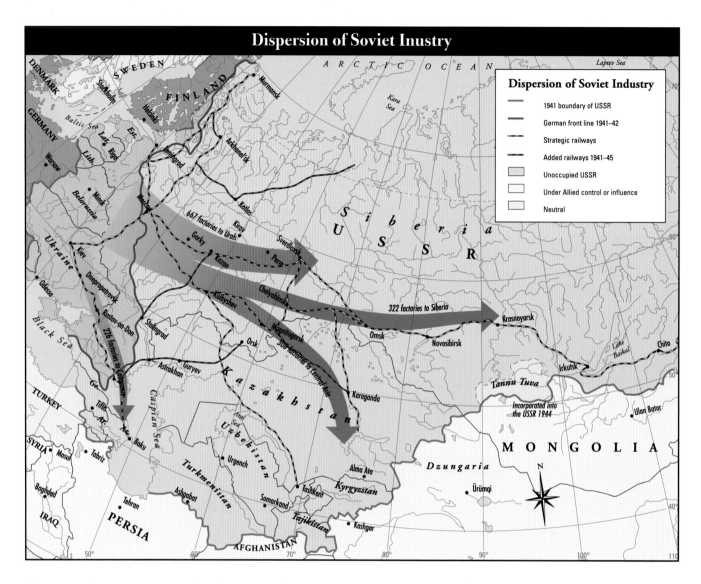

Dispersion of Soviet Inustry

Dispersion of Soviet Industry

——	1941 boundary of USSR
——	German front line 1941–42
—·—·—	Strategic railways
━━━	Added railways 1941–45
▨	Unoccupied USSR
▢	Under Allied control or influence
▨	Neutral

Above: With so much of European Russia in enemy hands, the Soviets moved their major war industries to safety east of the Urals. This titanic effort was completed in an astonishingly short time, and Soviet industry was soon out-producing the Germans in key weapons like tanks, small arms and aircraft.

coming summer offensive, codenamed Operation *Blau* (Blue). He set his revitalized armies, now numbering some 215 divisions, the task of destroying the last remaining enemy formations, and as far as possible, capturing the main sources of raw materials on which the German war economy depended.

All available forces were to be concentrated on the southern sector. Their mission was firstly to annihilate the enemy on the Don. Then they were to swing north and take Stalingrad, followed by a combined assault to conquer the oil-producing areas of the Caucasus. Lastly, they were to capture the passes through the Caucasus mountains, giving access to the Middle East.

Hitler was not the only dictator planning a knockout blow. The return of warmer weather was the signal for another Soviet offensive, but the attempt to recapture Kharkov failed dismally. Ten days and nights of hectic thrust and counter-thrust in open country turned into a master class in *Blitzkrieg*. The advancing Russians were outmanoeuvred by the superbly coordinated German air and ground forces. The *Luftwaffe* air fleets under Ritter von Greim dominated the skies. Swarms of Ju 88s, Stukas and Heinkel 111s pounded the Russian positions, protected by the world's most experienced fighter pilots and reinforced by Germany's Axis allies.

Three Russian armies were surrounded and annihilated. Marshal Timoshenko was summoned to Moscow to explain the loss of another 200,000 men. As the German Sixth and Seventeenth Armies shattered the Russian offensive at Kharkov, the Eleventh Army under the command of General Erich von Manstein broke through the heavily fortified Soviet positions on the Kerch peninsula. By April 1942, the Soviets had ferried 250,000 men into the Crimea, together with considerable tank and artillery support. Yet as in the previous year, the forces were committed piecemeal against overwhelming German opposition.

At dawn on 8 May, Manstein crossed the Kamenskoye isthmus to assault the positions covering Kerch. The nine German divisions were outnumbered two to one, but as usual the *Wehrmacht* commanders placed their strongest forces at the weakest point in the enemy front line. The sheer weight of German metal forced the Soviets back from Feodosia. The Panzers, supported by screaming Stukas, then drove through the waist of the peninsula towards Kerch itself. Between 15 and 20 May, the Caucasus front imploded and the Soviets were driven into the Black Sea. They left behind 170,000 prisoners, 1138 guns and 258 tanks.

Sevastopol

Not wishing to belittle his victory, Manstein described his enemy in his memoirs in much more moderate terms than did the Soviet high command, which vigorously criticized their bad positioning, inertia, and lack of communication between air and land forces.

With its flank protected, Eleventh Army doubled back to storm Sevastopol, home of the Soviet Black Sea Fleet. Manstein had received strong reinforcements. To oppose the Russian garrison of 106,000 sailors, soldiers and marines, he could call on 204,000 men, 720 tanks, 600 aircraft, 670 guns and 450 mortars, including the *Wehrmacht's* general reserve of siege artillery.

Armageddon preceded the assault on the fortress. Operations commenced with a five-day barrage, which reminded some older members of the army staff of Verdun, 25 years

---

RUSSIAN INDUSTRIAL MIGRATION

In 1941–42, as the Soviet Union's key industrial regions were overrun by the invaders, whole factories were uprooted and shipped to the Urals, to the deserts of Kazakhstan or the frozen tundra of Siberia. Over 1.5 million wagonloads made the journey, and workers – many of them women – struggled to set up machine tools literally in the middle of nowhere. Not only did they get the factories working again, but they also did so with unbelievable speed.

The Yak fighter plant in Moscow was dismantled and taken to Siberia, where production resumed in only a week. By early 1942, this factory was building more aircraft per month than it had done on its original site. From a far inferior base – Russia produced only a quarter as much steel as Germany – the Soviets were, by mid-1942, already outbuilding the invaders, and supplying their armies with more tanks, guns and aircraft than the *Wehrmacht* was receiving.

Above: The German occupation of European Russia was brutal. Reprisals for partisan attacks saw entire villages destroyed, their inhabitants driven out onto the steppe or even killed out of hand.

before. Manstein's experts used every piece of artillery they could bring to bear. Included in the heavy artillery pounding the Russian positions was both the massive 'Karl', a siege mortar with a calibre of 60cm (23.6in), and the largest gun ever made, the 80cm (31.4in) 'Gustav' railway gun. The *Luftwaffe* also played its part, dropping more than 20,000 tonnes (22,050 tons) of bombs on Sevastopol in three weeks – more than it dropped on the whole of England during the Blitz.

After the barrage, the German LIV Corps moved against the defences. The Soviets defended every yard of territory through the first weeks of June, demonstrating a tenacity that would be repeated to resounding effect at Stalingrad later that year. By the third week, Manstein was sufficiently worried that he not only threw in his last reserves, but also begged for reinforcements from the Seventeenth Army. The Soviet Navy continued to perform miracles in resupplying Sevastopol across the Black Sea. This supply route had become a killing ground for the *Luftwaffe* and *Kriegsmarine,* as they intercepted the vital transports. The relief efforts were born of desperation and eventually the sheer weight of material thrown against the Soviet defences began to tell.

The Germans finally breached the defences on the night of 28/29 June. During the next three days, the Soviets organized a Dunkirk-style evacuation to rescue as many as possible of the men, women and children who had survived the 250-day siege. The Germans had won, but were left with a gutted city, its buildings destroyed.

Although von Manstein was awarded a field marshal's baton for taking Sevastopol, his Eleventh Army was so depleted that he would have to leave the drive on Stalingrad to the unimaginative but hugely ambitious General Paulus. Paulus, a staff officer with little operational command experience, knew exactly where his fame and fortune were to be made, and that was at Stalingrad.

The Don and the Volga

Hitler moved his HQ to Vinnitsa in the Ukraine to oversee the next stage of the campaign. Army Group South, re-named Army Group B, included the Second and Sixth Armies, Fourth Panzer Army and Third Hungarian Army. It was to advance into the bend of the Don river then on to the Volga at Stalingrad.

The other claw in a gigantic pincer movement would be a new formation. Army Group A, comprising First Panzer Army, Seventeenth Army and Third Romanian Army would link up with Army Group B somewhere on the steppe west of the Volga, hopefully trapping another vast haul of Russian prisoners. Having gutted the Soviet armies again, Army Group A would then lunge south and east to overrun the Soviet oilfields.

On 28 June, the great summer offensive began. Army Group B, under the recalled Field Marshal Feodor von Bock, attacked on a 150km (93-mile) front. The spearhead

Below: Three partisans armed with the PPSh-41 submachinegun listen to orders. The partisan war was brutal, with no quarter given by either side. The Soviets set up a partisan command to coordinate the actions of tens of thousands of guerrillas behind German lines. German security units, generally drawn from the SS or the police, were particularly brutal in their actions.

Right: The siege of Sevastopol was decided when the Germans made use of some of the heaviest artillery pieces ever made to flatten the city before it was finally taken by ground assault.

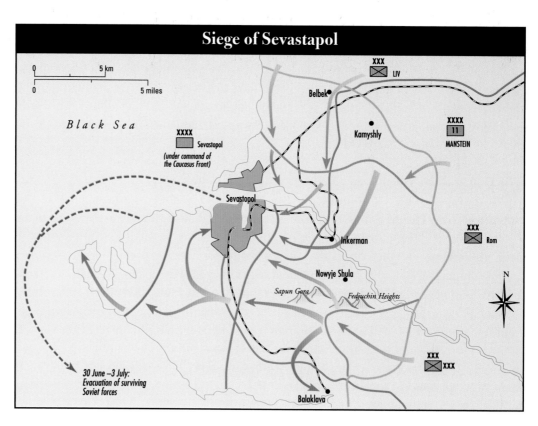

Siege of Sevastapol

Black Sea

Belbek

Kamyshly

LIV

XXXX
11
MANSTEIN

Sevastopol
(under command of
the Caucasus Front)

Sevastopol

Inkerman

Rom

Nowyje Shula

Sapun Gora

Fedjuchin Heights

N

30 June –3 July:
Evacuation of surviving
Soviet forces

Balaklava

Below: A flak crew provides security for troops advancing towards the Caucasus. Their weapons were as likely to be used against ground targets as against aircraft, as partisans regularly attacked the German lines of communication.

was General Hoth's Third Panzer Army. Paulus's Sixth Army extended the front a further 80km (50 miles) to the south. Two days later, Army Group A under General Wilhelm List burst over the Donetz bend and drove southwards to Proletarskaya and the Caucasus. The attacks were resoundingly successful. Hoth was in Voronezh by 3 July, though progress was not fast enough to satisfy Hitler and he replaced von Bock with Baron Maximilian von Weichs. Army Group B then poured down the Donets corridor to link up with von Kleist's armour pushing on Rostov. It seemed that the days of easy victory had returned.

The Russian forces were contemptuously swept aside. For the first time in many months, the ground favoured large-scale sweeping manoeuvres. Hundreds of miles of open rolling corn and steppe grass offered perfect country for the massed legions of German armour. Their advance was visible for miles: smoke from burning villages and dust kicked up by thousands of heavy vehicles signalled the irresistible onrush of a perfectly functioning war machine.

But then Hitler became too ambitious. He believed that the

Left: The crew of a 21cm (8.26in) Mrs 18 artillery piece load an enormous 113kg (250lb) shell as part of the bombardment of Sevastapol. Soldiers who had been frozen by the Russian winter only six months before were now being baked. Temperatures as von Kleist's panzer army approached the Caucasus mountains regularly exceeded 40°C, and tasks such as manning heavy artillery pieces became harder and harder.

Russians were finished and just needed one more devastating victory to bring the Soviet edifice low. On 13 July, aiming at another vast encirclement, he detached Hoth's armour, ordering it to swing southeast to link up with Army Group A's tanks, whose forces were now committed to an intense battle in the streets of Rostov. On 23 July, Rostov fell, but it ailed to yield the hoped-for booty. Stalin had finally learned the lesson of trading space for time, and he allowed his marshals to pull their forces back, rather than letting them be fatally surrounded. On the same day, Hitler issued the directive that arguably cost

Above: A German machine-gun crew take up position behind a wall on the outskirts of Stalingrad in the autumn of 1942. At this stage of the battle, many of the city's buildings were still intact.

him the war in the East, and with it sealed his empire's fate. Totally underestimating the opposing forces, he changed the plans for his two Army Groups. Rather than take Stalingrad and *then* attack the Caucasus, he opted to move on both objectives simultaneously. He compounded the error by making ruinous reductions in the forces available to the operations. The strategic reserve was sent to the four winds: 9th and 11th Panzer Divisions were assigned to General von Kluge, the *Grossdeutschland* Division was sent to Army Group Centre, *Leibstandarte*-SS was ordered to France, and the rested Eleventh Army was held back from taking part in the Caucasus drive.

A Stalling Advance

For the moment, everything still seemed to be going Hitler's way. The headlong advance across open country to the Volga was spearheaded by the Sixth Army, a veteran formation led in Poland and France by General von Reichenau, one of Hitler's strongest

supporters in the Wehrmacht. A vocal anti-Semite, von Reichenau had left his soldiers in no doubt as to their 'historic mission' to slaughter 'Asiatic inferiors', fighting talk that won him command of Army Group South when Hitler sacked von Rundstedt in December 1941. He did not live long to enjoy his promotion to field marshal, dying of a stroke soon afterwards. But his influence permeated the army he had led to victory for two years: the Sixth Army cut a swathe of destruction across Russia as it smashed its way east.

The only problems for the Germans were those of traffic control, for both Kleist and Hoth's Panzers arrived at the crossing of the Donetz simultaneously. In a series of acrimonious arguments, Kleist made it clear that he saw no reason why another Panzer army should be assigned to take the Caucasus. To prove the point, he speeded up his own pace once across the river and captured Proletarskaya.

But to the north, the advance had stagnated. Von Weichs had been left only with the Sixth Army to break through the Soviet forces barring the way to Stalingrad. He was forced to delay to await the arrival of the Italian Eighth Army, and lack of fuel stopped him employing all of his armour at any one time. Hitler relented, and sensing that Hoth's Panzers were doing more harm than good in the over-crowded roads south of the Don, he returned the forces to Army Group B on 30 July.

However, by that stage Hoth was already 140km (87 miles) south of Tsimlyansk, and strong Soviet forces were preventing a link up with Paulus. As Hoth's Panzers fought their way north, they were slowly being ground down, losing men and resources in a laborious war of attrition.

The End of Russian Retreat

The Sixth Army reached the banks of the Volga on 23 August. In spite of furious Soviet counterattacks, a defensive line was established upstream of Stalingrad. That night, Stalingrad was subjected to an air raid reminiscent of the heaviest London bombing. The bulk of the bombs dropped were incendiaries and the wooden buildings of the city burned in a spectacular holocaust. An assault on the city was now planned. But it was to prove an infinitely more difficult task, now that Stalingrad's defenders had had time to prepare the city's defences.

In the meantime, Army Group A had been making excellent progress. Six months after they had endured winter temperatures of -30°C (-22°F), German soldiers found themselves on the Kuban steppe, where the thermometer topped 40°C (104°F) in the shade. Inside the tanks of First Panzer Army, the heat was simply unbearable.

List's major worries were about supplies. It was impossible to satisfy the needs of 26 advancing divisions, some moving southwest, some south and some southeast – so much so that Colonel-General von Kleist jested: 'No Russians in front of us, no supplies behind

Map, page 183: The German summer offensive made good progress, with one thrust heading for the Caucasus and its vital oilfields, while another was directed against the city of Stalingrad.

us!' Jerry cans of petrol dropped from Ju 52 transports had to be brought up to the Panzers by camel transport.

The terrain slowed up fighting troops as well as supplies. Roads were rivers of dust, and the rivers were wide with unpredictable currents. Nevertheless, the SS *Wiking* Division forced the river Kuban in the face of intense resistance early in August. On 9 August, *Gruppe Ruoff* – Seventeenth Army and Third Rumanian Army under General Richard Ruoff – occupied simultaneously the port of Yeytsk on the Sea of Azov, Krasnovar on the Kuban and the blazing wreckage of the oil town of Maikop. Maikop's oil wells were so thoroughly sabotaged that they would not return to use until four years after the war.

Also on 9 August, First Panzer Army took Pyatigorsk at the bottom of the first foothills of the Caucasus, and patrols were sent out towards Astrakahn. On 21 August, a detachment of the elite 1st and 4th *Gebirgsjäger* mountain regiments planted the Swastika flag on the 5642m (18,510ft) summit of Mount Elbrus, and the rest of XLIX Mountain Corps advanced into the sub-tropical forests girding Sukhumi in Georgia. On the eastern side of the mountains, the river Terek was the last obstacle facing *Panzergruppe Kleist* in its breakneck advance.

Eventually the offensive reached what Clausewitz called the falling-off point, beyond which wear and tear take over from the initial drive and energy. Russian resistance was stiffening, and the German forces were now hundreds of kilometres past the last railheads. A desperate race followed, both sides hurrying forward ammunition, fuel, spare parts and more soldiers – always more soldiers – for one final battle before the *rasputitza* imposed nature's halt on campaigning.

Hitler, exasperated by the slow progress, removed List and took control of operations himself. Yet all the genius and dynamism with which he credited himself were unable to improve matters. With hindsight, it seems that Hitler may have been attempting the impossible, but Stalin was sufficiently alarmed by the series of reverses since the fall of Kerch to issue a famous order of the day on 28 July.

Below: Although the image of the Wehrmacht *which has passed into history is of a colossal mechanized juggernaut, the bulk of the forces involved in Russia were actually infantrymen, who marched for huge distances across the seemingly endless plains.*

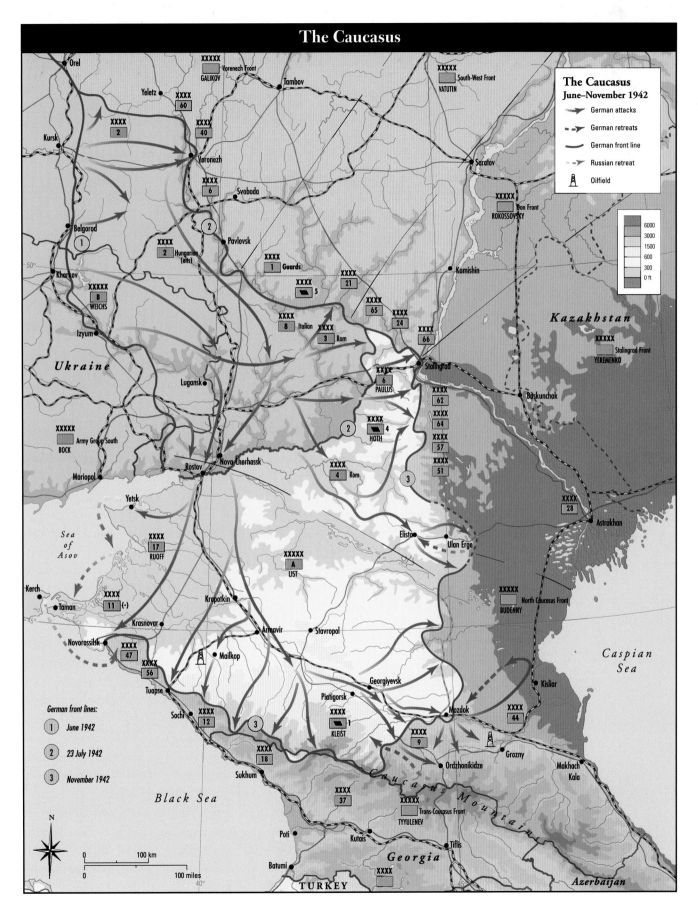

The Caucasus

The Caucasus
June–November 1942

- ⟶ German attacks
- ⤏ German retreats
- — German front line
- ⤏ Russian retreat
- ⛏ Oilfield

6000
3000
1500
600
300
0 ft

German front lines:

① June 1942

② 23 July 1942

③ November 1942

Orel
Yeletz
Kursk
XXXX 2
XXXX 60
GALIKOV XXXXX
Voronezh Front
Tambov
XXXXX VATUTIN
South-West Front
Saratov
XXXX 40
Belgorod
①
XXXX 6
Svoboda
②
Pavlovsk
XXXXX ROKOSSOVSKY
Don Front
Kharkov
XXXXX B WEICHS
XXXX 2 Hungarian (elts)
XXXX 1 Guards
XXXX 21
Kamishin
Kazakhstan
Izyum
XXXX 8 Italian
XXXX 3 Rom
XXXX 65
XXXX 24
XXXX 66
XXXX 5
Ukraine
Lugansk
Stalingrad
XXXX 6 PAULUS
XXXXX YEREMENKO
Stalingrad Front
XXXX 62
Baskunchak
XXXXX Army Group South BOCK
②
XXXX 4 HOTH
XXXX 64
Nova Cherkassk
Rostov
XXXX 4 Rom
③
XXXX 57
XXXX 51
Mariopol
Yetsk
XXXX 28
Astrakhan
Sea of Asov
XXXX 17 RUOFF
XXXXX A LIST
Elista
Ulan Erge
Kerch
Taman
XXXX 11 (-)
Krasnovar
Caspian Sea
XXXXX North Caucasus Front BUDENNY
Novorossilsk
XXXX 47
XXXX 56
Kropotkin
Armavir
Stavropol
Mailkop ⛏
Georgiyevsk
Kisliar
Tuapse
Sochi
XXXX 12
③
Piatigorsk
XXXX 1 KLEIST
Mozdok
XXXX 44
Grozny ⛏
XXXX 9
XXXX 18
Sukhum
Ordzhonikidze
Makhach Kala
Caucasus Mountains
XXXX 37
XXXXX Trans-Caucasus Front TYYULENEV
Black Sea
Poti
Kutais
Tiflis
Batumi
XXXX
Georgia
TURKEY
Azerbaijan

N

100 km

100 miles

Right: While one man keeps watch, his comrades take the opportunity to have a meal. All supplies for the soldiers had to be brought across the Volga.

'Every inch of territory we concede strengthens the enemy and weakens the defence of our country. If we do not stop the retreat, we shall be left with no grain, fuel, metal, workshops, factories or railways. Therefore the moment has come to stop the retreat: not another step back!'

The Battle of Stalingrad

In Stalingrad, the order had the desired effect. The city had half a million inhabitants, and much of the civilian population had been marched out to dig trenches and anti-tank ditches. But these were not the only German worry. German intelligence had not warned the units taking part that Stalingrad sprawled for more than 30km (19 miles) along the Volga and that, in places, the western edge of the city was more than 8km (5 miles) from the bank of the river.

The time for taking the city by *coup de main* had passed. Paulus's makeshift attack could have succeeded only if it met an enemy that was not only beaten but whose morale was extremely low. From the very first engagements in the increasingly bitter street fighting, it was clear to the Germans that the Russians had recovered beyond anyone's expectations.

On 16 September, General von Richthofen, now commander of *Luftflotte IV,* wrote in his diary: 'With a little effort, the town should fall in two days'. Less than a week later, he noted, with more justification: 'September the 2nd. In the town itself progress is desperately slow. The 6th Army will never finish the job at this rate'.

The Russian soldiers, spurred on by patriotic propaganda, were now fighting in circumstances in which their own natural talents were an advantage, and their lack of armour and mobility did not matter. They fought from holes burrowed in rubble, from the blackened caverns of burned-out offices, from behind parapets of gaunt towering blocks; they fought for every yard of every street and every alleyway in the city.

Here, all the Panzers could do was to creep over the wasteland of a city devastated by their own efforts. Unable to see the hidden enemy, their fate was to be blasted by liquid fire, or their tracks blown off by grenades. Armoured vehicles are virtually defenceless once immobilized. And once the tanks were stopped, German infantry were mown down by machine-gun fire as they sought protection behind their vehicles.

In Berlin, Hitler was already proclaiming the victory in Stalingrad, and poured as many reinforcements as possible into the inferno. By contrast, the Russians fed in just enough troops to keep the Germans occupied, and to resist their best efforts. In the meantime, the mass of men and arms accumulating in reserve were being held back for a different purpose.

This was finally revealed on 19 November. The last of six major attacks by the Sixth Army had been repulsed, and the weary German troops were licking their wounds. Surprise was near total when the Soviets unleashed massive barrages north and south of Stalingrad. The Red Army had finally learned the lessons of *Blitzkrieg*. This time their attacks would be launched at the weakest part of the German line – Paulus' thinly held flanks, protected only by Romanian and Italian formations. The battle for Stalingrad had entered a new and desperate phase. General Paulus thought he had the city of Stalingrad within his grasp. But his confidence was shattered when he received alarming reports from the units guarding his flanks. Soviet forces were attacking in unbelievable strength.

To the north, German divisions were being engulfed by wave upon wave of massed Soviet armour, heavily supported by even larger numbers of aircraft and artillery pieces.

Below: The German 6th Army commanded by General Paulus reached the Volga at Stalingrad at the end of August. The Wehrmacht High Command expected the city to fall quickly, but the Soviet defenders fought street by street, building by building to thwart their expectations.

On 20 November, the Soviets attacked in the south, with equal effect. By 23 November, the encirclement was complete. Some 300,000 Axis soldiers were trapped inside Stalingrad.

Paulus reported that his Sixth Army had enough food for only a week and that fuel and ammunition was running low. His senior commanders begged him to order a breakout, but Paulus' superior, Field Marshal von Manstein, refused to hear of it. Hitler insisted that *'Festung Stalingrad'* – Fortress Stalingrad – hold out until relieved. The expression 'fortress' gave false comfort; the troops had no proper fortifications, just the holes in the frozen ground they had managed to excavate with their remaining explosives.

The temperature sank remorselessly. Blizzards swept across the steppe. Huddled in underground bunkers, the Sixth Army counted the days until a relief operation rescued them. Fighting rations were reduced to 200g (7oz) of horsemeat and 200g (7oz) of bread per day. Support troops received half that, and there was nothing at all for Soviet prisoners held inside the pocket. Yet the ordinary soldiers believed, against mounting evidence to the contrary, that Hitler would get them out. Manstein failed to relieve the trapped army. He sent Hoth to blast a way through the Soviet lines on 12 December, and in a week of desperate fighting, his Panzer corps got close enough to see the horizon lit up at night, flares rising and falling over the pocket. But the Soviets attacked the Italian and Romanian armies along the River Chir, north-west of Stalingrad. Another great breakthrough was achieved, and Hoth's relief force was compelled to turn away and meet the new threat. The Sixth Army was abandoned. Stalin ordered the pocket crushed in

Below: German prisoners-of-war after the capture of Stalingrad were tansported to the rear in the most appalling weather conditions. Few were to survive captivity.

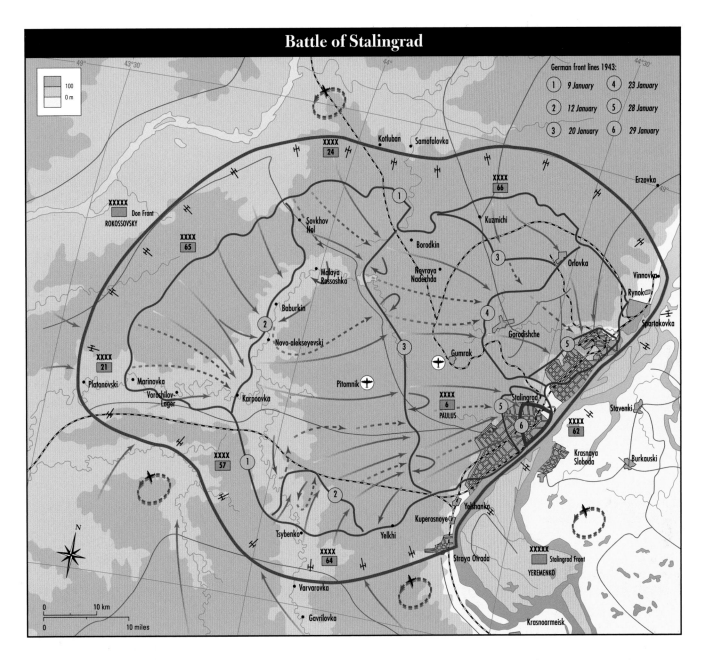

Battle of Stalingrad

German front lines 1943:

1 9 January   4 23 January
2 12 January   5 28 January
3 20 January   6 29 January

100
0 m

XXXXX Don Front
ROKOSSOVSKY

XXXX 24
XXXX 66
XXXX 65
XXXX 21
XXXX 57
XXXX 6 PAULUS
XXXX 62
XXXX 64

XXXXX Stalingrad Front
YEREMENKO

Kotluban Samofalovka
Erzovka
Kuzmichi
Sovkhov Nol
Borodkin
Navraya Nadexhda
Orlovka
Vinnovka
Rynok
Malaya Rossoshka
Spartakovka
Baburkin
Gorodishche
Novo-alekseyevski
Gumrak
Stalingrad
Platonovski
Marinovka
Voroshilov-Lager
Karpoovka
Pitomnik
Stavenki
Krasnaya Sloboda
Burkauski
Tsybenko
Yelkhi
Yelshanka
Kuperosnoye
Straya Otrada
Varvarovka
Gavrilovka
Krasnoarmeisk

N

0   10 km
0   10 miles

January, and a renewed Soviet Blitzkrieg broke into the perimeter west of the city. Some 25,000 sick and wounded Germans were evacuated, but a far greater number of men died as frostbitten limbs and wounds turned gangrenous. Basic medicines such as anaesthetic ran out. No rations were given to the wounded after 11 January. Hitler promoted Paulus to full general and then to field marshal, on the tacit understanding that no German field marshal had ever been taken alive. But Paulus refused to commit suicide, and surrendered himself and his staff on 30 January. Small parties of troops broke out onto the steppe, trying to make their way back to safety. Some were spotted from time to time by Luftwaffe reconnaissance flights. However, none made it back to the German lines.

Of the 300,000 German soldiers surrounded in Stalingrad, only 91,000 survived to surrender, and half of these would be dead before spring. Only 5000 would ever return from Soviet captivity, many of them not until the 1950s.

Above: The Sixth Army was quickly encircled: when Marshal Zhukov launched Operation Uranus on 19 November 1942, massive artillery barrages north and south of the city heralded equally massive attacks, which within four days had trapped Paulus' army in a ring of steel.

Appendix: guide to map symbols

Below is a guide to the symbols used to designate the different types of military units featured on the maps.

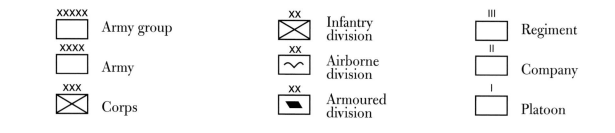

Bibliography

Beevor, Anthony. *Stalingrad.* London: Viking, 1998.

Bishop, Chris. *Encyclopedia of Weapons of WWII.* New York: Metro Books, 1998.

Bishop, Chris. *SS Hell on the Western Front.* St. Paul, Minn: Motorbooks International, 2003.

Bond, Brian. *Britain, France and Belgium 1939–1940.* London: Brassey 1990.

Churchill, Winston. *The Second World War.* London: Cassell, 1949.

Command Magazine. *Hitler's Army: The Evolution and Structure of German Forces, 1933–1945.* Cambridge, Massachussetts: DaCapo Press, 2000.

Deighton, Len. *Blitzkrieg.* London: Jonathan Cape, 1979.

Drury, Ian and Bishop, Chris. *Great Battles of the 20th Century.* London: Hamlyn, 1988.

Erickson, John. *The Road to Stalingrad.* London: Weidenfeldt & Nicholson, 1975.

Guderian, Heinz. *Panzer Leader.* London: Arrow, 1990.

Guderian, Heinz. *Achtung Panzer.* London: Arms and Armour, 1992.

Macintyre, Donald. *The Battle of the Atlantic.* London: Pan Books, 1969.

Marix Evans, Martin. *The Fall of France.* Oxford: Osprey, 2000.

Mitcham, Samuel W. *Hitler's Field Marshals.* London: William Heinemann, 1988.

Padfield, Peter. *War Beneath the Sea.* Hoboken, New Jersey: Wiley, 1998.

Pitt, Barrie. *The Crucible of War.* London: Cassell Military, 2001.

Pitt, Barrie. *The Military History of World War II.* London: Temple Press/Aerospace, 1987.

Rommel, Erwin (ed. Liddell-Hart, Basil). *The Rommel Papers.* London: Collins, 1953.

Seaton, Albert. *The German Army 1933–1945.* New York: New American Library, 1982.

Shirer, William L. *The Rise and Fall of the Third Reich.* New York: Simon and Schuster, 1960.

Showell, Jak P. Mallman. *U-Boat Commanders and Crews 1935–1945.* Malmsbury: The Crowood Press, 1998.

Trevor-Roper, Hugh (Ed). *Hitler's War Directives.* London: Sidgwick and Jackson, 1964.

Von Mellenthin, F.W. *Panzer Battles 1939–1945.* London: Cassell, 1955.

Index